MAT **GROOM** • MARGUERITE **BENNETT** • MOISÉS **HIDALGO** • ANNA KEKOVSKY **CHANDRA**
RAÚL **ANGULO** • SARA **ANTONELLINI** • FABI **MARQUES**

MIGHTY MORPHIN

VOLUME SIX

D1264999

Published by

BOOM!
STUDIOS

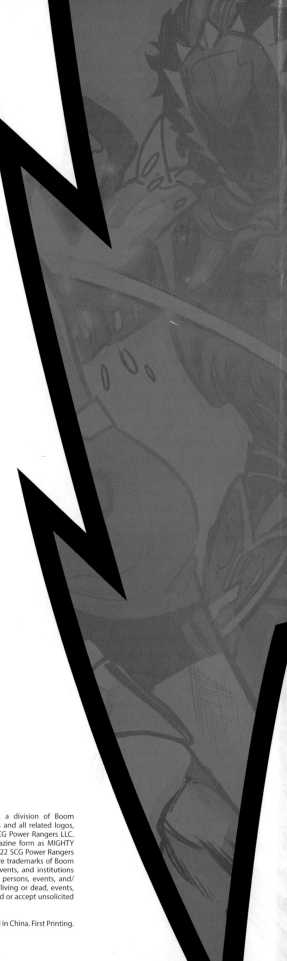

SERIES DESIGNER
MADISON GOYETTE

COLLECTION DESIGNER
VERONICA GUTIERREZ

COLLECTION EDITOR
ALLYSON GRONOWITZ

ASSISTANT EDITOR
GWEN WALLER

SERIES EDITOR
DAFNA PLEBAN

HASBRO SPECIAL THANKS
ED LANE, TAYLA REO,
AND **MICHAEL KELLY**

Ross Richie Chairman & Founder
Jen Harned CFO
Matt Gagnon Editor-in-Chief
Filip Sablik President, Publishing & Marketing
Stephen Christy President, Development
Adam Yoelin Senior Vice President, Film
Lance Kreiter Vice President, Licensing & Merchandising
Bryce Carlson Vice President, Editorial & Creative Strategy
Hunter Gorinson Vice President, Business Development
Josh Hayes Vice President, Sales
Sierra Hahn Executive Editor
Eric Harburn Executive Editor
Ryan Matsunaga Director, Marketing
Stephanie Lazarski Director, Operations
Mette Norkjaer Director, Development
Elyse Strandberg Manager, Finance
Michelle Ankley Manager, Production Design
Cheryl Parker Manager, Human Resources
Breanna Sarpy Manager, Digital Marketing & Advertising
Dafna Pleban Senior Editor
Shantel LaRocque Senior Editor
Jon Moisan Acquisition Editor
Elizabeth Brei Editor
Kathleen Wisneski Editor
Sophie Philips-Roberts Editor
Allyson Gronowitz Editor
Ramiro Portnoy Associate Editor
Gavin Gronenthal Assistant Editor
Gwen Waller Assistant Editor
Kenzie Rzonca Assistant Editor
Maya Bollinger Assistant Editor
Rey Netschke Editorial Assistant
Marie Krupina Design Lead
Crystal White Design Lead
Grace Park Design Coordinator
Madison Goyette Production Designer
Veronica Gutierrez Production Designer
Jessy Gould Production Designer
Nancy Mojica Production Designer
Samantha Knapp Production Design Assistant
Esther Kim Marketing Lead
Amanda Lawson Marketing Coordinator
Alex Lorenzen Marketing Coordinator, Copywriter
Grecia Martinez Marketing Assistant, Digital
Harley Salbacka Sales Lead
Ashley Troub Consumer Sales Coordinator
Greg Hopkins Retail Sales Coordinator
Manny Castellanos Sales Coordinator
Megan Christopher Operations Lead
Rodrigo Hernandez Operations Lead
Nicholas Romeo Operations Coordinator
Michelle Flores Operations Assistant
Jason Lee Senior Accountant
Faizah Bashir Business Analyst
Amber Peters Staff Accountant
Tiffany Thomas Accounts Payable Clerk
Michel Lichand Executive Assistant
Diane Payne Publishing Administrative Assistant

Licensed by:

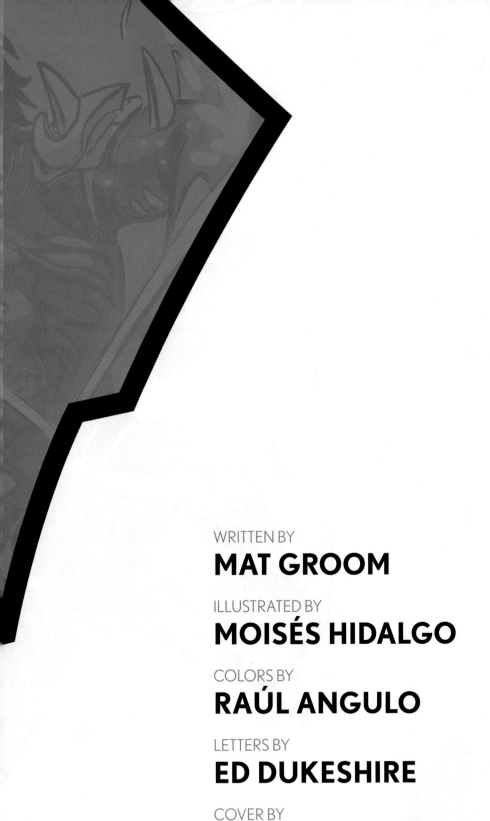

WRITTEN BY
MAT GROOM

ILLUSTRATED BY
MOISÉS HIDALGO

COLORS BY
RAÚL ANGULO

LETTERS BY
ED DUKESHIRE

COVER BY
INHYUK LEE

CHAPTER
TWENTY-ONE

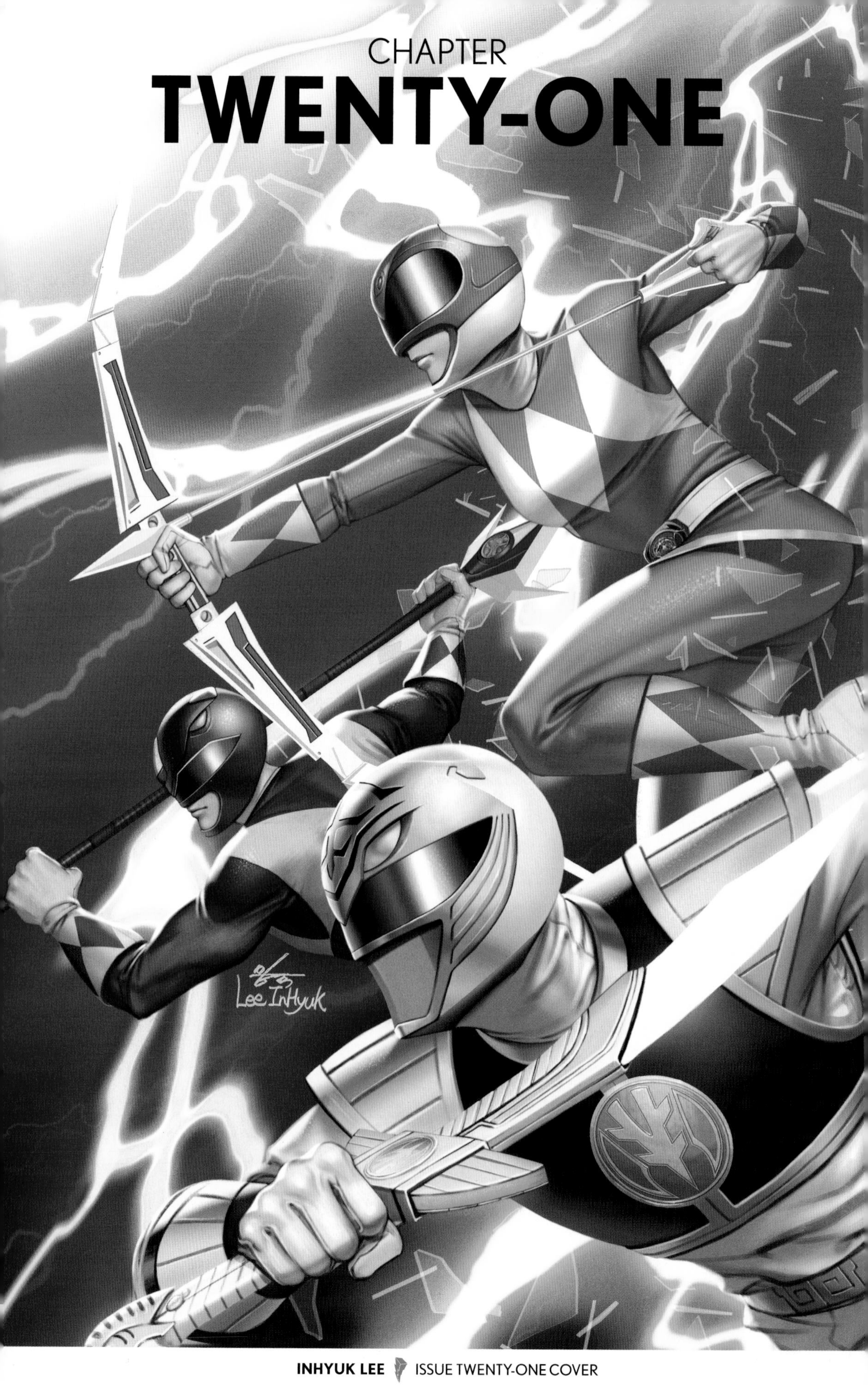
Lee InHyuk

INHYUK LEE ISSUE TWENTY-ONE COVER

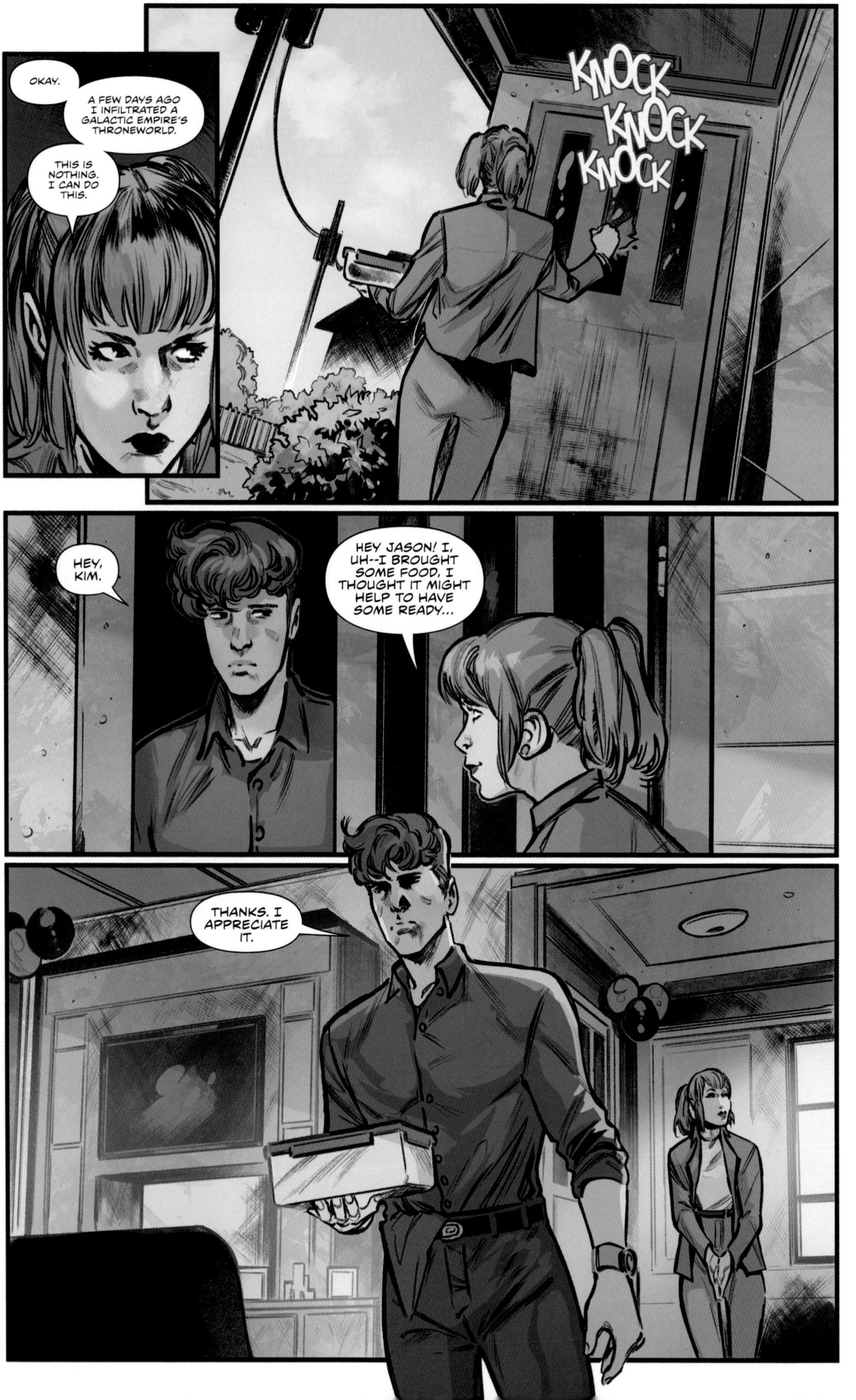
OKAY.
A FEW DAYS AGO I INFILTRATED A GALACTIC EMPIRE'S THRONEWORLD.
THIS IS NOTHING. I CAN DO THIS.
KNOCK KNOCK KNOCK
HEY, KIM.
HEY JASON! I, UH--I BROUGHT SOME FOOD, I THOUGHT IT MIGHT HELP TO HAVE SOME READY...
THANKS. I APPRECIATE IT.

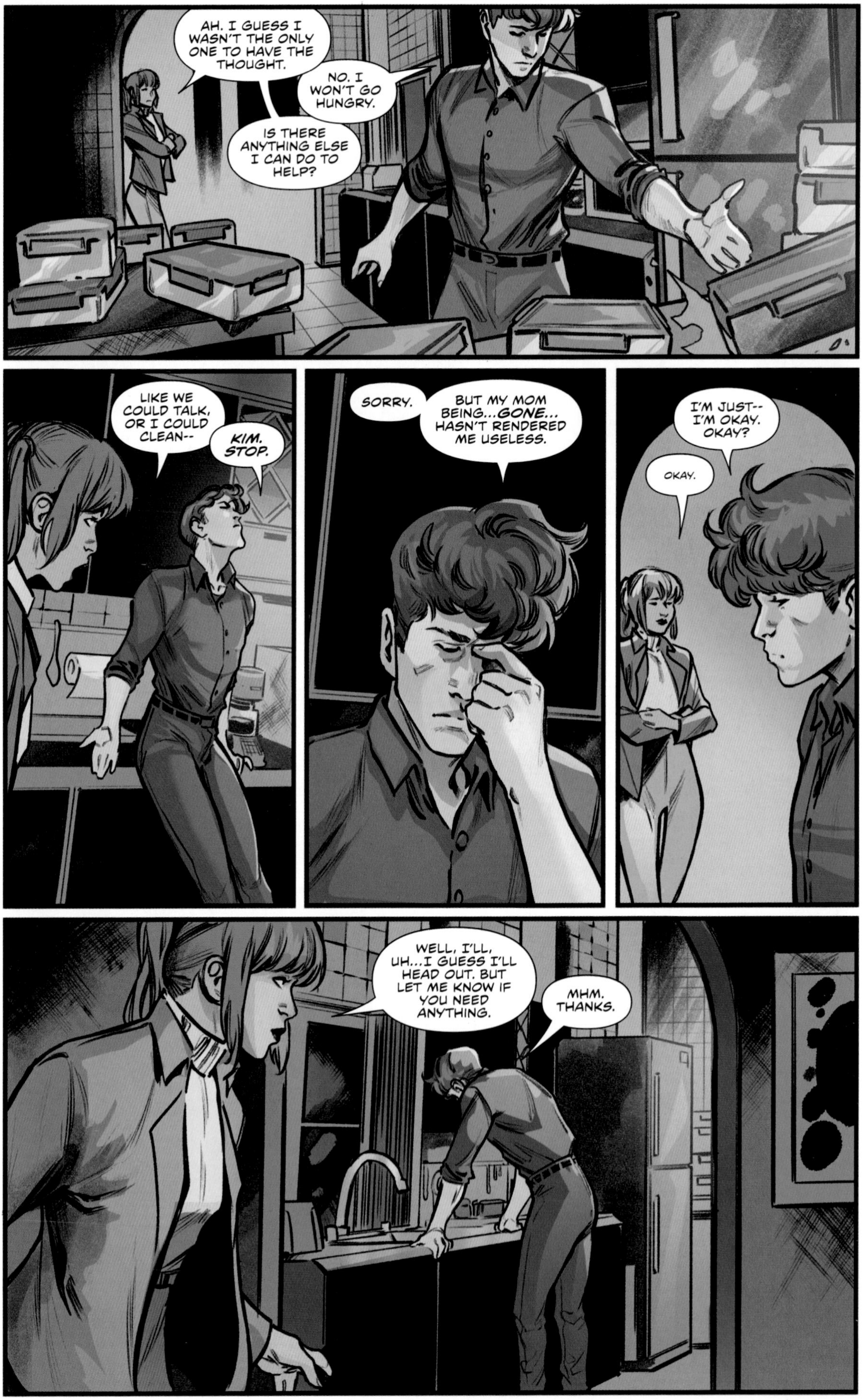
AH. I GUESS I WASN'T THE ONLY ONE TO HAVE THE THOUGHT.
NO. I WON'T GO HUNGRY.
IS THERE ANYTHING ELSE I CAN DO TO HELP?
LIKE WE COULD TALK, OR I COULD CLEAN--
KIM. STOP.
SORRY.
BUT MY MOM BEING...GONE... HASN'T RENDERED ME USELESS.
I'M JUST-- I'M OKAY. OKAY?
OKAY.
WELL, I'LL, UH...I GUESS I'LL HEAD OUT. BUT LET ME KNOW IF YOU NEED ANYTHING.
MHM. THANKS.

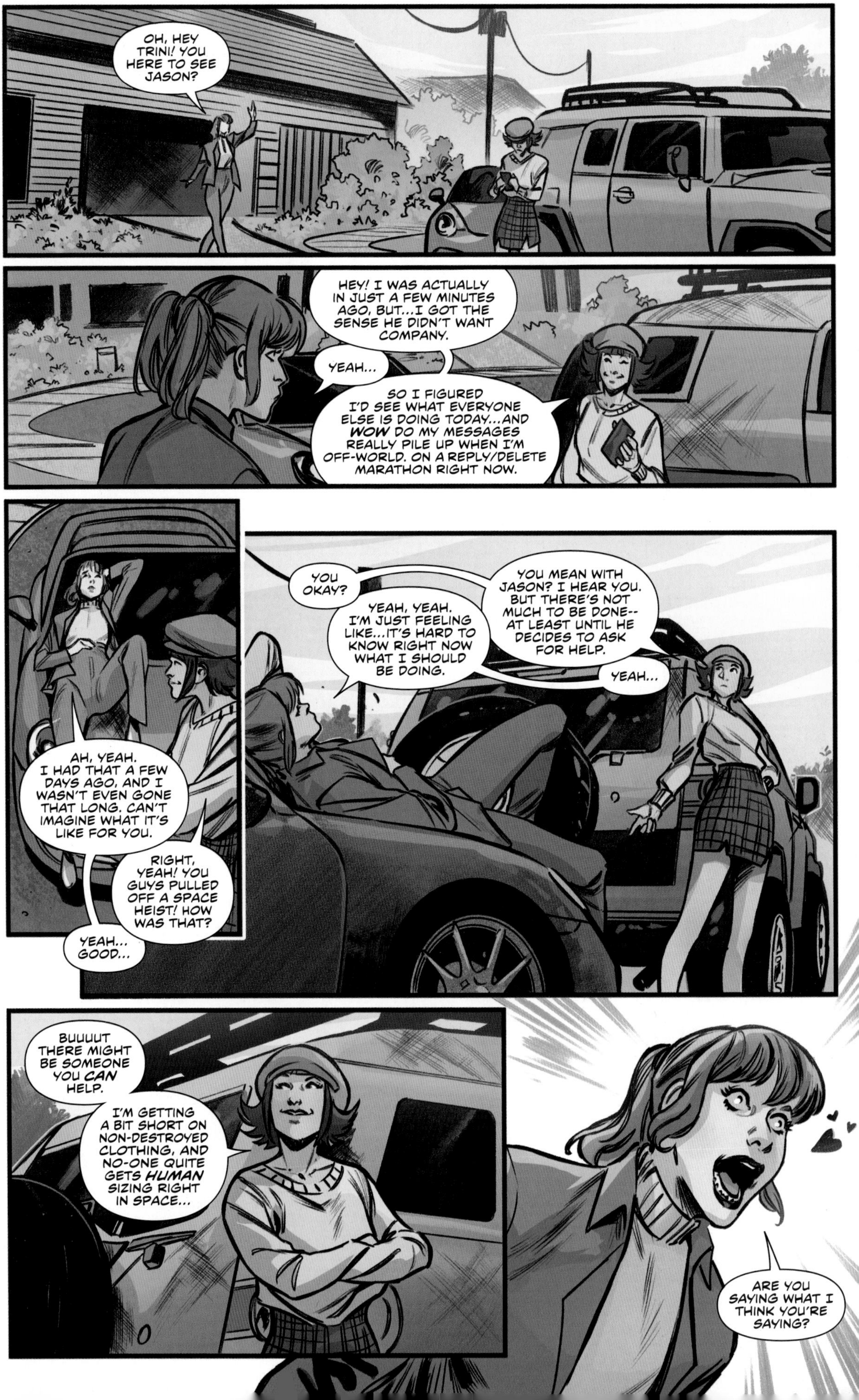
OH, HEY TRINI! YOU HERE TO SEE JASON?
HEY! I WAS ACTUALLY IN JUST A FEW MINUTES AGO, BUT...I GOT THE SENSE HE DIDN'T WANT COMPANY.
YEAH...
SO I FIGURED I'D SEE WHAT EVERYONE ELSE IS DOING TODAY...AND WOW DO MY MESSAGES REALLY PILE UP WHEN I'M OFF-WORLD. ON A REPLY/DELETE MARATHON RIGHT NOW.
AH, YEAH. I HAD THAT A FEW DAYS AGO, AND I WASN'T EVEN GONE THAT LONG. CAN'T IMAGINE WHAT IT'S LIKE FOR YOU.
RIGHT, YEAH! YOU GUYS PULLED OFF A SPACE HEIST! HOW WAS THAT?
YEAH... GOOD...
YOU OKAY?
YEAH, YEAH. I'M JUST FEELING LIKE...IT'S HARD TO KNOW RIGHT NOW WHAT I SHOULD BE DOING.
YOU MEAN WITH JASON? I HEAR YOU. BUT THERE'S NOT MUCH TO BE DONE-- AT LEAST UNTIL HE DECIDES TO ASK FOR HELP.
YEAH...
BUUUUT THERE MIGHT BE SOMEONE YOU CAN HELP.
I'M GETTING A BIT SHORT ON NON-DESTROYED CLOTHING, AND NO-ONE QUITE GETS HUMAN SIZING RIGHT IN SPACE...
ARE YOU SAYING WHAT I THINK YOU'RE SAYING?

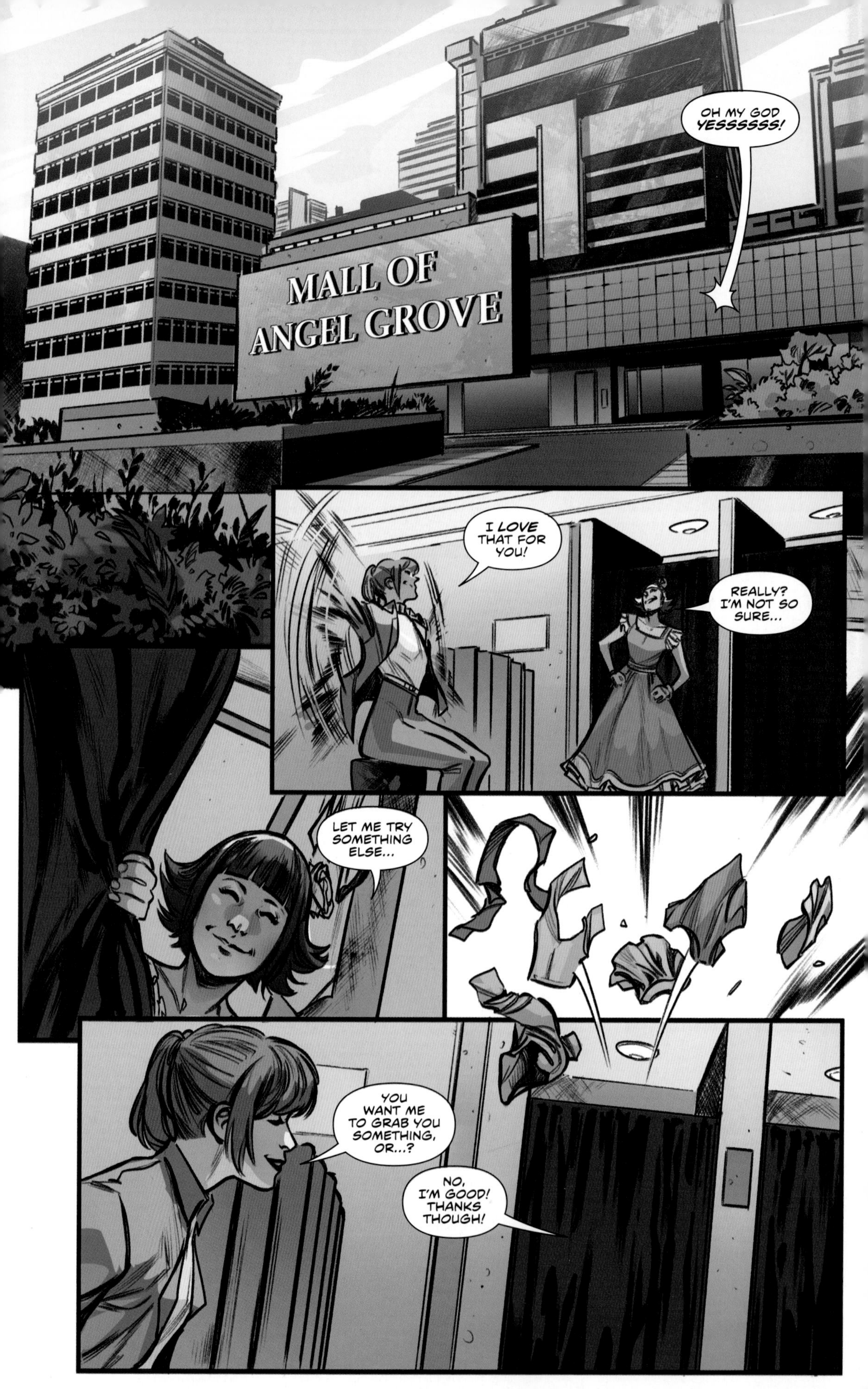
MALL OF ANGEL GROVE
OH MY GOD YESSSSSS!
I LOVE THAT FOR YOU!
REALLY? I'M NOT SO SURE...
LET ME TRY SOMETHING ELSE...
YOU WANT ME TO GRAB YOU SOMETHING, OR...?
NO, I'M GOOD! THANKS THOUGH!

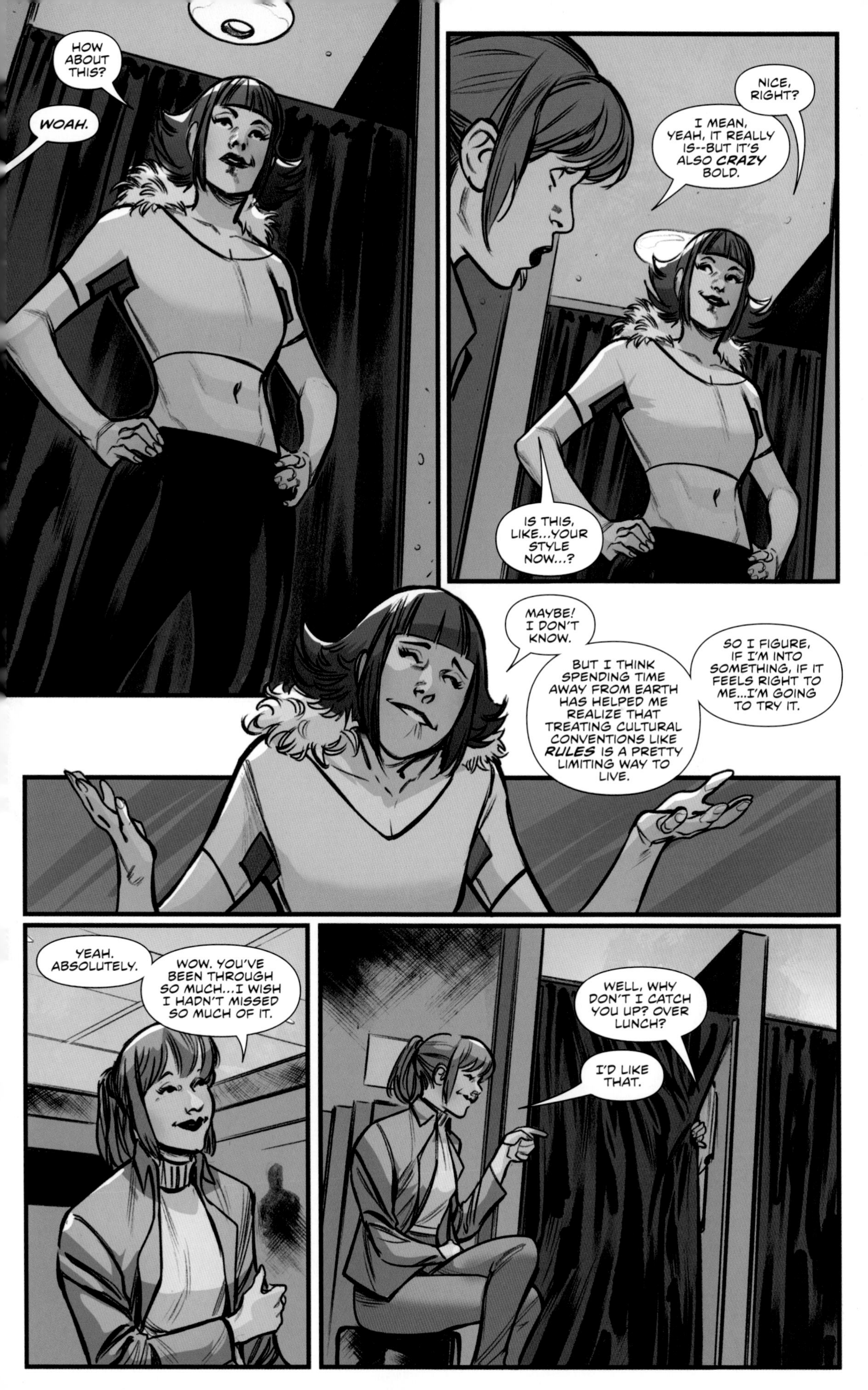
HOW ABOUT THIS?
WOAH.
NICE, RIGHT?
I MEAN, YEAH, IT REALLY IS--BUT IT'S ALSO CRAZY BOLD.
IS THIS, LIKE...YOUR STYLE NOW...?
MAYBE! I DON'T KNOW.
BUT I THINK SPENDING TIME AWAY FROM EARTH HAS HELPED ME REALIZE THAT TREATING CULTURAL CONVENTIONS LIKE RULES IS A PRETTY LIMITING WAY TO LIVE.
SO I FIGURE, IF I'M INTO SOMETHING, IF IT FEELS RIGHT TO ME...I'M GOING TO TRY IT.
YEAH. ABSOLUTELY.
WOW. YOU'VE BEEN THROUGH SO MUCH...I WISH I HADN'T MISSED SO MUCH OF IT.
WELL, WHY DON'T I CATCH YOU UP? OVER LUNCH?
I'D LIKE THAT.

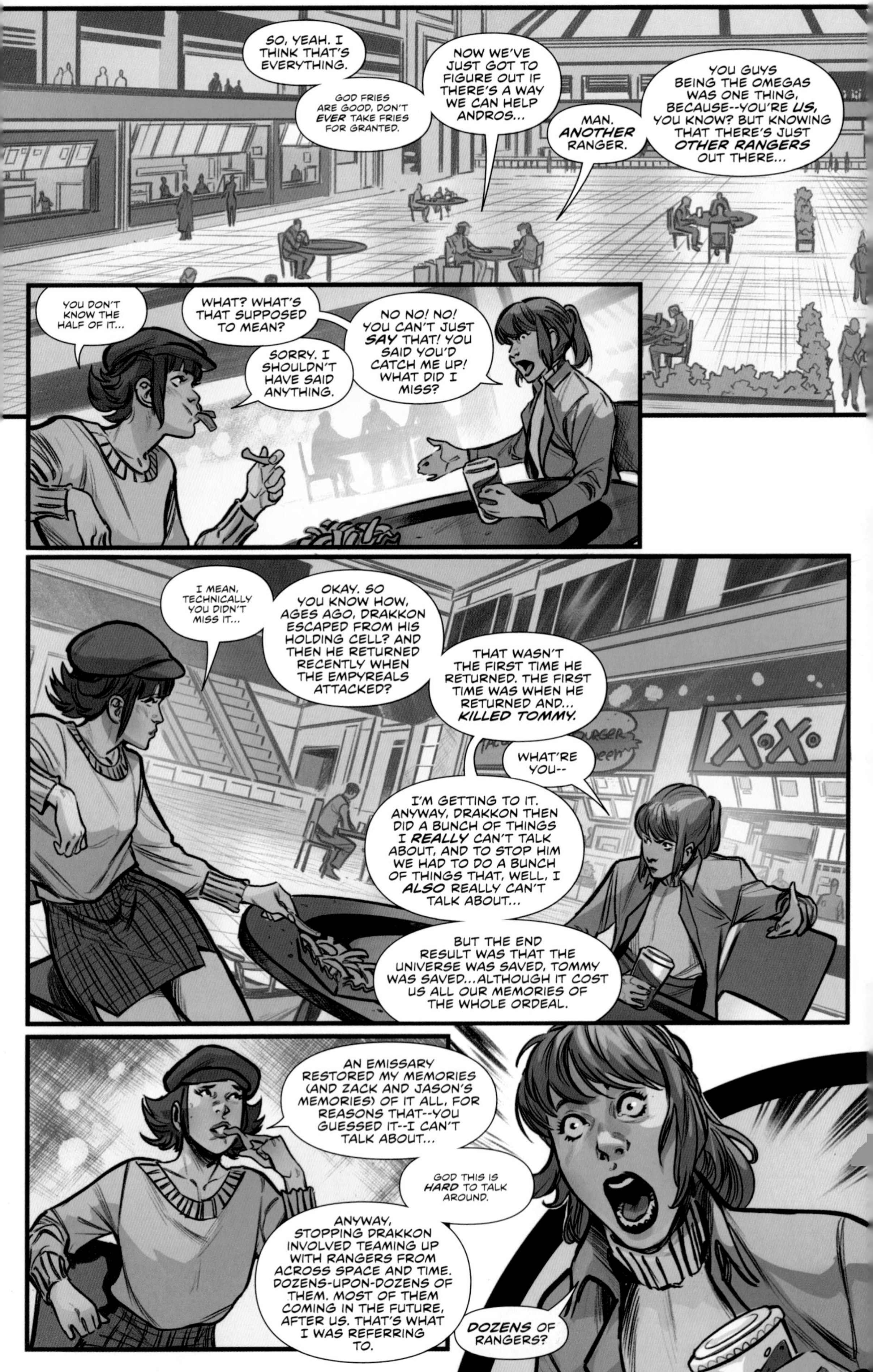
SO, YEAH. I THINK THAT'S EVERYTHING.
GOD FRIES ARE GOOD, DON'T EVER TAKE FRIES FOR GRANTED.
NOW WE'VE JUST GOT TO FIGURE OUT IF THERE'S A WAY WE CAN HELP ANDROS...
MAN. ANOTHER RANGER.
YOU GUYS BEING THE OMEGAS WAS ONE THING, BECAUSE--YOU'RE US, YOU KNOW? BUT KNOWING THAT THERE'S JUST OTHER RANGERS OUT THERE...
YOU DON'T KNOW THE HALF OF IT...
WHAT? WHAT'S THAT SUPPOSED TO MEAN?
SORRY. I SHOULDN'T HAVE SAID ANYTHING.
NO NO! NO! YOU CAN'T JUST SAY THAT! YOU SAID YOU'D CATCH ME UP! WHAT DID I MISS?
I MEAN, TECHNICALLY YOU DIDN'T MISS IT...
OKAY. SO YOU KNOW HOW, AGES AGO, DRAKKON ESCAPED FROM HIS HOLDING CELL? AND THEN HE RETURNED RECENTLY WHEN THE EMPYREALS ATTACKED?
THAT WASN'T THE FIRST TIME HE RETURNED. THE FIRST TIME WAS WHEN HE RETURNED AND... KILLED TOMMY.
WHAT'RE YOU--
I'M GETTING TO IT. ANYWAY, DRAKKON THEN DID A BUNCH OF THINGS I REALLY CAN'T TALK ABOUT, AND TO STOP HIM WE HAD TO DO A BUNCH OF THINGS THAT, WELL, I ALSO REALLY CAN'T TALK ABOUT...
BUT THE END RESULT WAS THAT THE UNIVERSE WAS SAVED, TOMMY WAS SAVED...ALTHOUGH IT COST US ALL OUR MEMORIES OF THE WHOLE ORDEAL.
AN EMISSARY RESTORED MY MEMORIES (AND ZACK AND JASON'S MEMORIES) OF IT ALL, FOR REASONS THAT--YOU GUESSED IT--I CAN'T TALK ABOUT...
GOD THIS IS HARD TO TALK AROUND.
ANYWAY, STOPPING DRAKKON INVOLVED TEAMING UP WITH RANGERS FROM ACROSS SPACE AND TIME. DOZENS-UPON-DOZENS OF THEM. MOST OF THEM COMING IN THE FUTURE, AFTER US. THAT'S WHAT I WAS REFERRING TO.
DOZENS OF RANGERS?

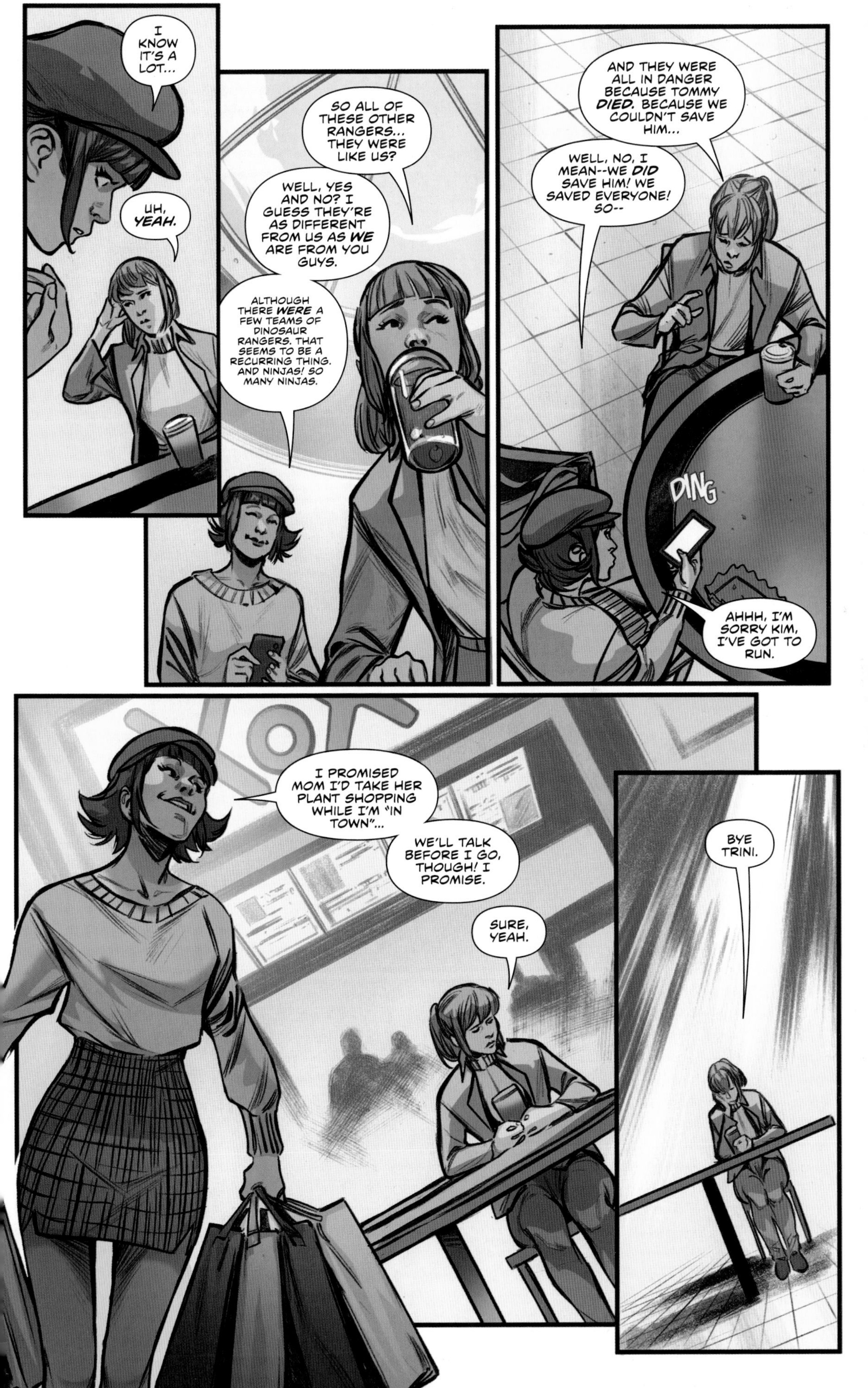
I KNOW IT'S A LOT...
UH, YEAH.
SO ALL OF THESE OTHER RANGERS... THEY WERE LIKE US?
WELL, YES AND NO? I GUESS THEY'RE AS DIFFERENT FROM US AS WE ARE FROM YOU GUYS.
ALTHOUGH THERE WERE A FEW TEAMS OF DINOSAUR RANGERS. THAT SEEMS TO BE A RECURRING THING. AND NINJAS! SO MANY NINJAS.
AND THEY WERE ALL IN DANGER BECAUSE TOMMY DIED. BECAUSE WE COULDN'T SAVE HIM...
WELL, NO, I MEAN--WE DID SAVE HIM! WE SAVED EVERYONE! SO--
DING
AHHH, I'M SORRY KIM, I'VE GOT TO RUN.
I PROMISED MOM I'D TAKE HER PLANT SHOPPING WHILE I'M "IN TOWN"...
WE'LL TALK BEFORE I GO, THOUGH! I PROMISE.
SURE, YEAH.
BYE TRINI.

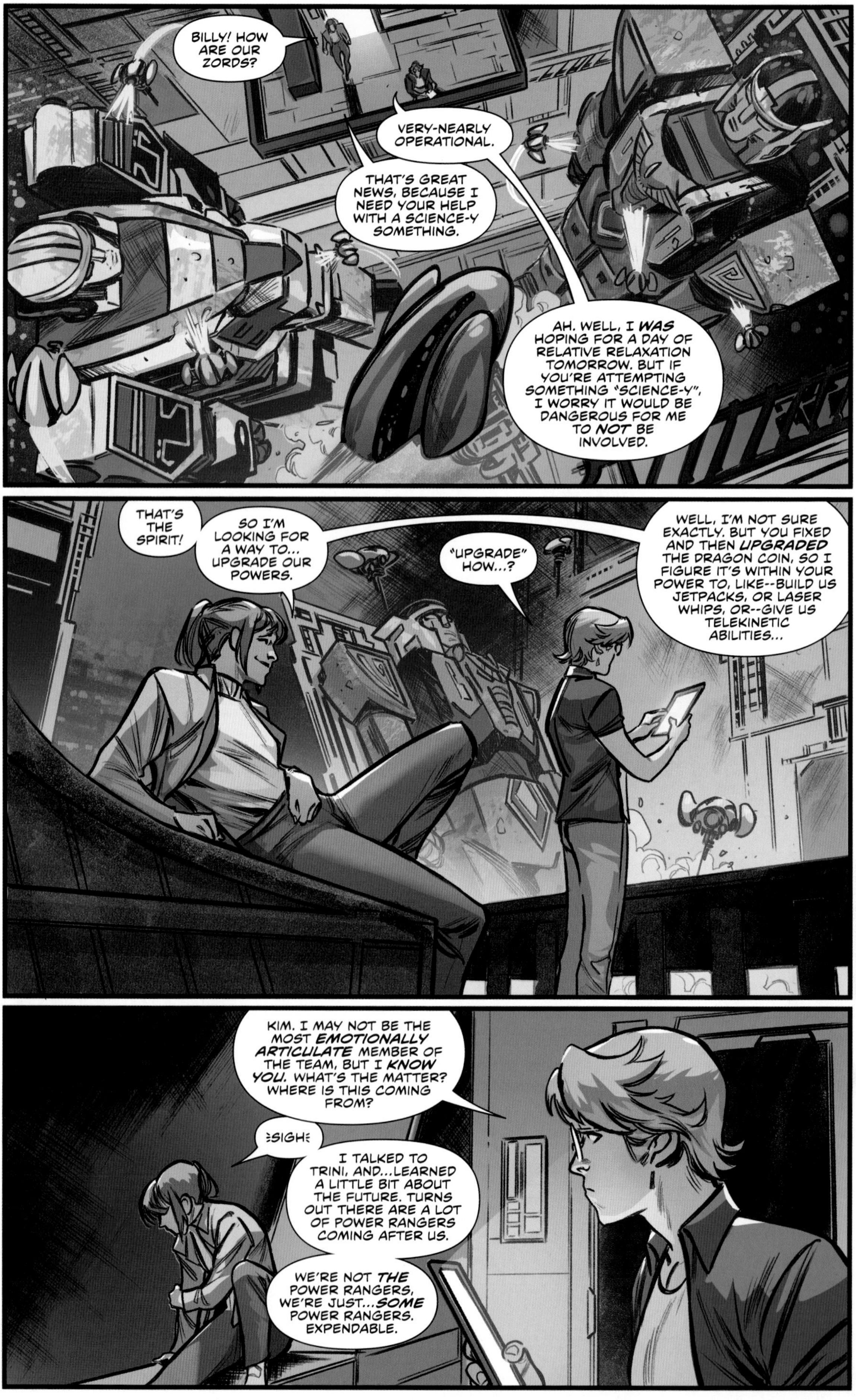

BILLY! HOW ARE OUR ZORDS?
VERY-NEARLY OPERATIONAL.
THAT'S GREAT NEWS, BECAUSE I NEED YOUR HELP WITH A SCIENCE-Y SOMETHING.
AH. WELL, I WAS HOPING FOR A DAY OF RELATIVE RELAXATION TOMORROW. BUT IF YOU'RE ATTEMPTING SOMETHING "SCIENCE-Y", I WORRY IT WOULD BE DANGEROUS FOR ME TO NOT BE INVOLVED.
THAT'S THE SPIRIT!
SO I'M LOOKING FOR A WAY TO... UPGRADE OUR POWERS.
"UPGRADE" HOW...?
WELL, I'M NOT SURE EXACTLY. BUT YOU FIXED AND THEN UPGRADED THE DRAGON COIN, SO I FIGURE IT'S WITHIN YOUR POWER TO, LIKE--BUILD US JETPACKS, OR LASER WHIPS, OR--GIVE US TELEKINETIC ABILITIES...
KIM. I MAY NOT BE THE MOST EMOTIONALLY ARTICULATE MEMBER OF THE TEAM, BUT I KNOW YOU. WHAT'S THE MATTER? WHERE IS THIS COMING FROM?
SIGH
I TALKED TO TRINI, AND...LEARNED A LITTLE BIT ABOUT THE FUTURE. TURNS OUT THERE ARE A LOT OF POWER RANGERS COMING AFTER US.
WE'RE NOT THE POWER RANGERS, WE'RE JUST...SOME POWER RANGERS. EXPENDABLE.

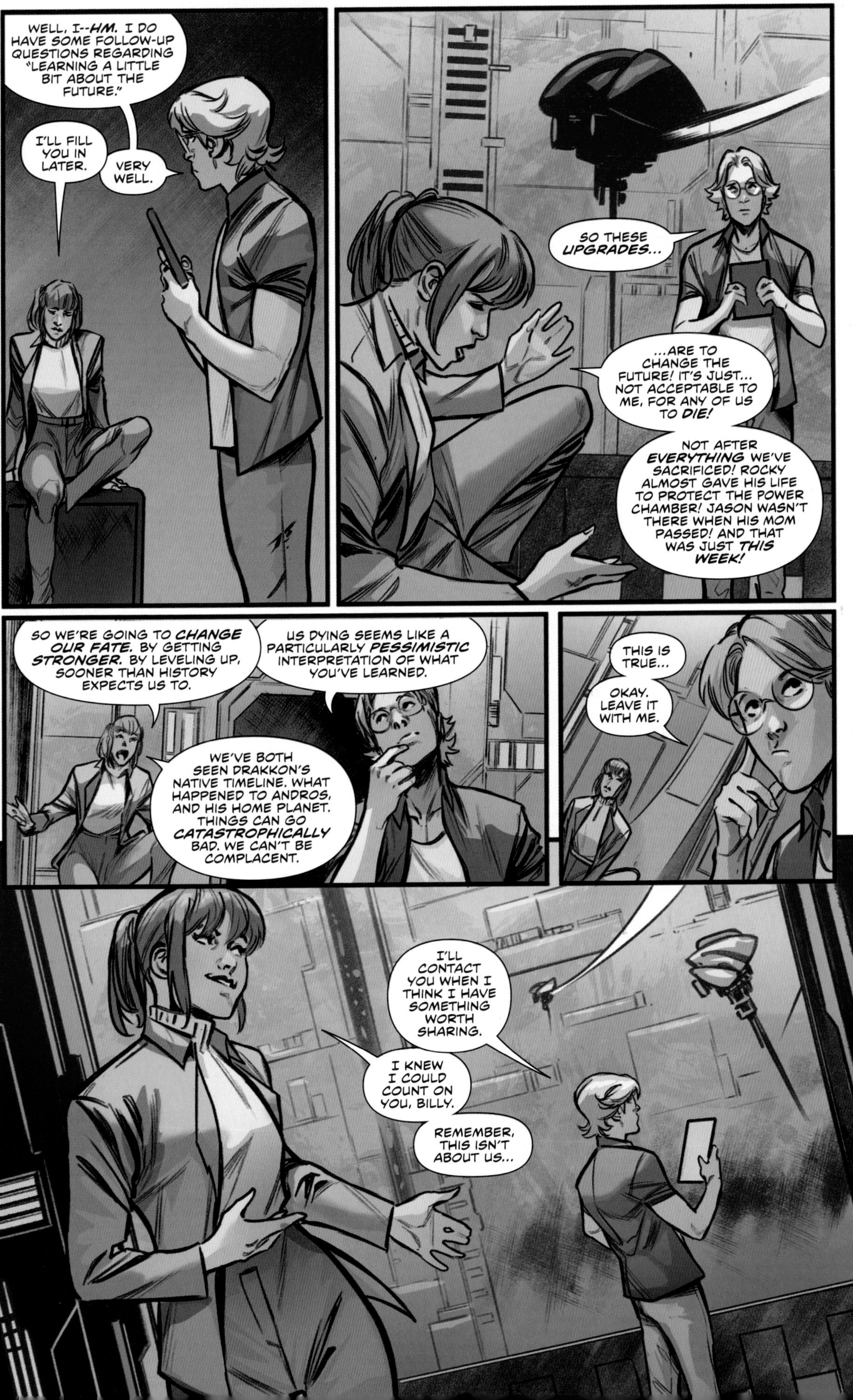
WELL, I--HM. I DO HAVE SOME FOLLOW-UP QUESTIONS REGARDING "LEARNING A LITTLE BIT ABOUT THE FUTURE."
I'LL FILL YOU IN LATER.
VERY WELL.
SO THESE UPGRADES...
...ARE TO CHANGE THE FUTURE! IT'S JUST... NOT ACCEPTABLE TO ME, FOR ANY OF US TO DIE!
NOT AFTER EVERYTHING WE'VE SACRIFICED! ROCKY ALMOST GAVE HIS LIFE TO PROTECT THE POWER CHAMBER! JASON WASN'T THERE WHEN HIS MOM PASSED! AND THAT WAS JUST THIS WEEK!
SO WE'RE GOING TO CHANGE OUR FATE. BY GETTING STRONGER. BY LEVELING UP, SOONER THAN HISTORY EXPECTS US TO.
US DYING SEEMS LIKE A PARTICULARLY PESSIMISTIC INTERPRETATION OF WHAT YOU'VE LEARNED.
WE'VE BOTH SEEN DRAKKON'S NATIVE TIMELINE. WHAT HAPPENED TO ANDROS, AND HIS HOME PLANET. THINGS CAN GO CATASTROPHICALLY BAD. WE CAN'T BE COMPLACENT.
THIS IS TRUE...
OKAY. LEAVE IT WITH ME.
I'LL CONTACT YOU WHEN I THINK I HAVE SOMETHING WORTH SHARING.
I KNEW I COULD COUNT ON YOU, BILLY.
REMEMBER, THIS ISN'T ABOUT US...

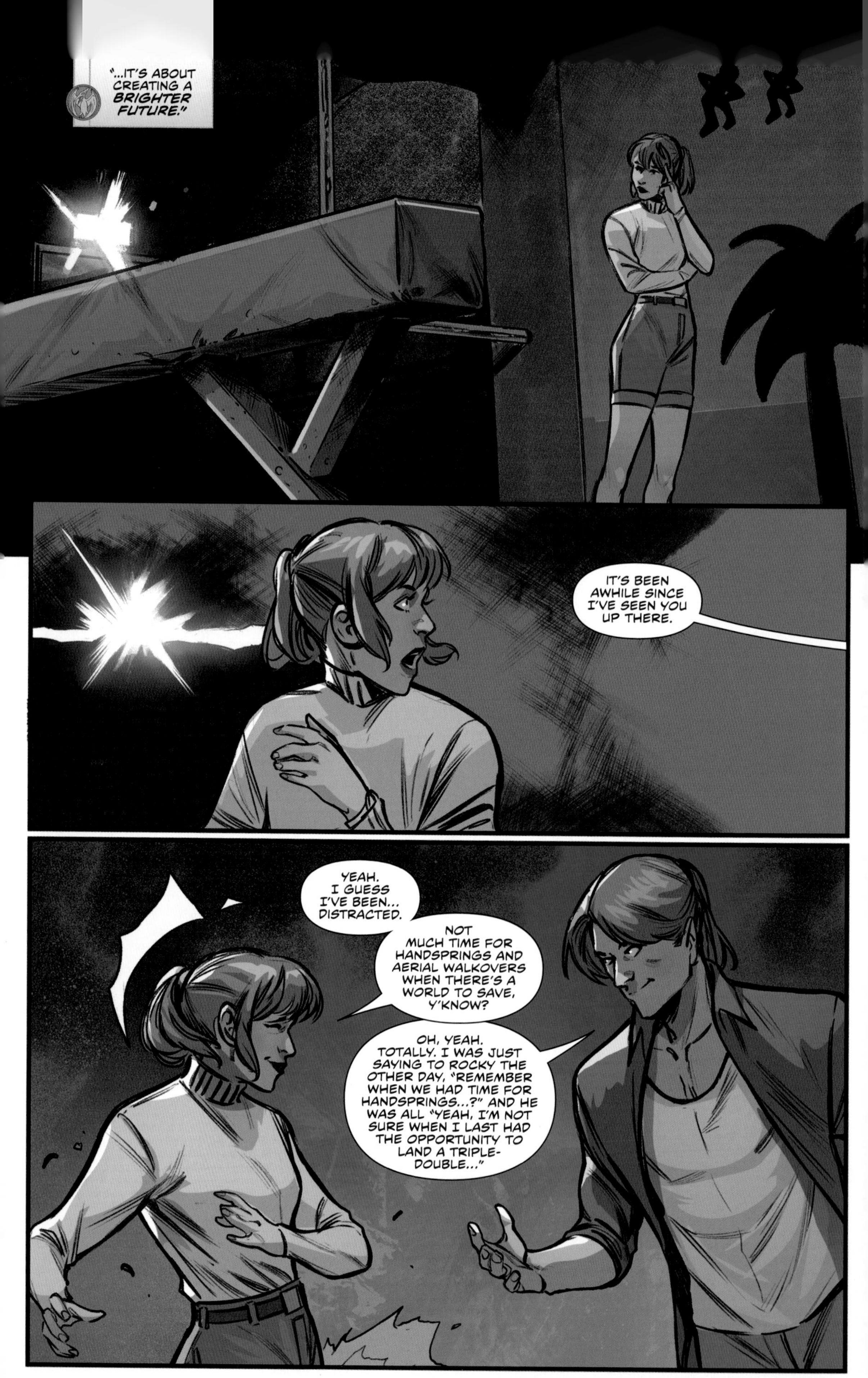
"...IT'S ABOUT CREATING A BRIGHTER FUTURE."
IT'S BEEN AWHILE SINCE I'VE SEEN YOU UP THERE.
YEAH. I GUESS I'VE BEEN... DISTRACTED.
NOT MUCH TIME FOR HANDSPRINGS AND AERIAL WALKOVERS WHEN THERE'S A WORLD TO SAVE, Y'KNOW?
OH, YEAH. TOTALLY. I WAS JUST SAYING TO ROCKY THE OTHER DAY, "REMEMBER WHEN WE HAD TIME FOR HANDSPRINGS...?" AND HE WAS ALL "YEAH, I'M NOT SURE WHEN I LAST HAD THE OPPORTUNITY TO LAND A TRIPLE-DOUBLE..."

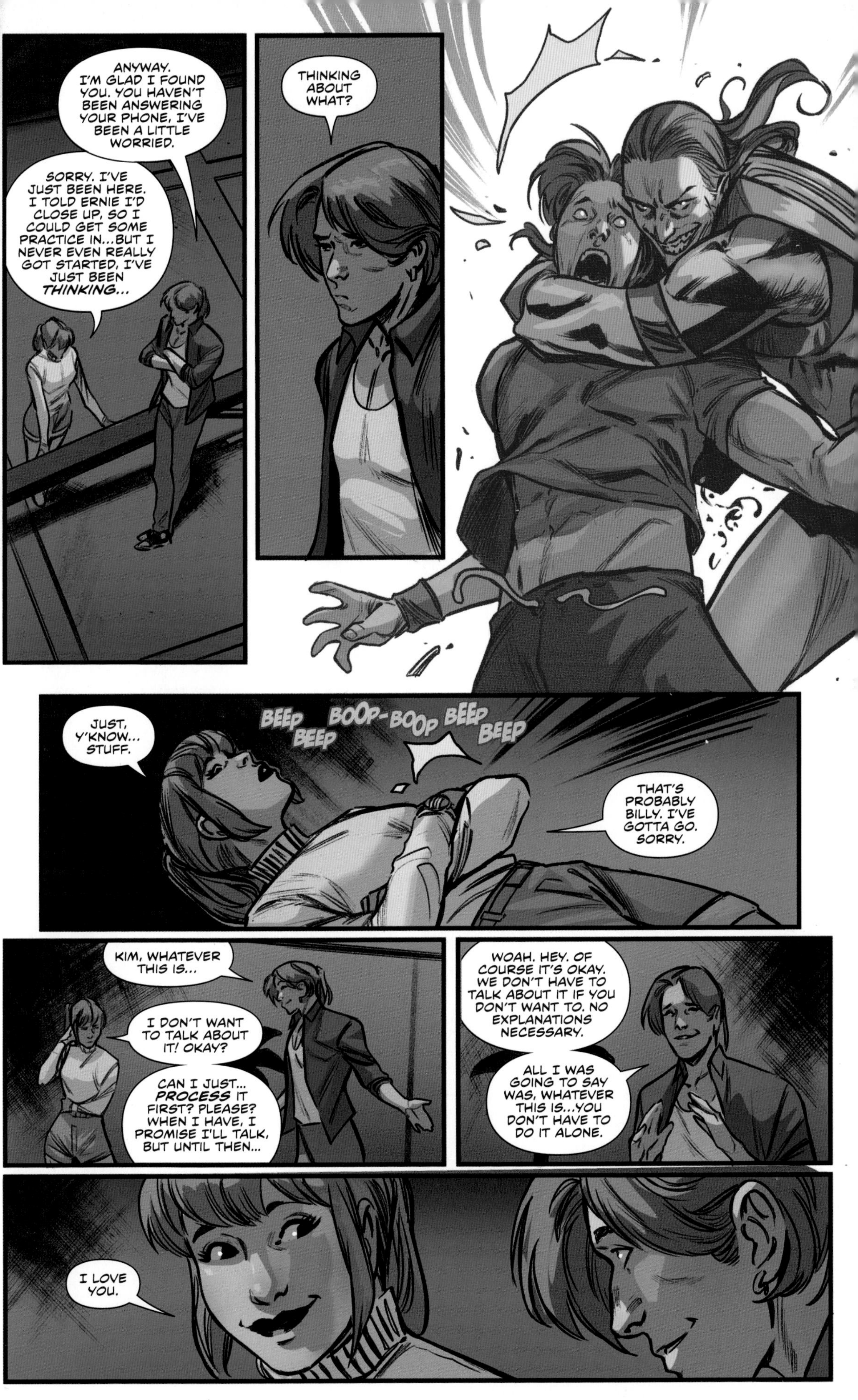
ANYWAY. I'M GLAD I FOUND YOU. YOU HAVEN'T BEEN ANSWERING YOUR PHONE, I'VE BEEN A LITTLE WORRIED.
SORRY. I'VE JUST BEEN HERE. I TOLD ERNIE I'D CLOSE UP, SO I COULD GET SOME PRACTICE IN...BUT I NEVER EVEN REALLY GOT STARTED, I'VE JUST BEEN *THINKING...*
THINKING ABOUT WHAT?
JUST, Y'KNOW... STUFF.
BEEP BEEP BOOP-BOOP BEEP BEEP
THAT'S PROBABLY BILLY. I'VE GOTTA GO. SORRY.
KIM, WHATEVER THIS IS...
I DON'T WANT TO TALK ABOUT IT! OKAY?
CAN I JUST... *PROCESS* IT FIRST? PLEASE? WHEN I HAVE, I PROMISE I'LL TALK, BUT UNTIL THEN...
WOAH. HEY. OF COURSE IT'S OKAY. WE DON'T HAVE TO TALK ABOUT IT IF YOU DON'T WANT TO. NO EXPLANATIONS NECESSARY.
ALL I WAS GOING TO SAY WAS, WHATEVER THIS IS...YOU DON'T HAVE TO DO IT ALONE.
I LOVE YOU.

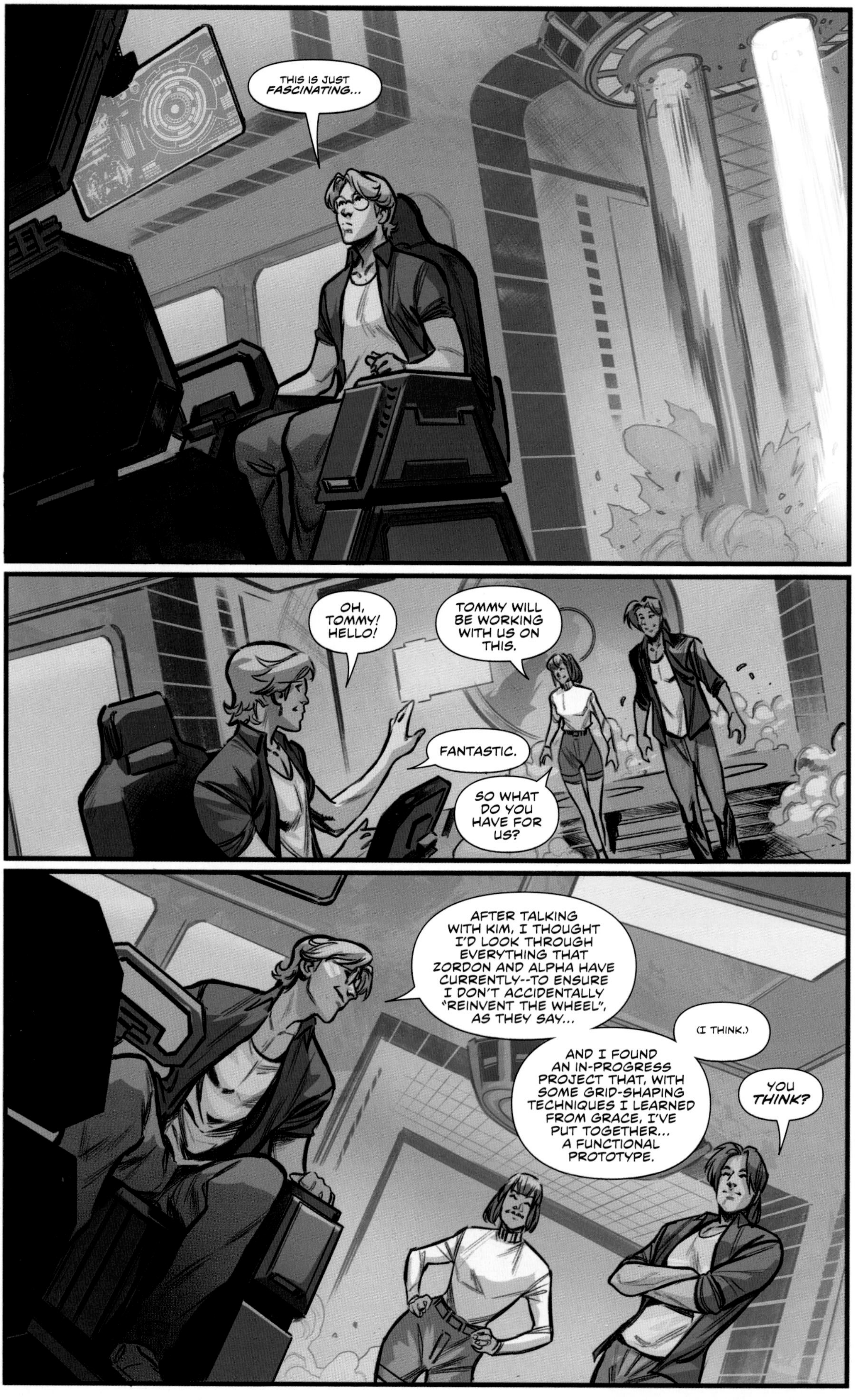
THIS IS JUST *FASCINATING*...
OH, TOMMY! HELLO!
TOMMY WILL BE WORKING WITH US ON THIS.
FANTASTIC.
SO WHAT DO YOU HAVE FOR US?
AFTER TALKING WITH KIM, I THOUGHT I'D LOOK THROUGH EVERYTHING THAT ZORDON AND ALPHA HAVE CURRENTLY--TO ENSURE I DON'T ACCIDENTALLY "REINVENT THE WHEEL", AS THEY SAY...
(I THINK.)
AND I FOUND AN IN-PROGRESS PROJECT THAT, WITH SOME GRID-SHAPING TECHNIQUES I LEARNED FROM GRACE, I'VE PUT TOGETHER... A FUNCTIONAL PROTOTYPE.
YOU *THINK?*

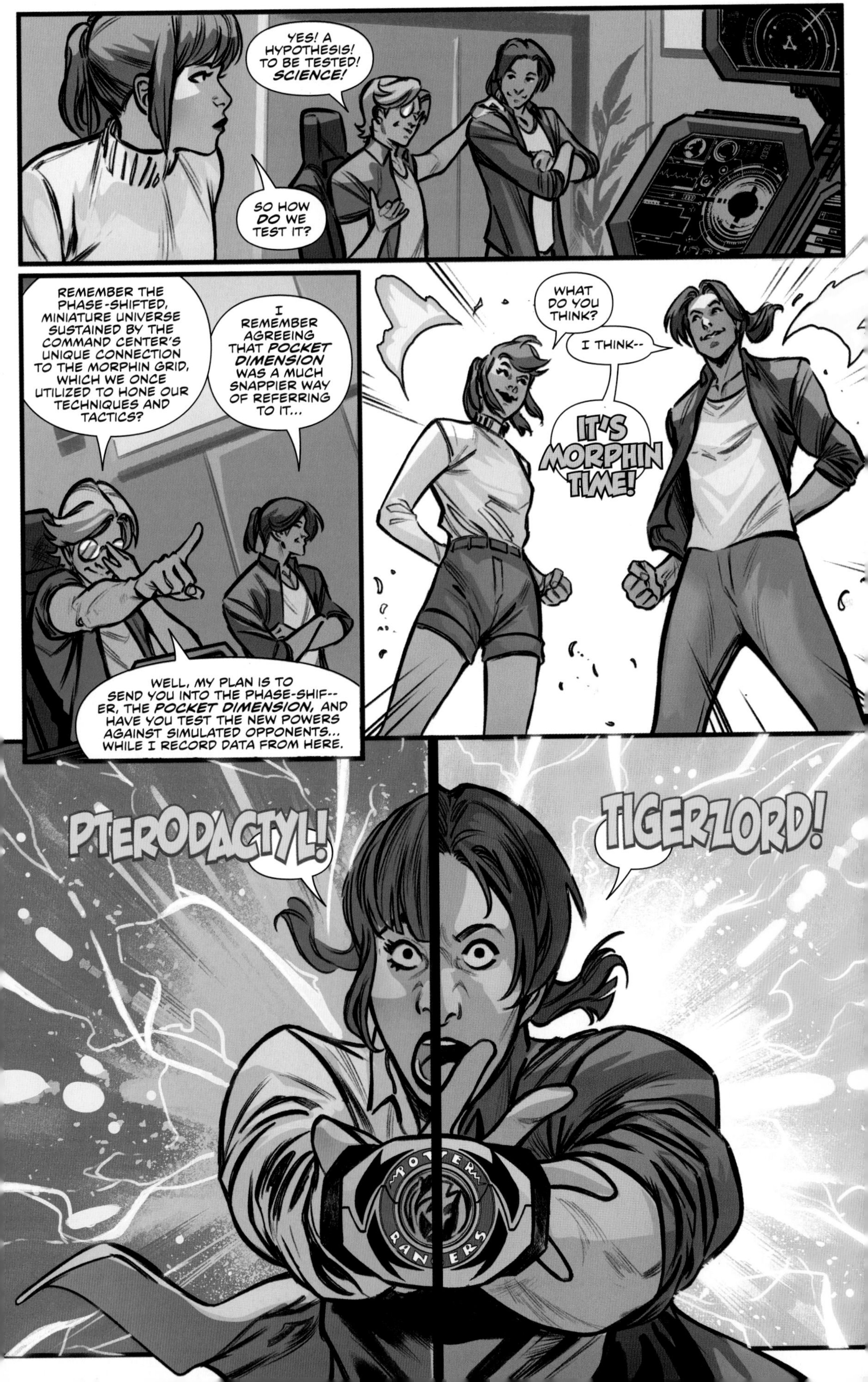
YES! A HYPOTHESIS! TO BE TESTED! *SCIENCE!*
SO HOW *DO* WE TEST IT?
REMEMBER THE PHASE-SHIFTED, MINIATURE UNIVERSE SUSTAINED BY THE COMMAND CENTER'S UNIQUE CONNECTION TO THE MORPHIN GRID, WHICH WE ONCE UTILIZED TO HONE OUR TECHNIQUES AND TACTICS?
I REMEMBER AGREEING THAT *POCKET DIMENSION* WAS A MUCH SNAPPIER WAY OF REFERRING TO IT...
WELL, MY PLAN IS TO SEND YOU INTO THE PHASE-SHIF-- ER, THE *POCKET DIMENSION,* AND HAVE YOU TEST THE NEW POWERS AGAINST SIMULATED OPPONENTS... WHILE I RECORD DATA FROM HERE.
WHAT DO YOU THINK?
I THINK--
IT'S MORPHIN TIME!
PTERODACTYL!
TIGERZORD!
POWER RANGERS

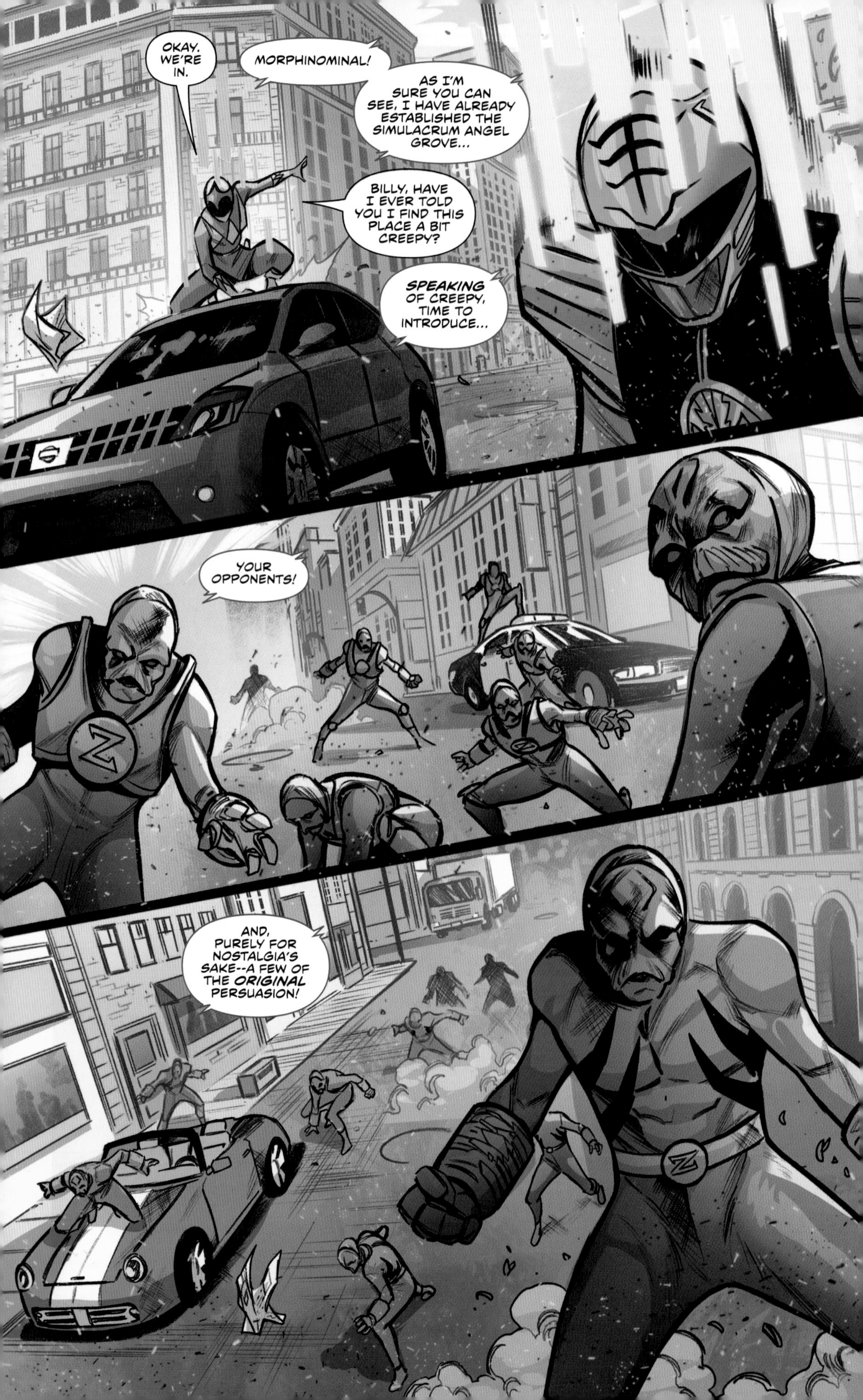
OKAY. WE'RE IN.
MORPHINOMINAL!
AS I'M SURE YOU CAN SEE, I HAVE ALREADY ESTABLISHED THE SIMULACRUM ANGEL GROVE...
BILLY, HAVE I EVER TOLD YOU I FIND THIS PLACE A BIT CREEPY?
SPEAKING OF CREEPY, TIME TO INTRODUCE...
YOUR OPPONENTS!
AND, PURELY FOR NOSTALGIA'S SAKE--A FEW OF THE ORIGINAL PERSUASION!

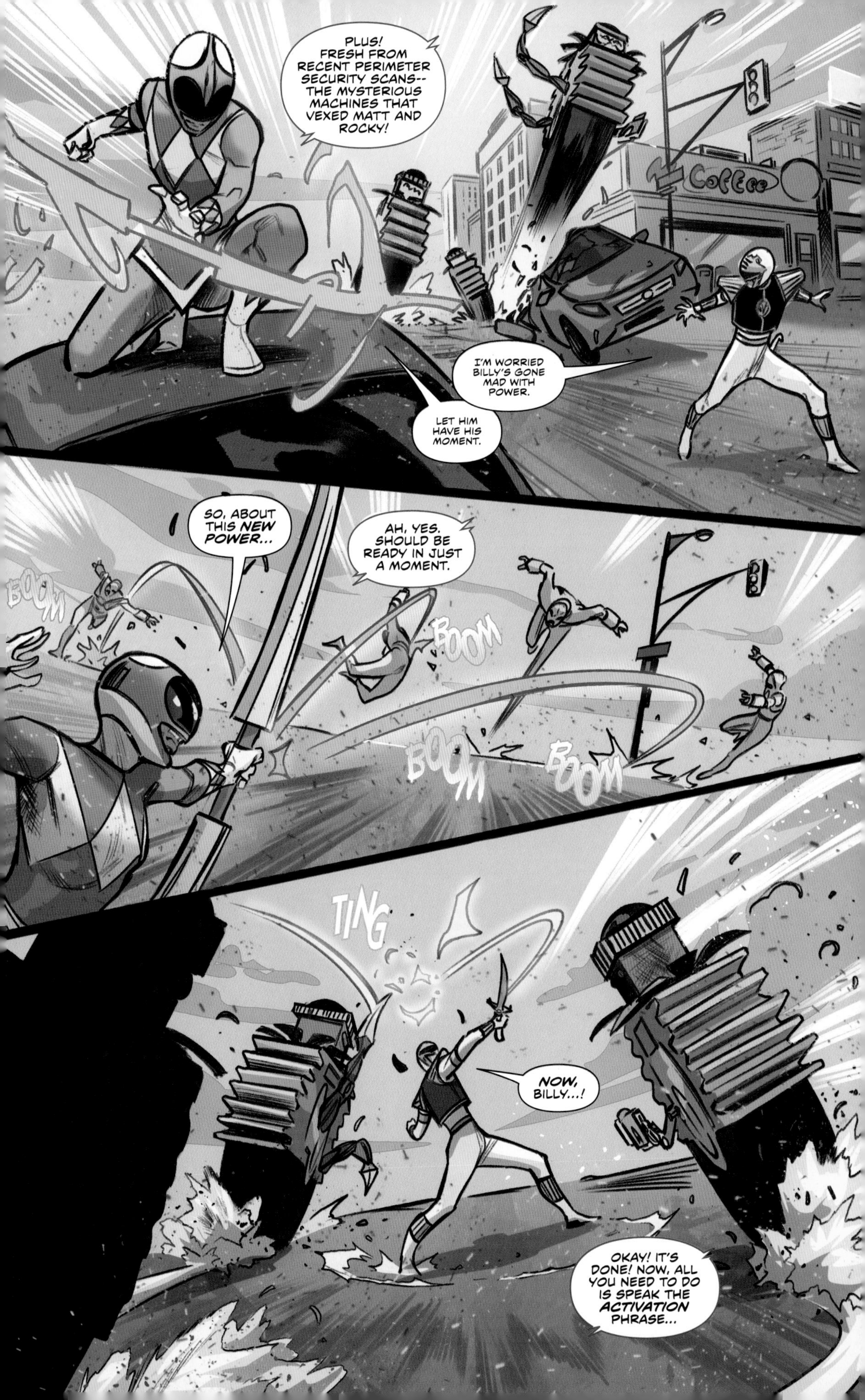
PLUS! FRESH FROM RECENT PERIMETER SECURITY SCANS-- THE MYSTERIOUS MACHINES THAT VEXED MATT AND ROCKY!
CoFFee
I'M WORRIED BILLY'S GONE MAD WITH POWER.
LET HIM HAVE HIS MOMENT.
SO, ABOUT THIS *NEW POWER*...
AH, YES. SHOULD BE READY IN JUST A MOMENT.
BOOM
BOOM
BOOM
BOOM
TING
NOW, BILLY...!
OKAY! IT'S DONE! NOW, ALL YOU NEED TO DO IS SPEAK THE *ACTIVATION* PHRASE...

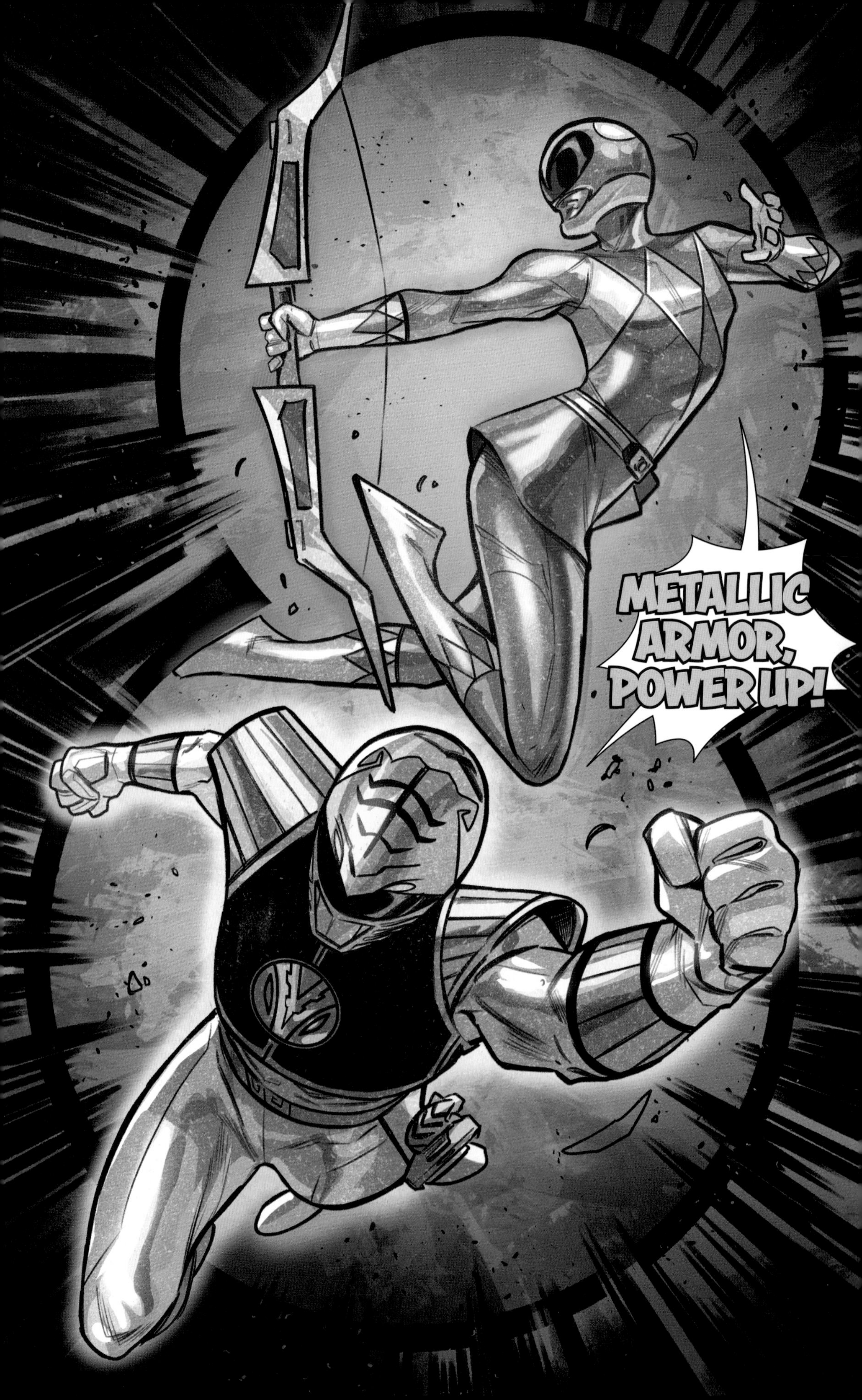
METALLIC ARMOR, POWER UP!

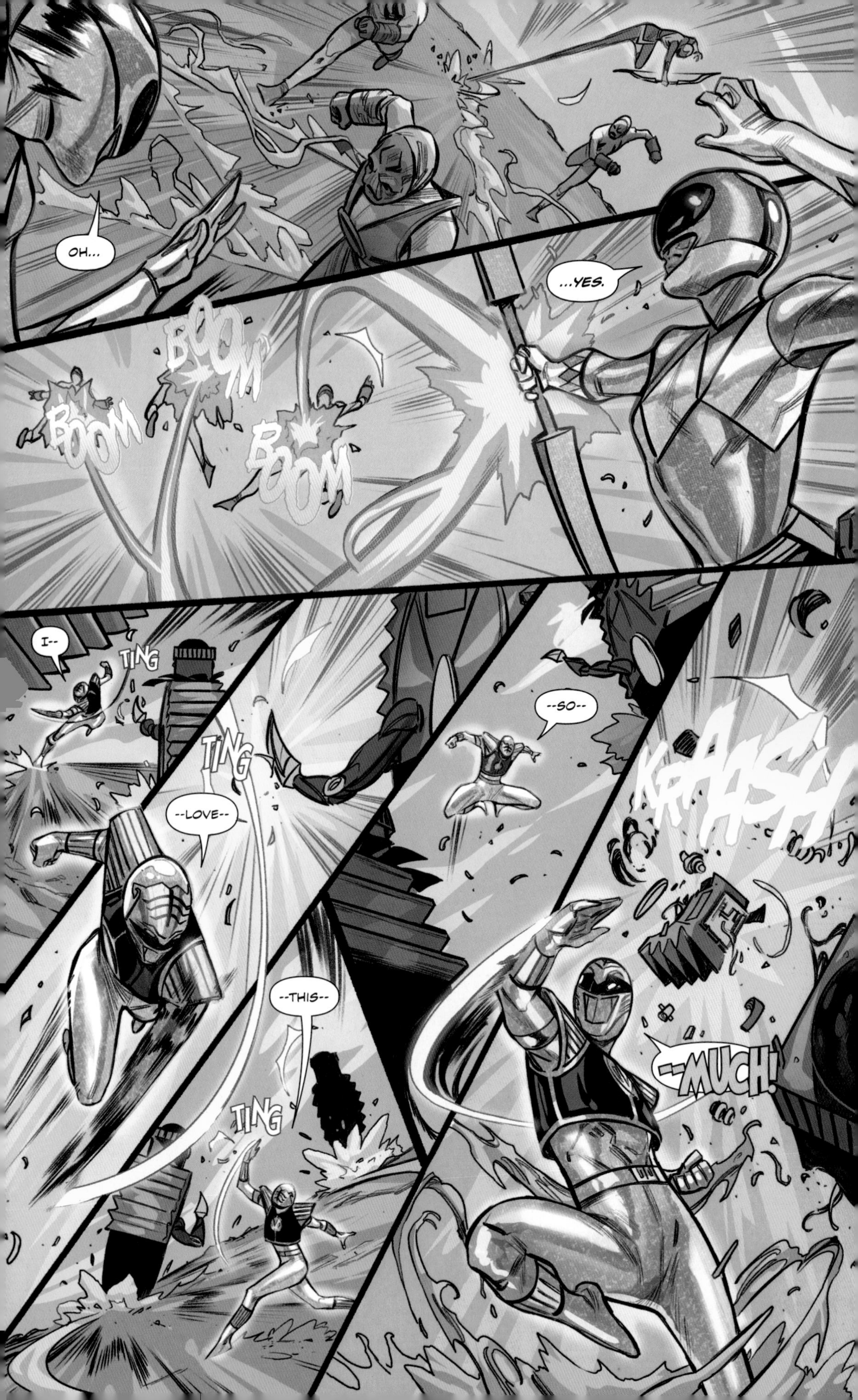
OH...
...YES.
BOOM
BOOM
BOOM
I--
TING
TING
--LOVE--
TING
--THIS--
--SO--
KRAASH
--MUCH!

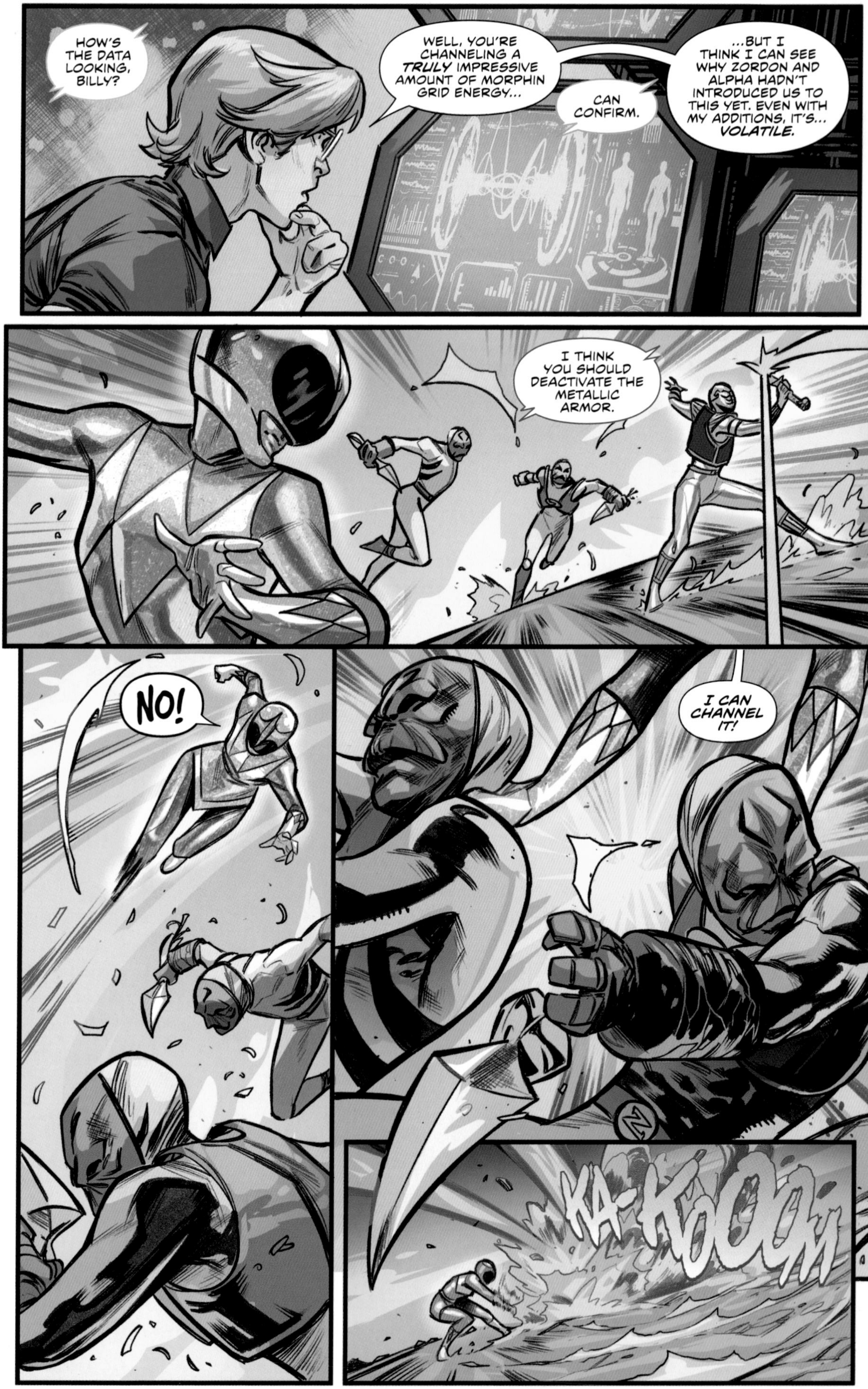
HOW'S THE DATA LOOKING, BILLY?
WELL, YOU'RE CHANNELING A TRULY IMPRESSIVE AMOUNT OF MORPHIN GRID ENERGY...
...BUT I THINK I CAN SEE WHY ZORDON AND ALPHA HADN'T INTRODUCED US TO THIS YET. EVEN WITH MY ADDITIONS, IT'S... VOLATILE.
CAN CONFIRM.
I THINK YOU SHOULD DEACTIVATE THE METALLIC ARMOR.
NO!
I CAN CHANNEL IT!
KA-KOOOM

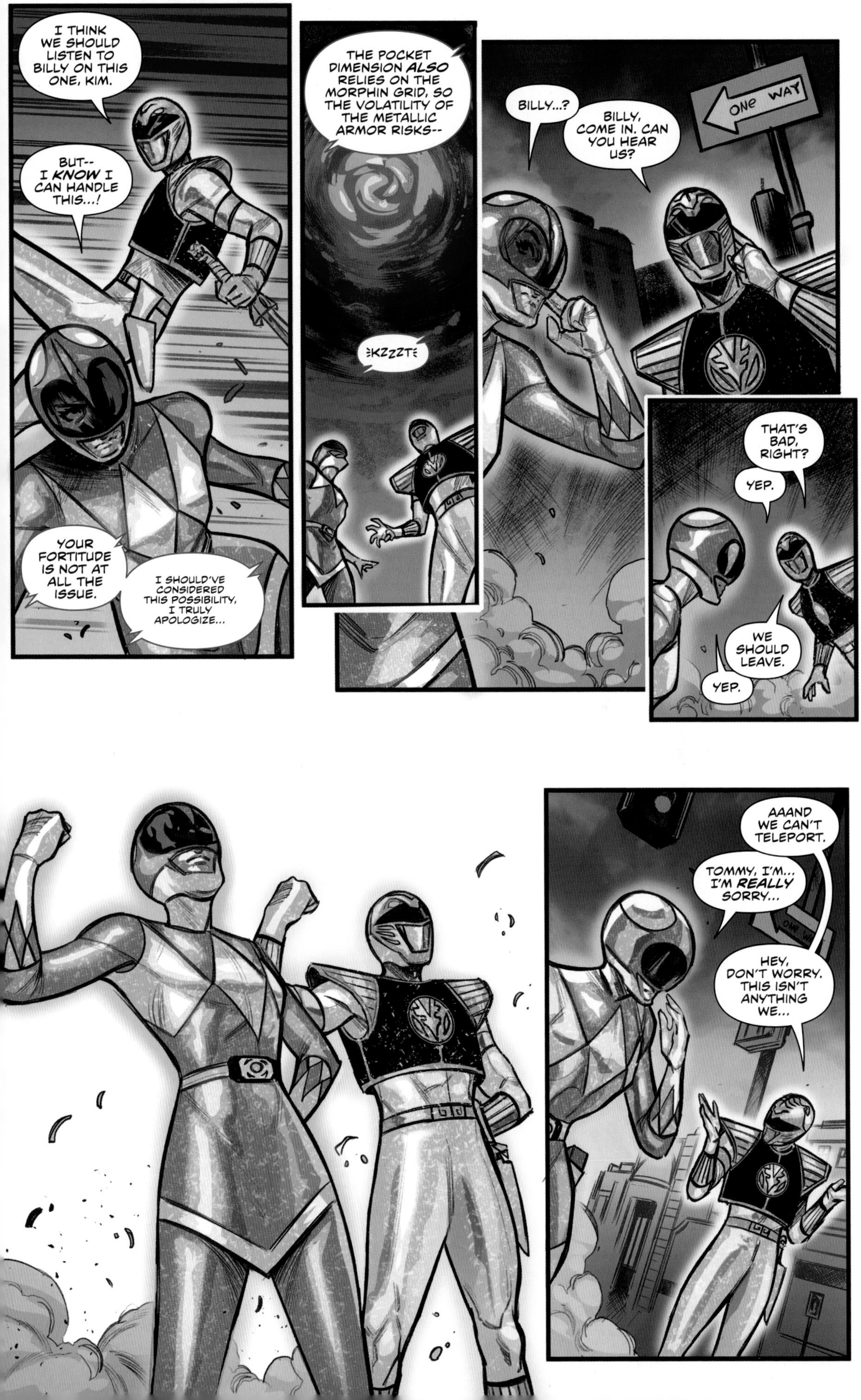
I THINK WE SHOULD LISTEN TO BILLY ON THIS ONE, KIM.
BUT-- I KNOW I CAN HANDLE THIS...!
YOUR FORTITUDE IS NOT AT ALL THE ISSUE.
I SHOULD'VE CONSIDERED THIS POSSIBILITY, I TRULY APOLOGIZE...
THE POCKET DIMENSION ALSO RELIES ON THE MORPHIN GRID, SO THE VOLATILITY OF THE METALLIC ARMOR RISKS--
KZZZT
BILLY...?
BILLY, COME IN. CAN YOU HEAR US?
ONE WAY
THAT'S BAD, RIGHT?
YEP.
WE SHOULD LEAVE.
YEP.
AAAND WE CAN'T TELEPORT.
TOMMY, I'M... I'M REALLY SORRY...
HEY, DON'T WORRY. THIS ISN'T ANYTHING WE...

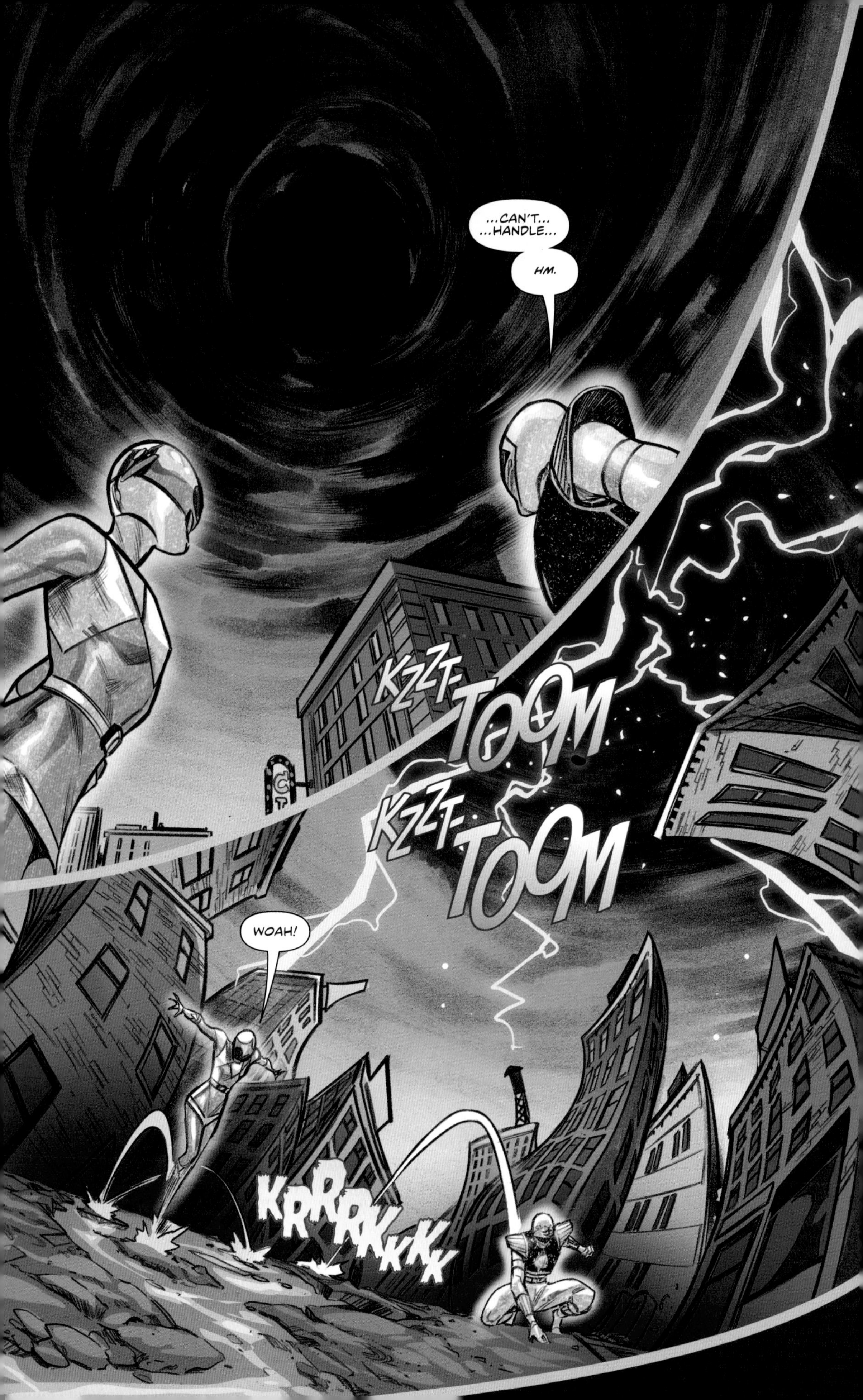
...CAN'T... ...HANDLE...
HM.
KZZT-TOOM
KZZT-TOOM
WOAH!
KRRRKKKK

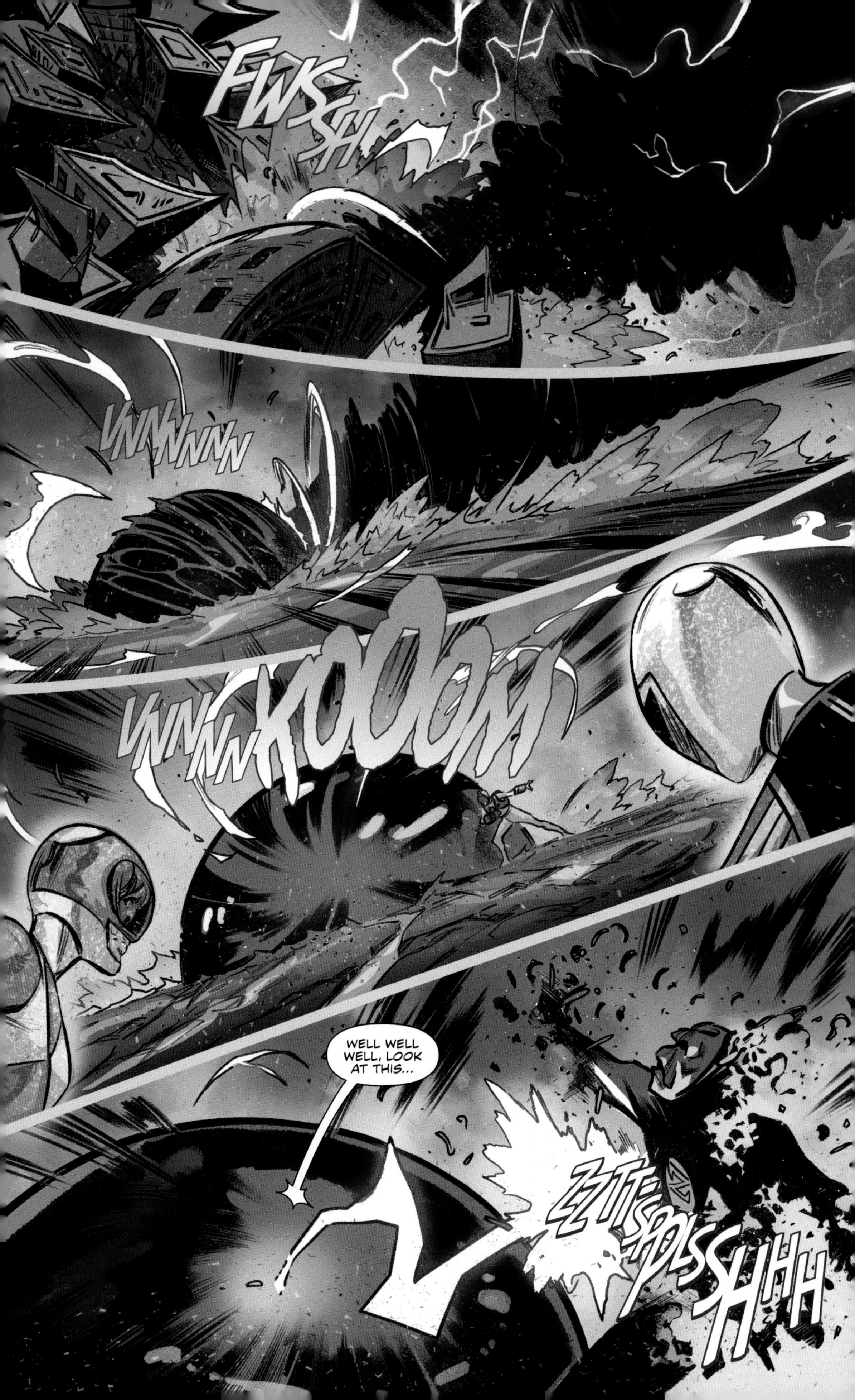
FWSSH
VNNNNNN
VNNNNNKOOOOM
WELL WELL WELL, LOOK AT THIS...
ZZTTSPLSSHHH

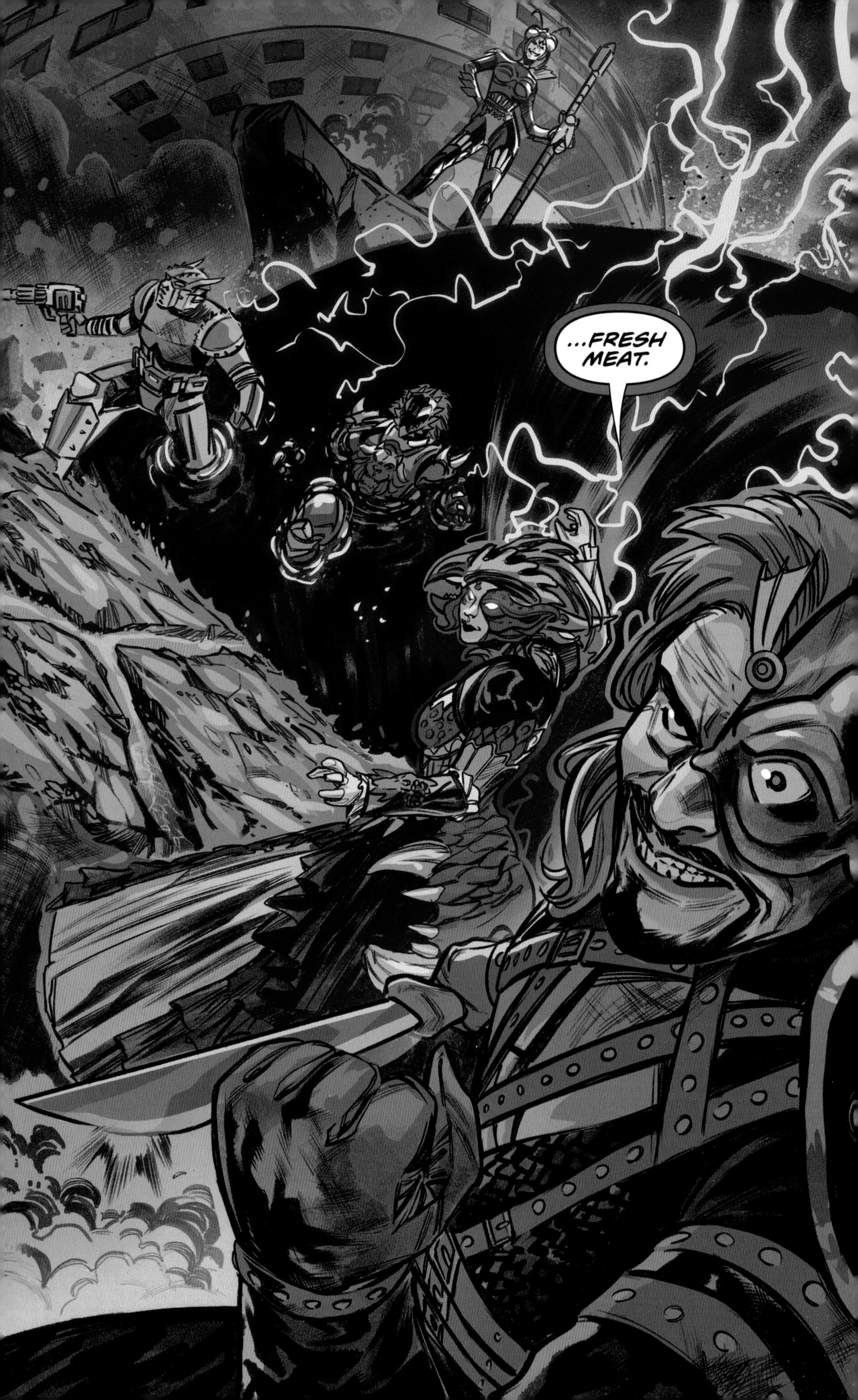
...FRESH MEAT.

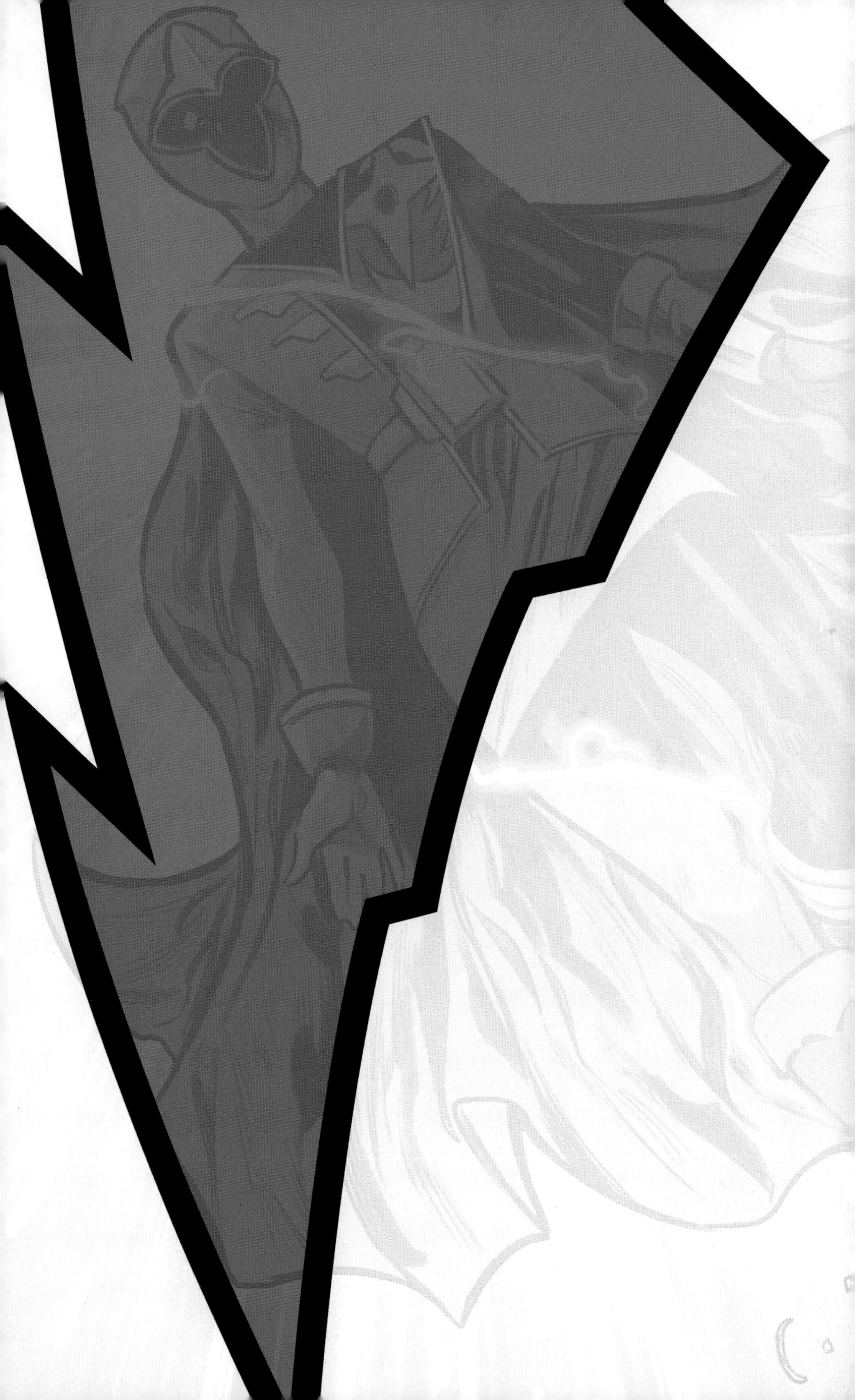

CHAPTER TWENTY-TWO

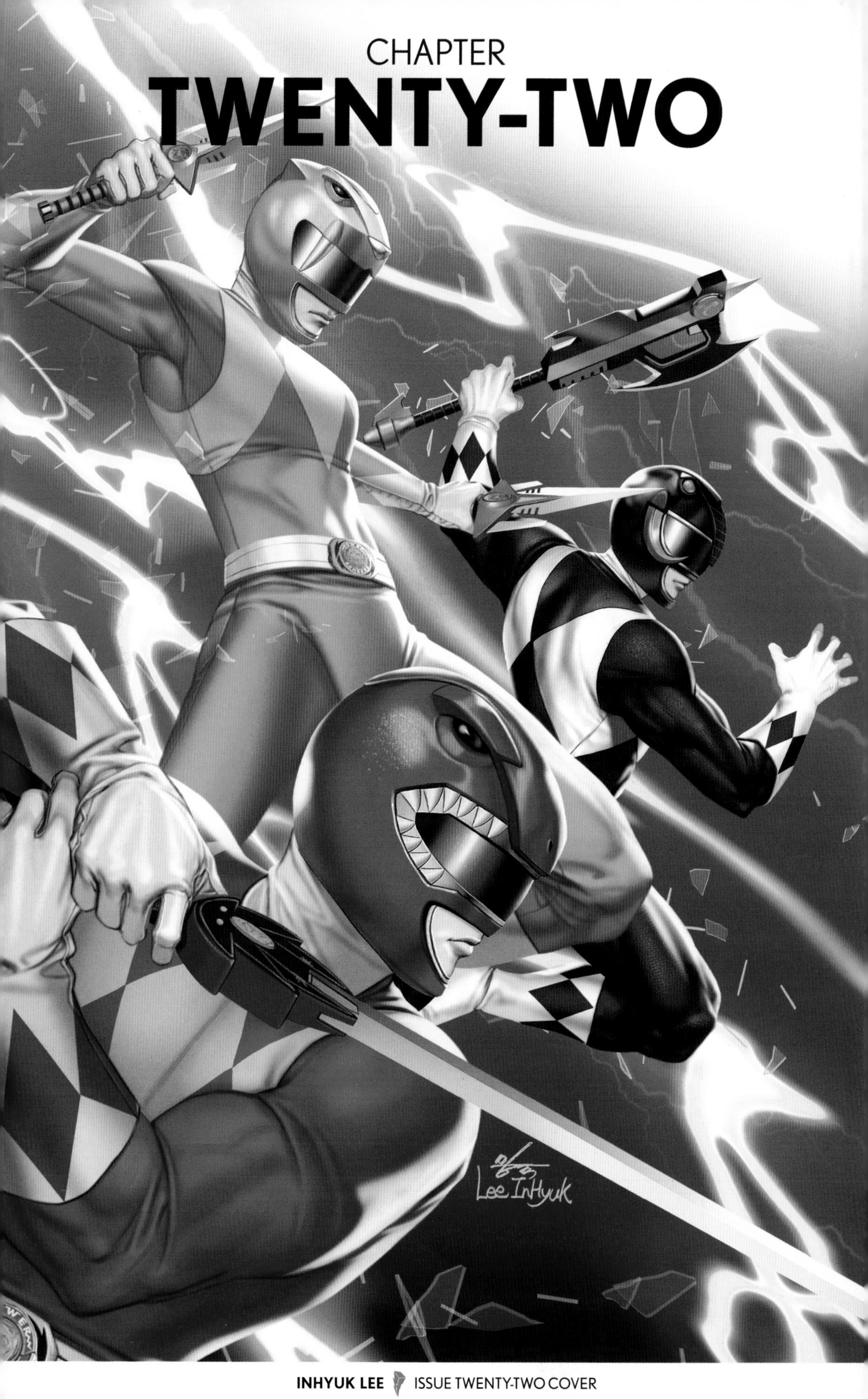
Lee InHyuk

INHYUK LEE | ISSUE TWENTY-TWO COVER

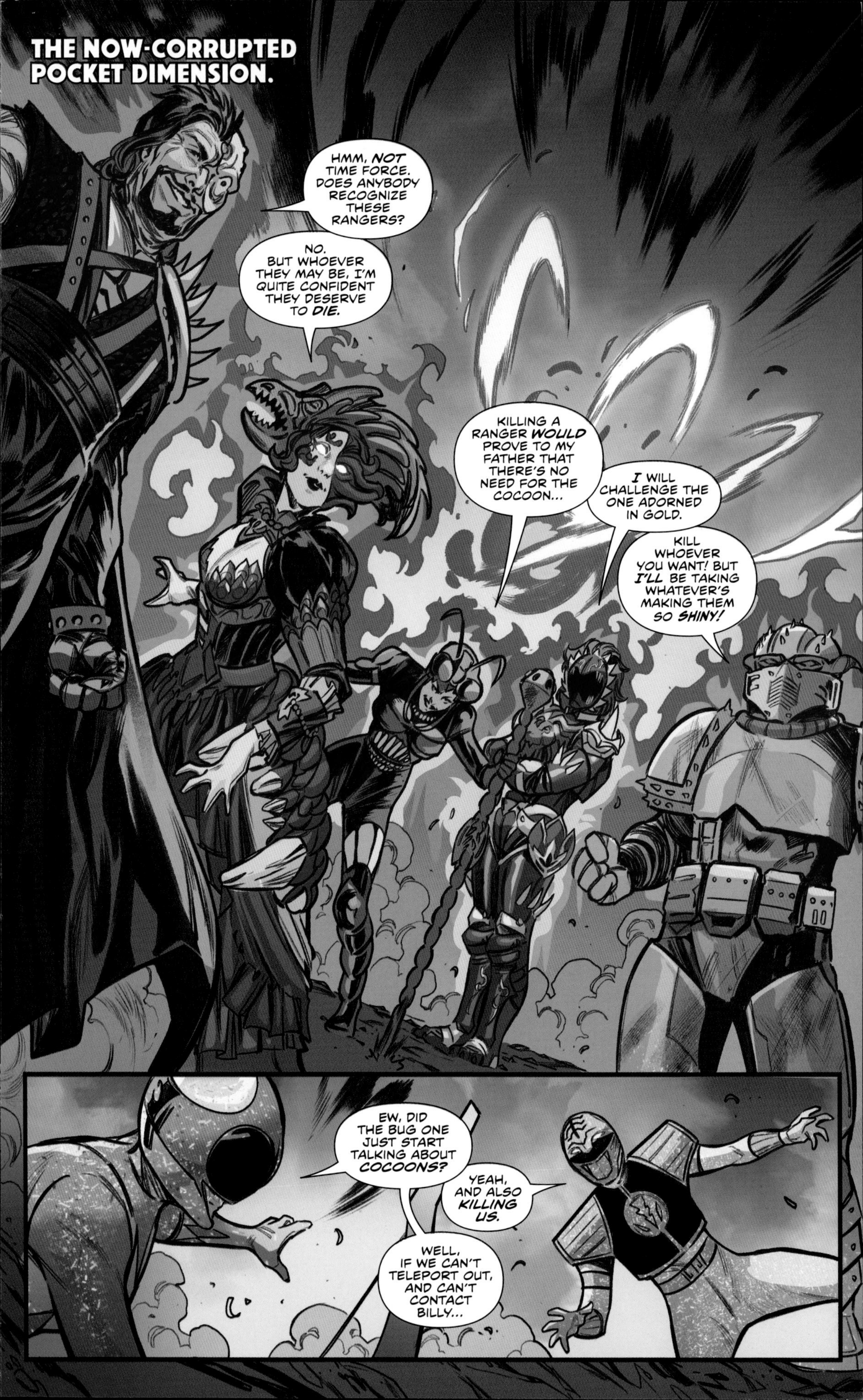
THE NOW-CORRUPTED POCKET DIMENSION.
HMM, NOT TIME FORCE. DOES ANYBODY RECOGNIZE THESE RANGERS?
NO. BUT WHOEVER THEY MAY BE, I'M QUITE CONFIDENT THEY DESERVE TO DIE.
KILLING A RANGER WOULD PROVE TO MY FATHER THAT THERE'S NO NEED FOR THE COCOON...
I WILL CHALLENGE THE ONE ADORNED IN GOLD.
KILL WHOEVER YOU WANT! BUT I'LL BE TAKING WHATEVER'S MAKING THEM SO SHINY!
EW, DID THE BUG ONE JUST START TALKING ABOUT COCOONS?
YEAH, AND ALSO KILLING US.
WELL, IF WE CAN'T TELEPORT OUT, AND CAN'T CONTACT BILLY...

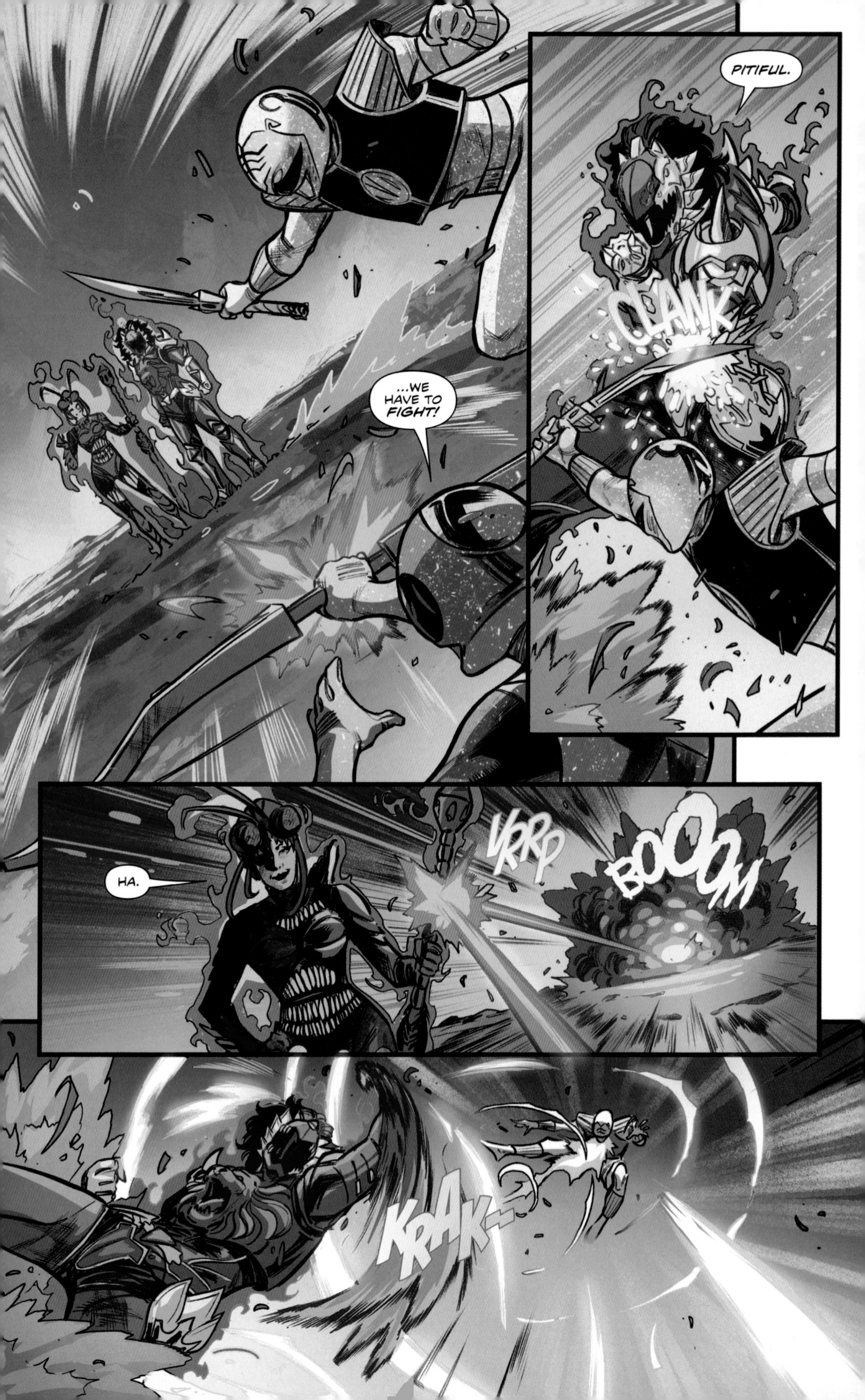
...WE HAVE TO FIGHT!
PITIFUL.
CLANK
HA.
VRRP
BOOOOM
KRAK--

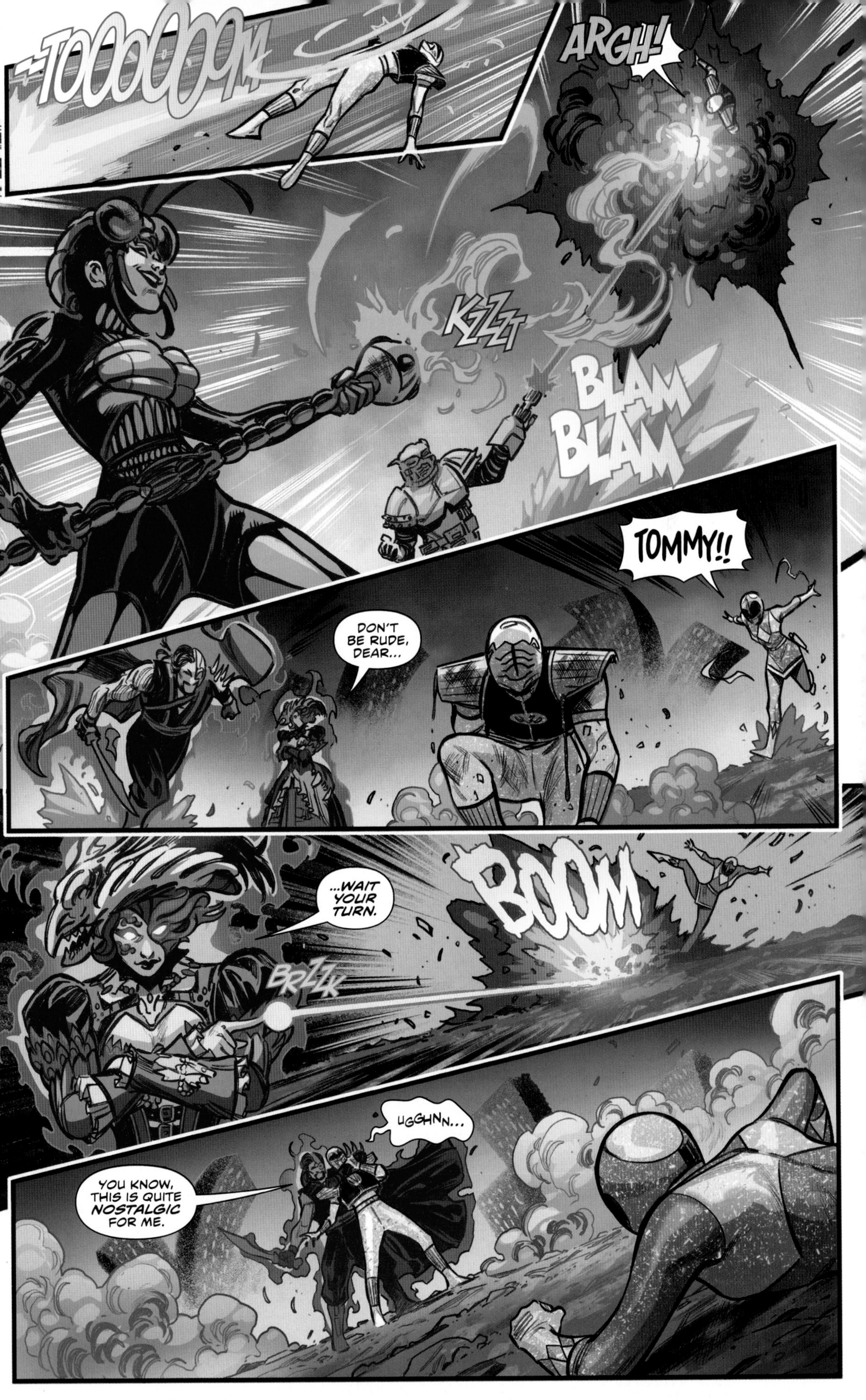
TOOOOOOM
ARGH!
KZZZT
BLAM BLAM
TOMMY!!
DON'T BE RUDE, DEAR...
...WAIT YOUR TURN.
BOOM
BRZZK
UGGHNN...
YOU KNOW, THIS IS QUITE NOSTALGIC FOR ME.

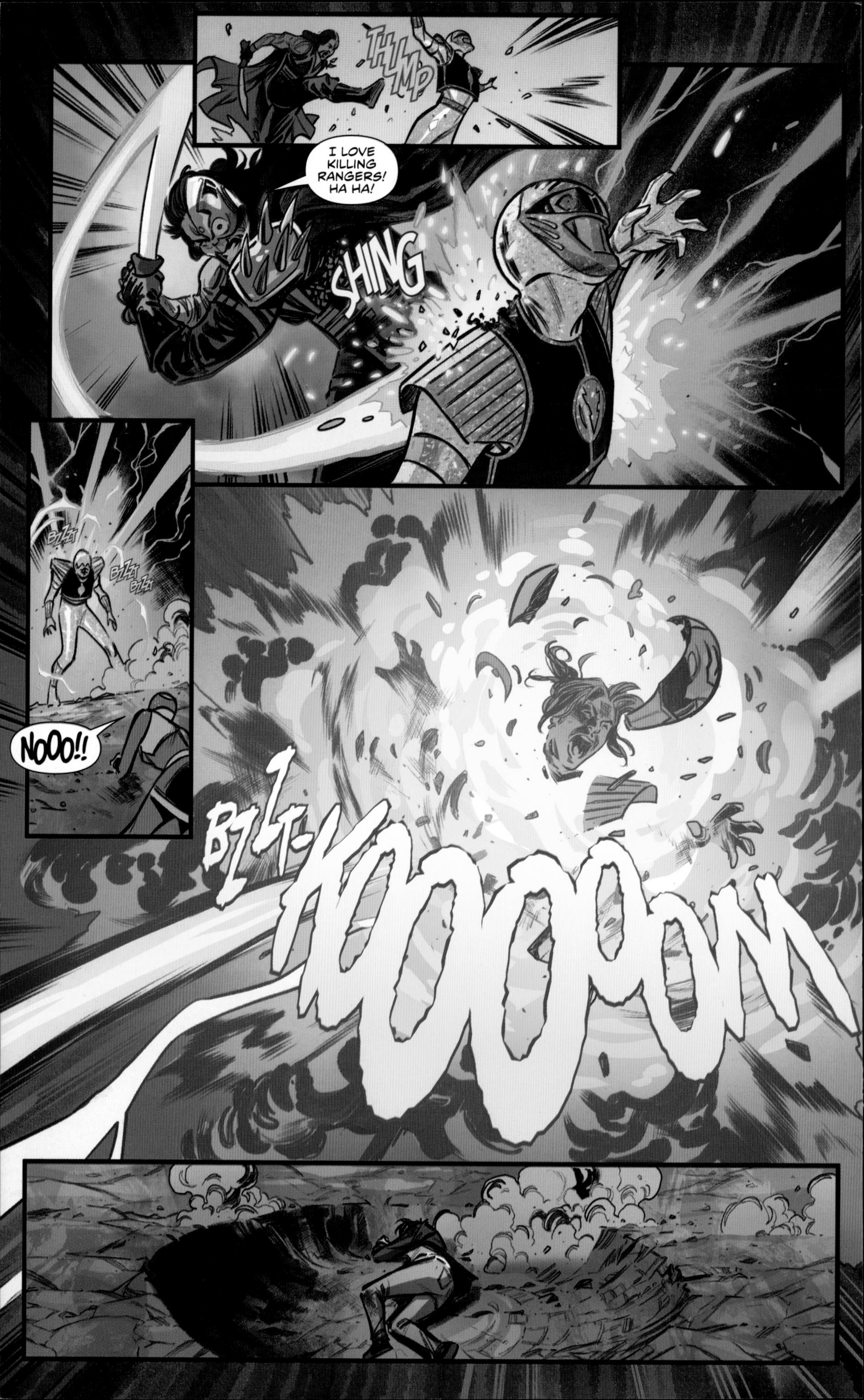
THUMP
I LOVE KILLING RANGERS! HA HA!
SHING
BZZZT
BZZZT BZZZT
NOOO!!
BZZT-KOOOOOM

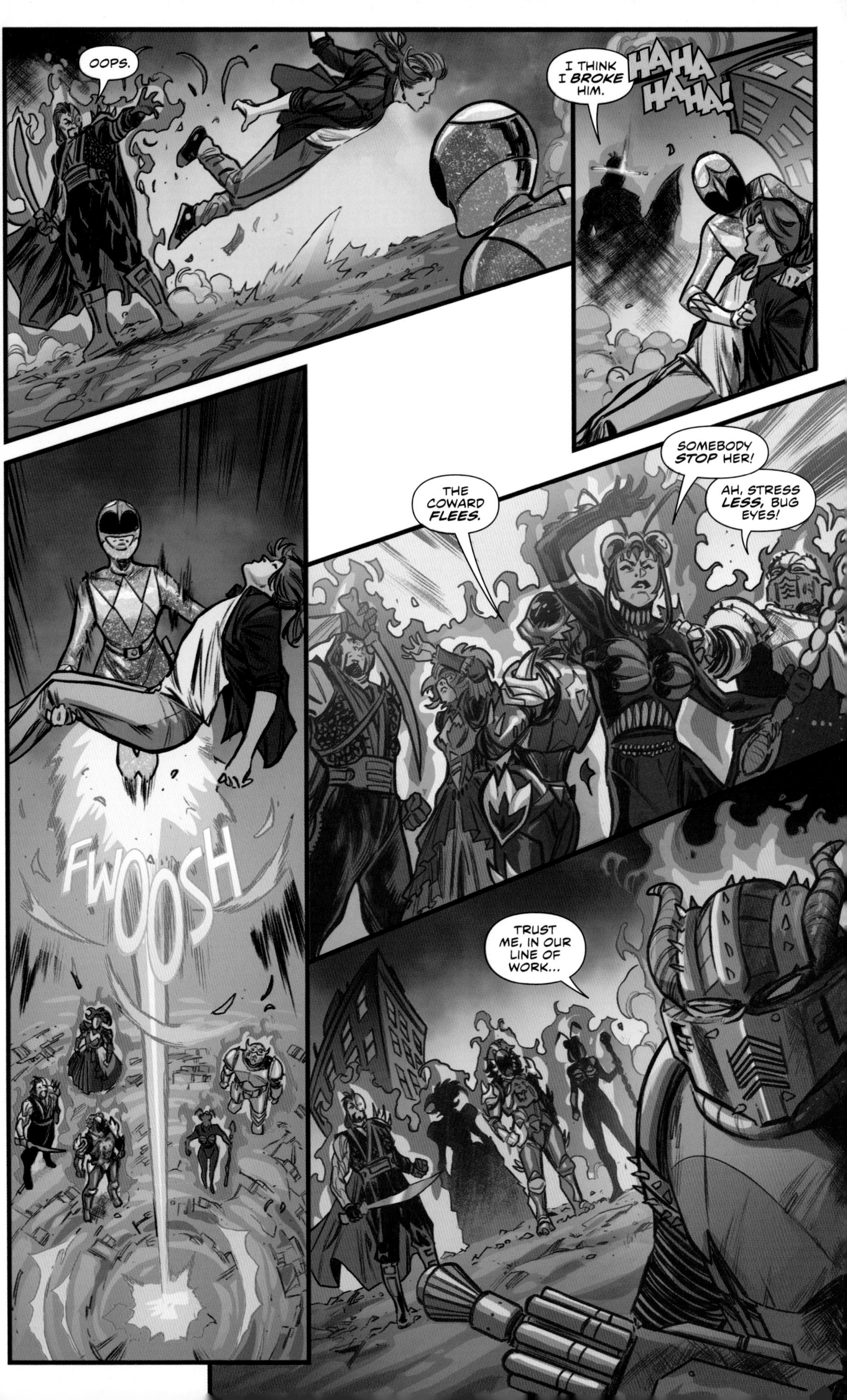
OOPS.
I THINK I BROKE HIM.
HAHA HAHA!
FWOOSH
THE COWARD FLEES.
SOMEBODY STOP HER!
AH, STRESS LESS, BUG EYES!
TRUST ME, IN OUR LINE OF WORK...

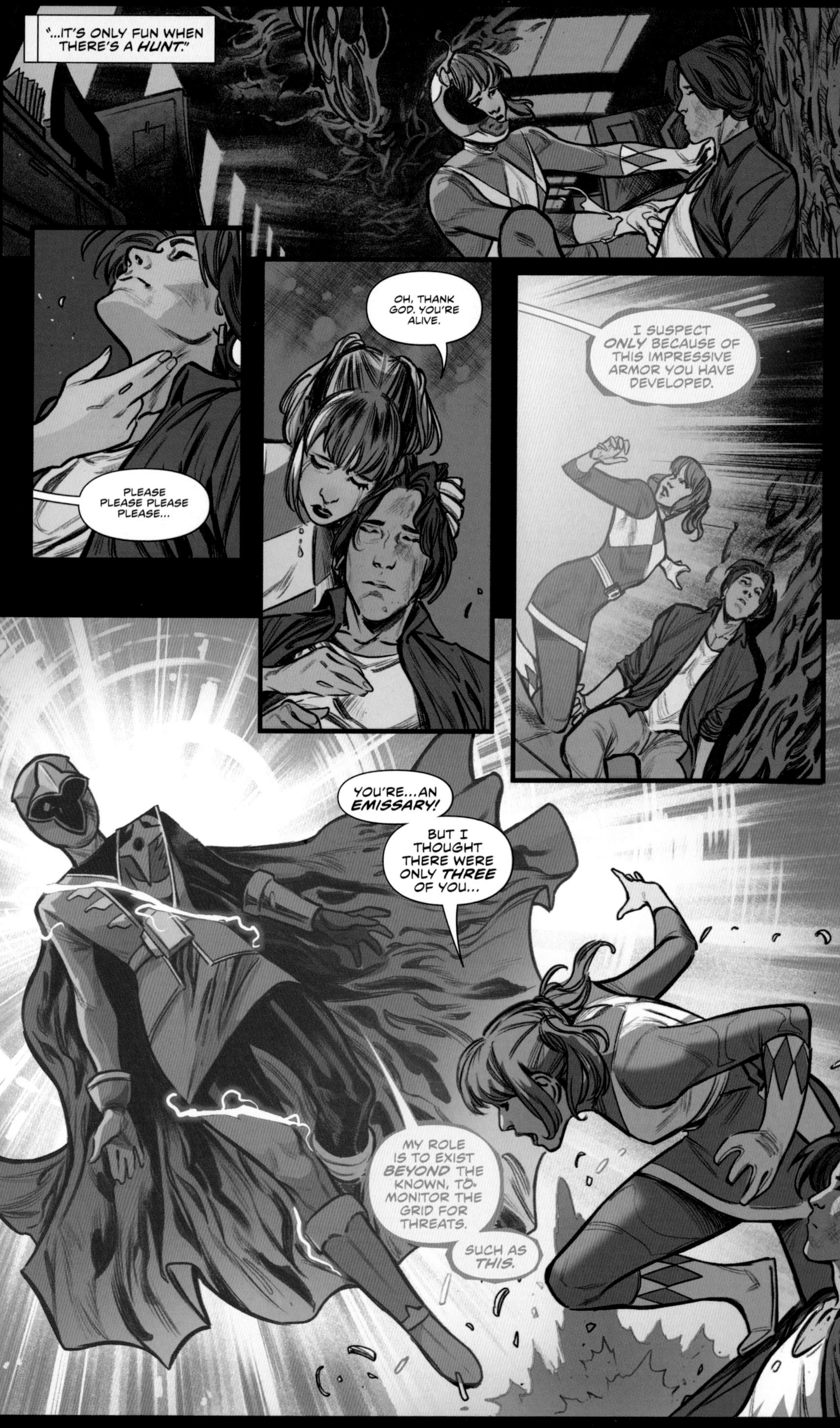
"...IT'S ONLY FUN WHEN THERE'S A HUNT."
PLEASE PLEASE PLEASE PLEASE...
OH, THANK GOD. YOU'RE ALIVE.
I SUSPECT ONLY BECAUSE OF THIS IMPRESSIVE ARMOR YOU HAVE DEVELOPED.
YOU'RE...AN EMISSARY!
BUT I THOUGHT THERE WERE ONLY THREE OF YOU...
MY ROLE IS TO EXIST BEYOND THE KNOWN, TO MONITOR THE GRID FOR THREATS.
SUCH AS THIS.

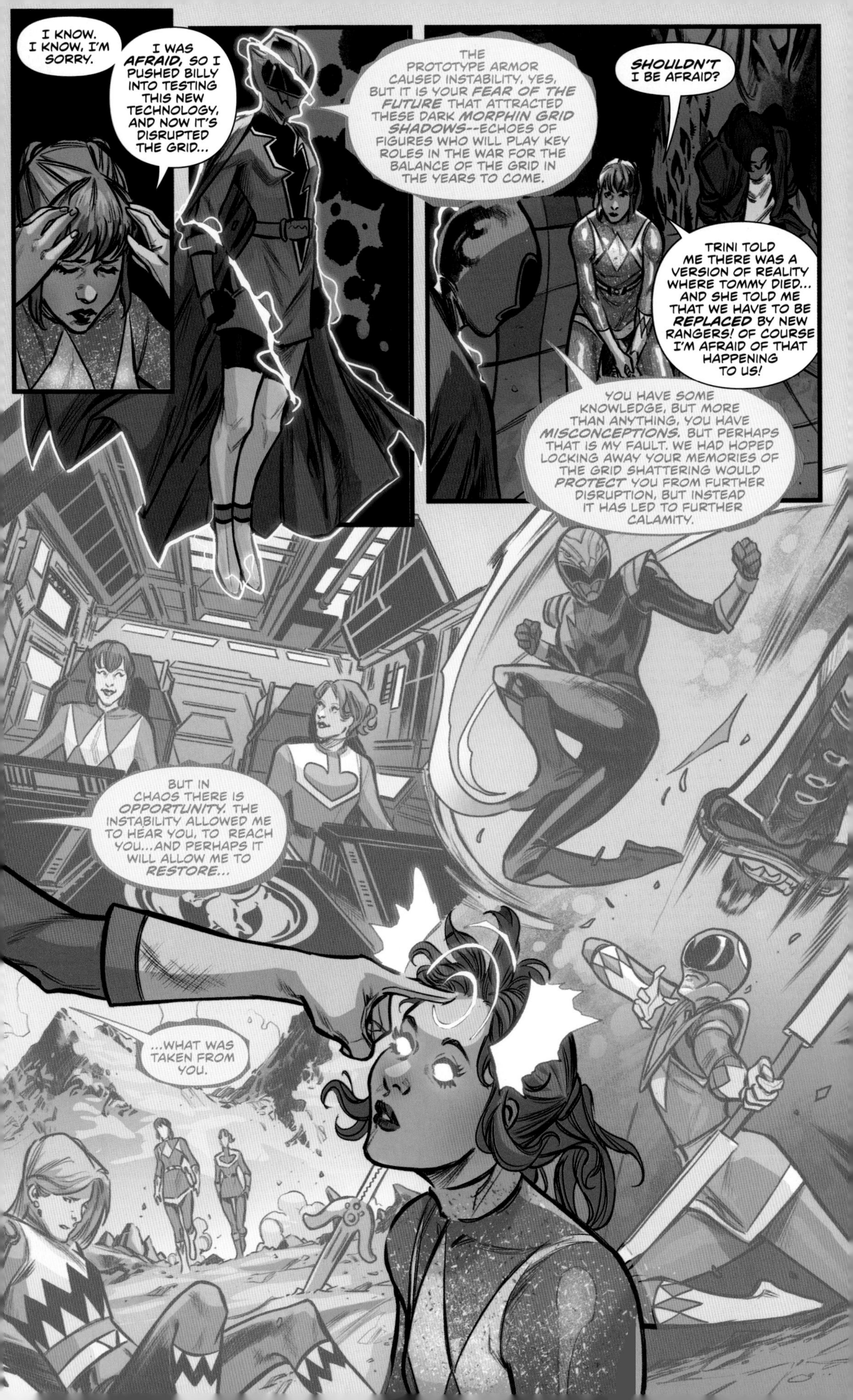
I KNOW. I KNOW, I'M SORRY.
I WAS AFRAID, SO I PUSHED BILLY INTO TESTING THIS NEW TECHNOLOGY, AND NOW IT'S DISRUPTED THE GRID...
THE PROTOTYPE ARMOR CAUSED INSTABILITY, YES, BUT IT IS YOUR FEAR OF THE FUTURE THAT ATTRACTED THESE DARK MORPHIN GRID SHADOWS--ECHOES OF FIGURES WHO WILL PLAY KEY ROLES IN THE WAR FOR THE BALANCE OF THE GRID IN THE YEARS TO COME.
SHOULDN'T I BE AFRAID?
TRINI TOLD ME THERE WAS A VERSION OF REALITY WHERE TOMMY DIED... AND SHE TOLD ME THAT WE HAVE TO BE REPLACED BY NEW RANGERS! OF COURSE I'M AFRAID OF THAT HAPPENING TO US!
YOU HAVE SOME KNOWLEDGE, BUT MORE THAN ANYTHING, YOU HAVE MISCONCEPTIONS. BUT PERHAPS THAT IS MY FAULT. WE HAD HOPED LOCKING AWAY YOUR MEMORIES OF THE GRID SHATTERING WOULD PROTECT YOU FROM FURTHER DISRUPTION, BUT INSTEAD IT HAS LED TO FURTHER CALAMITY.
BUT IN CHAOS THERE IS OPPORTUNITY. THE INSTABILITY ALLOWED ME TO HEAR YOU, TO REACH YOU...AND PERHAPS IT WILL ALLOW ME TO RESTORE...
...WHAT WAS TAKEN FROM YOU.

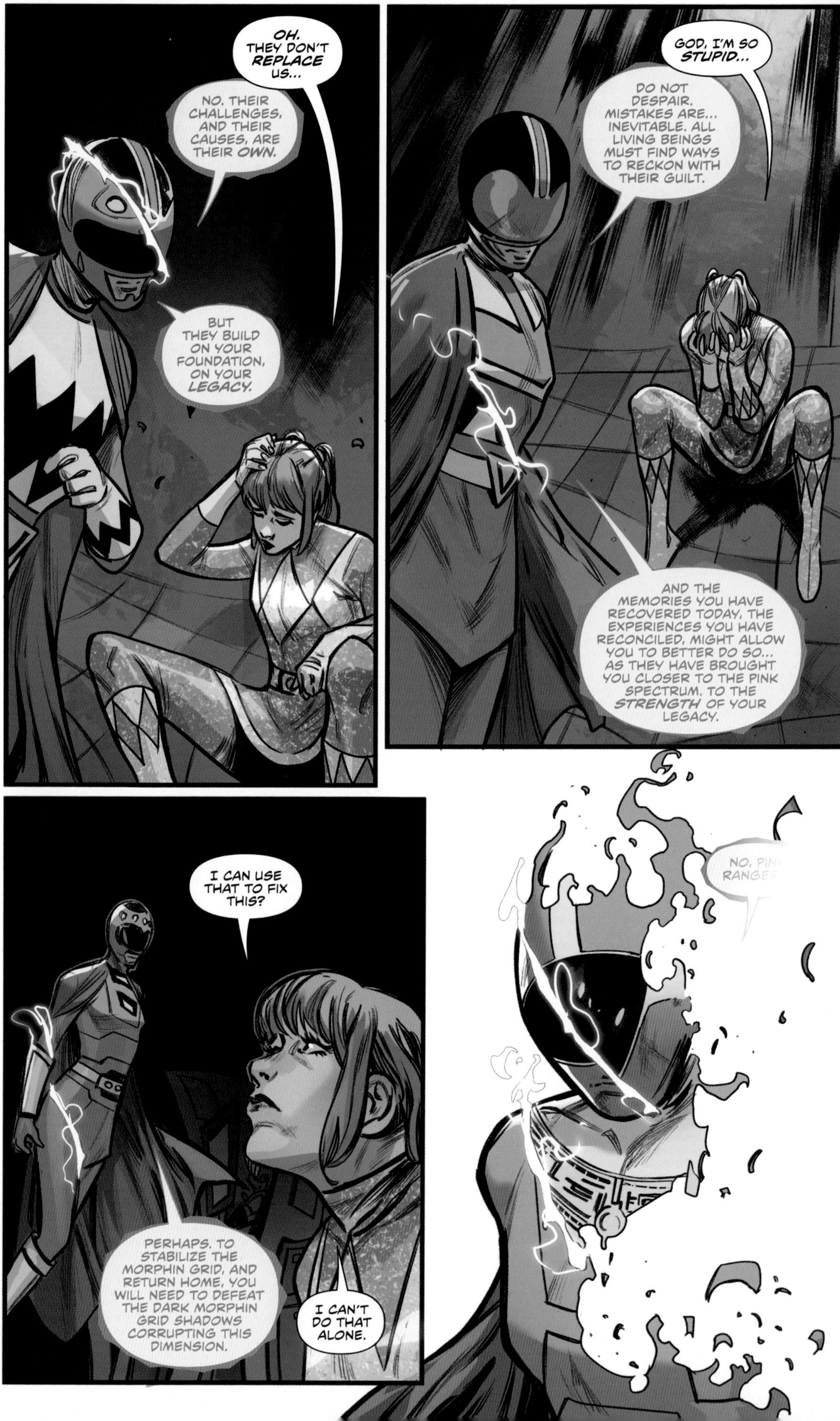
OH. THEY DON'T REPLACE US...
NO. THEIR CHALLENGES, AND THEIR CAUSES, ARE THEIR OWN.
BUT THEY BUILD ON YOUR FOUNDATION, ON YOUR LEGACY.
GOD, I'M SO STUPID...
DO NOT DESPAIR. MISTAKES ARE... INEVITABLE. ALL LIVING BEINGS MUST FIND WAYS TO RECKON WITH THEIR GUILT.
AND THE MEMORIES YOU HAVE RECOVERED TODAY, THE EXPERIENCES YOU HAVE RECONCILED, MIGHT ALLOW YOU TO BETTER DO SO... AS THEY HAVE BROUGHT YOU CLOSER TO THE PINK SPECTRUM. TO THE STRENGTH OF YOUR LEGACY.
I CAN USE THAT TO FIX THIS?
PERHAPS. TO STABILIZE THE MORPHIN GRID, AND RETURN HOME, YOU WILL NEED TO DEFEAT THE DARK MORPHIN GRID SHADOWS CORRUPTING THIS DIMENSION.
I CAN'T DO THAT ALONE.
NO, PIN
RANGE

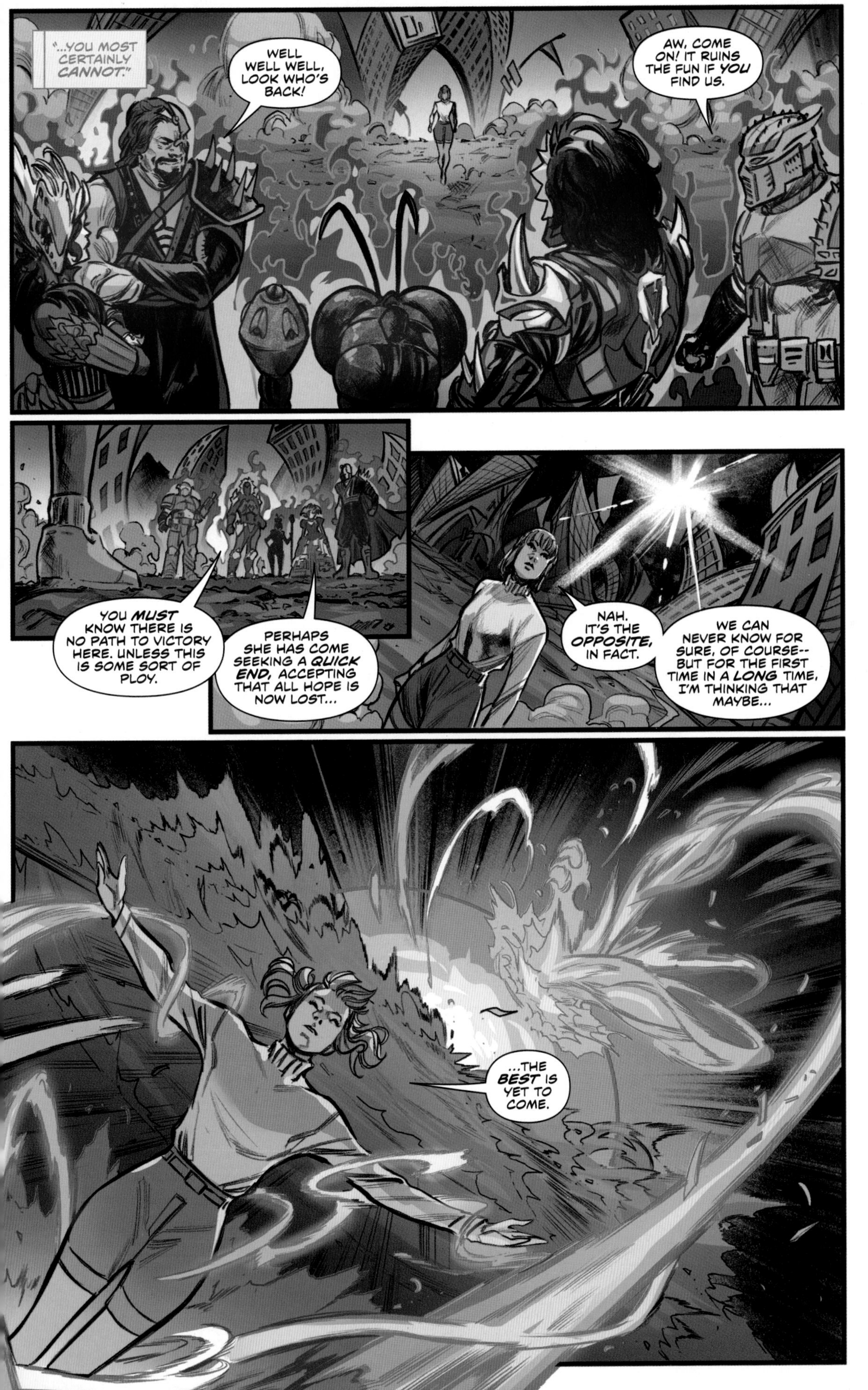
"...YOU MOST CERTAINLY CANNOT."
WELL WELL WELL, LOOK WHO'S BACK!
AW, COME ON! IT RUINS THE FUN IF YOU FIND US.
YOU MUST KNOW THERE IS NO PATH TO VICTORY HERE. UNLESS THIS IS SOME SORT OF PLOY.
PERHAPS SHE HAS COME SEEKING A QUICK END, ACCEPTING THAT ALL HOPE IS NOW LOST...
NAH. IT'S THE OPPOSITE, IN FACT.
WE CAN NEVER KNOW FOR SURE, OF COURSE-- BUT FOR THE FIRST TIME IN A LONG TIME, I'M THINKING THAT MAYBE...
...THE BEST IS YET TO COME.

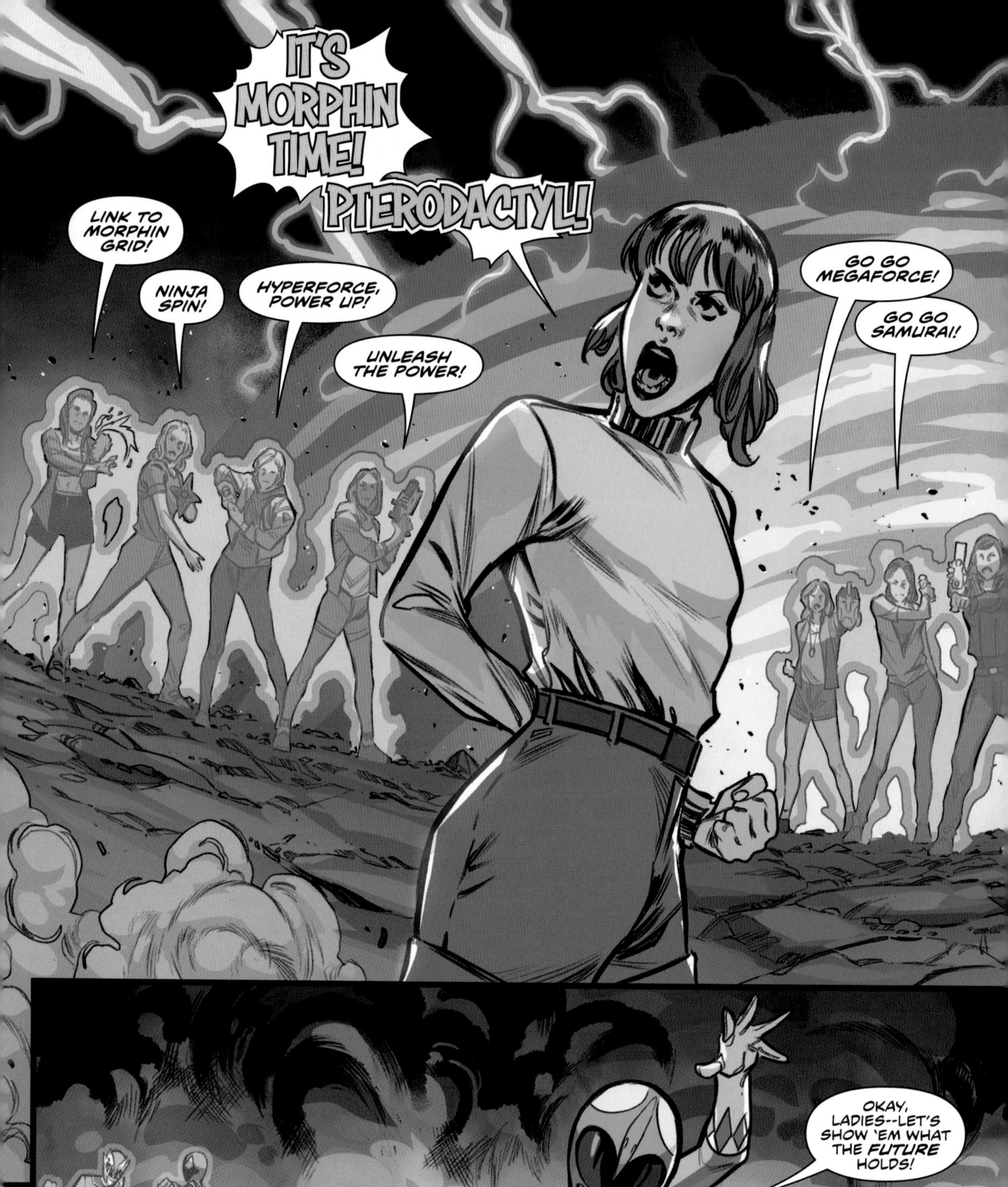
IT'S MORPHIN TIME! PTERODACTYL!
LINK TO MORPHIN GRID!
NINJA SPIN!
HYPERFORCE, POWER UP!
UNLEASH THE POWER!
GO GO MEGAFORCE!
GO GO SAMURAI!

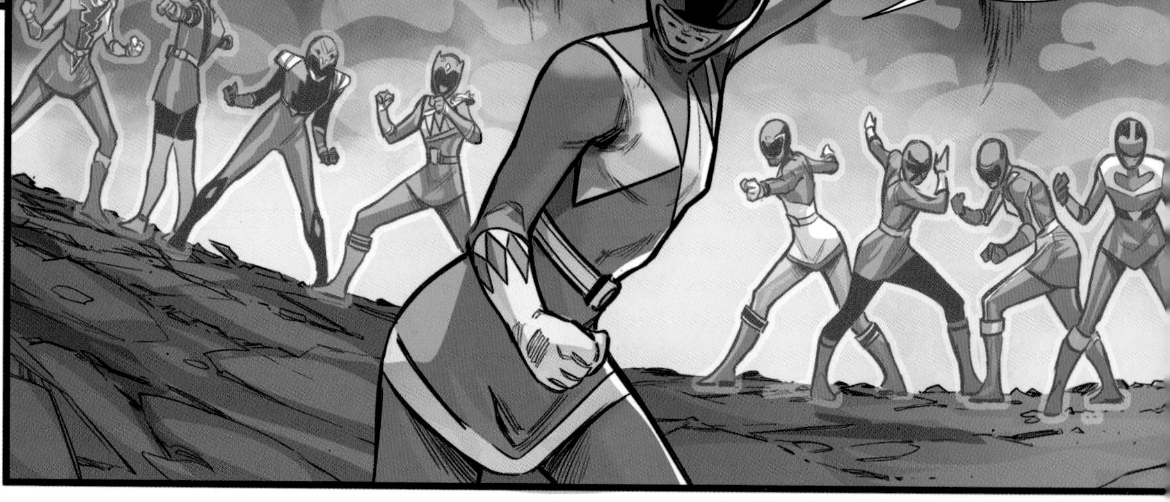
OKAY, LADIES--LET'S SHOW 'EM WHAT THE *FUTURE* HOLDS!

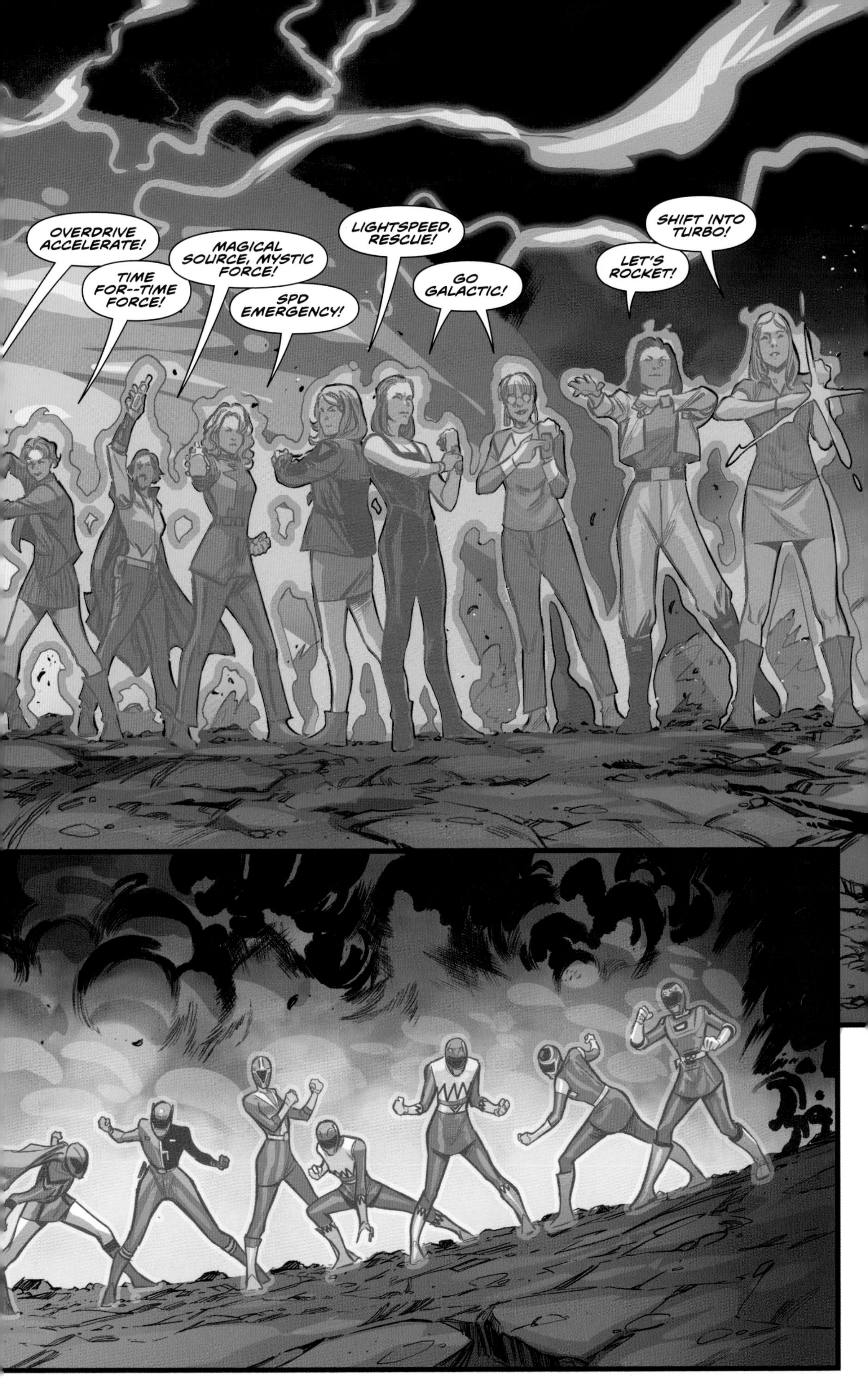
OVERDRIVE ACCELERATE!
TIME FOR--TIME FORCE!
MAGICAL SOURCE, MYSTIC FORCE!
SPD EMERGENCY!
LIGHTSPEED, RESCUE!
GO GALACTIC!
LET'S ROCKET!
SHIFT INTO TURBO!

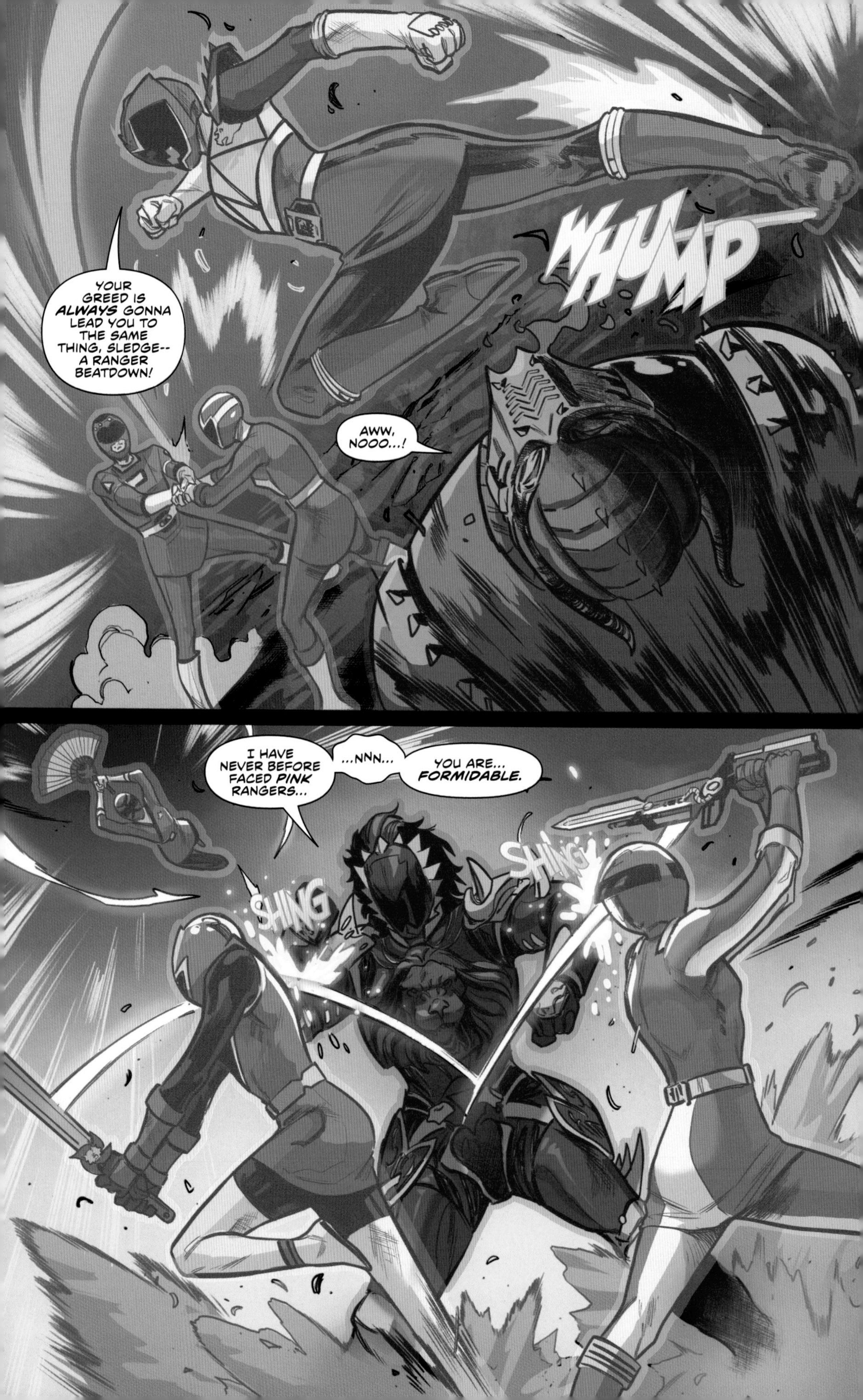
YOUR GREED IS ALWAYS GONNA LEAD YOU TO THE SAME THING, SLEDGE-- A RANGER BEATDOWN!
WHUMP
AWW, NOOO...!
I HAVE NEVER BEFORE FACED PINK RANGERS...
...NNN...
YOU ARE... FORMIDABLE.
SHING
SHING

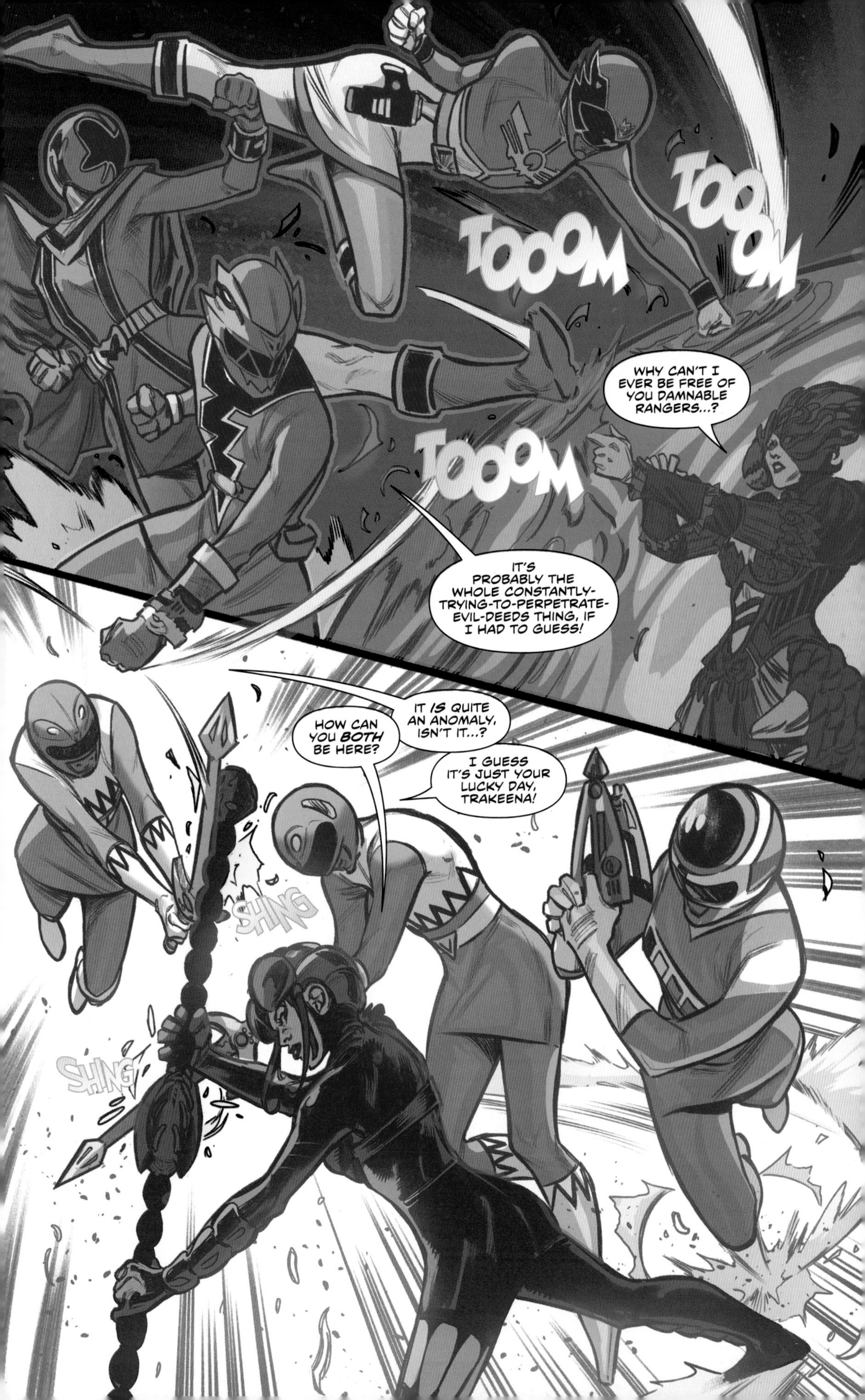
TOOOM
TOOOM
WHY CAN'T I EVER BE FREE OF YOU DAMNABLE RANGERS...?
TOOOM
IT'S PROBABLY THE WHOLE CONSTANTLY-TRYING-TO-PERPETRATE-EVIL-DEEDS THING, IF I HAD TO GUESS!
HOW CAN YOU *BOTH* BE HERE?
IT *IS* QUITE AN ANOMALY, ISN'T IT...?
I GUESS IT'S JUST YOUR LUCKY DAY, TRAKEENA!
SHING
SHING

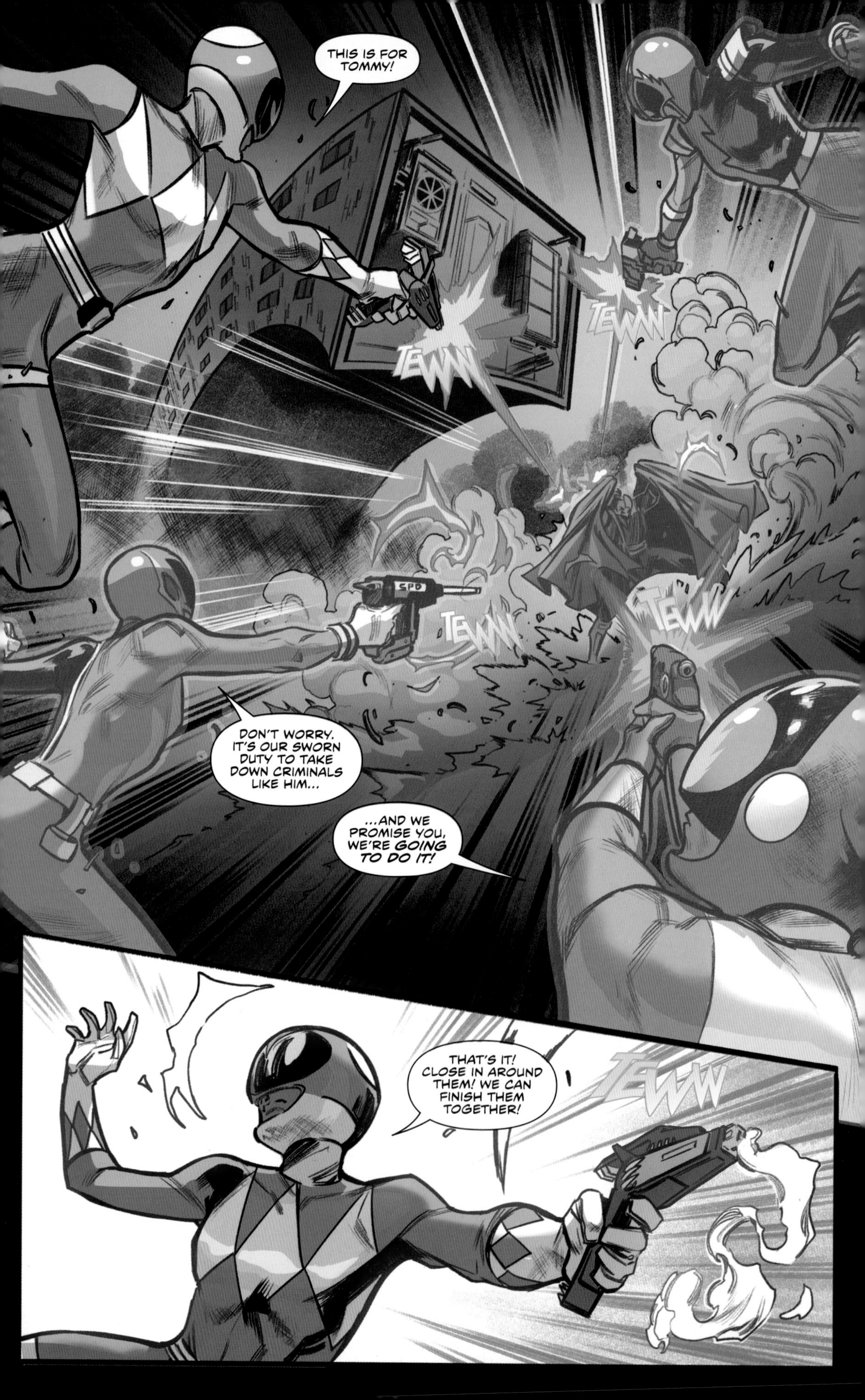
THIS IS FOR TOMMY!
TEWW
TEWW
TEWW
TEWW
DON'T WORRY. IT'S OUR SWORN DUTY TO TAKE DOWN CRIMINALS LIKE HIM...
...AND WE PROMISE YOU, WE'RE *GOING TO DO IT!*
TEWW
THAT'S IT! CLOSE IN AROUND THEM! WE CAN FINISH THEM TOGETHER!

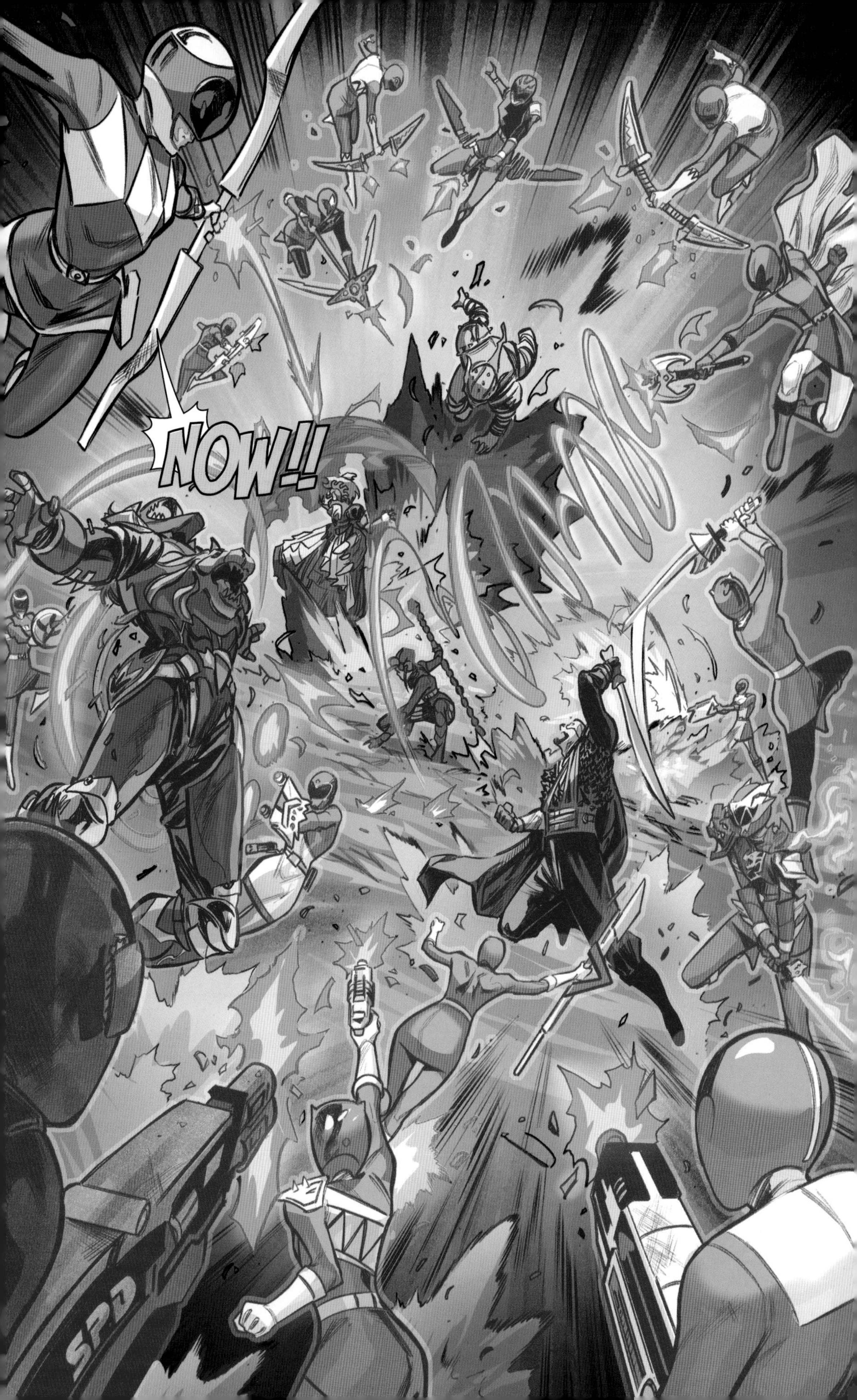
NOW!!
SPD

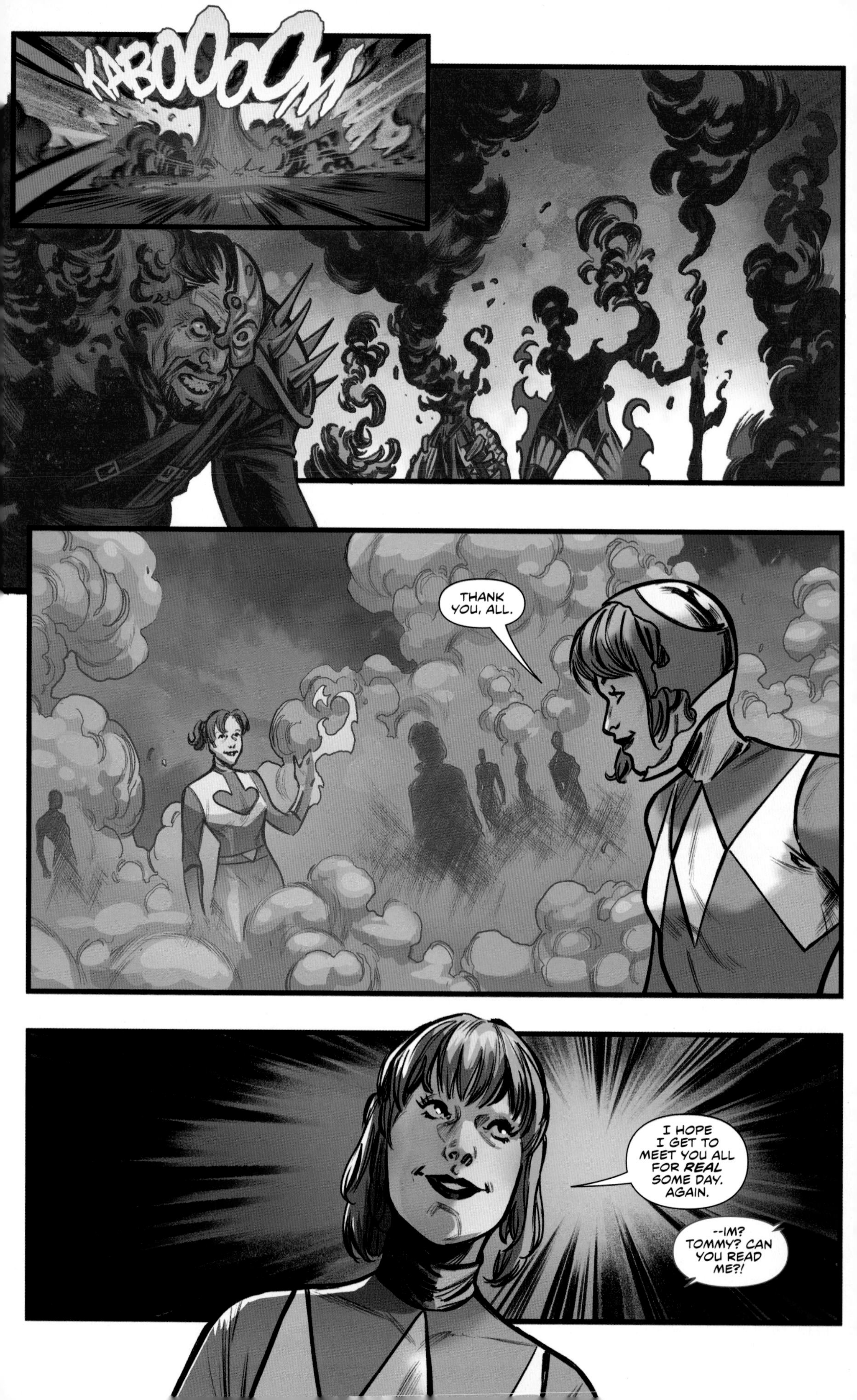
KABOOOOM
THANK YOU, ALL.
I HOPE I GET TO MEET YOU ALL FOR REAL SOME DAY. AGAIN.
--IM? TOMMY? CAN YOU READ ME?!

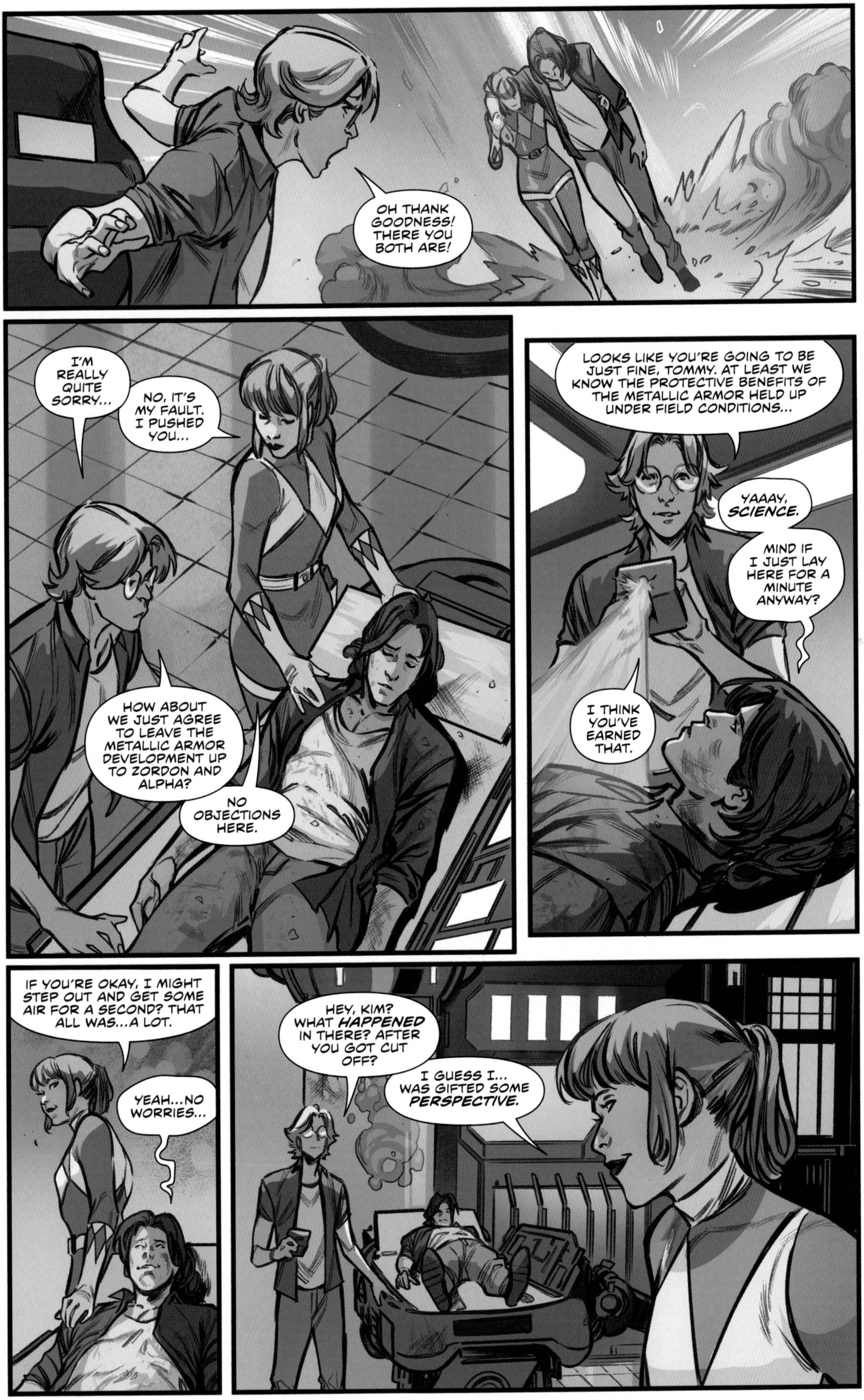
OH THANK GOODNESS! THERE YOU BOTH ARE!
I'M REALLY QUITE SORRY...
NO, IT'S MY FAULT. I PUSHED YOU...
HOW ABOUT WE JUST AGREE TO LEAVE THE METALLIC ARMOR DEVELOPMENT UP TO ZORDON AND ALPHA?
NO OBJECTIONS HERE.
LOOKS LIKE YOU'RE GOING TO BE JUST FINE, TOMMY. AT LEAST WE KNOW THE PROTECTIVE BENEFITS OF THE METALLIC ARMOR HELD UP UNDER FIELD CONDITIONS...
YAAAY, SCIENCE.
MIND IF I JUST LAY HERE FOR A MINUTE ANYWAY?
I THINK YOU'VE EARNED THAT.
IF YOU'RE OKAY, I MIGHT STEP OUT AND GET SOME AIR FOR A SECOND? THAT ALL WAS...A LOT.
YEAH...NO WORRIES...
HEY, KIM? WHAT HAPPENED IN THERE? AFTER YOU GOT CUT OFF?
I GUESS I... WAS GIFTED SOME PERSPECTIVE.

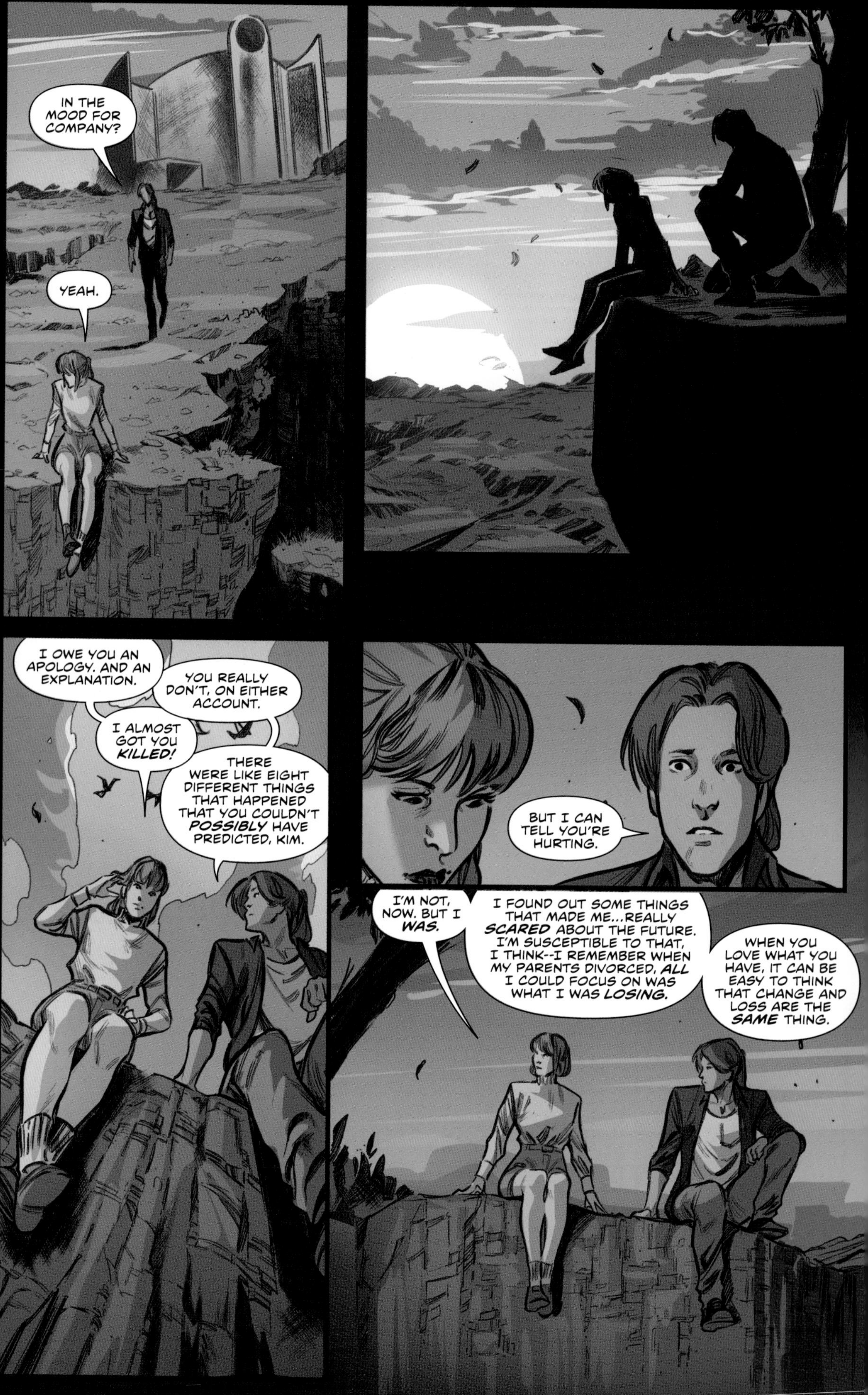
IN THE MOOD FOR COMPANY?
YEAH.
I OWE YOU AN APOLOGY. AND AN EXPLANATION.
YOU REALLY DON'T, ON EITHER ACCOUNT.
I ALMOST GOT YOU KILLED!
THERE WERE LIKE EIGHT DIFFERENT THINGS THAT HAPPENED THAT YOU COULDN'T POSSIBLY HAVE PREDICTED, KIM.
BUT I CAN TELL YOU'RE HURTING.
I'M NOT, NOW. BUT I WAS.
I FOUND OUT SOME THINGS THAT MADE ME...REALLY SCARED ABOUT THE FUTURE. I'M SUSCEPTIBLE TO THAT, I THINK--I REMEMBER WHEN MY PARENTS DIVORCED, ALL I COULD FOCUS ON WAS WHAT I WAS LOSING.
WHEN YOU LOVE WHAT YOU HAVE, IT CAN BE EASY TO THINK THAT CHANGE AND LOSS ARE THE SAME THING.

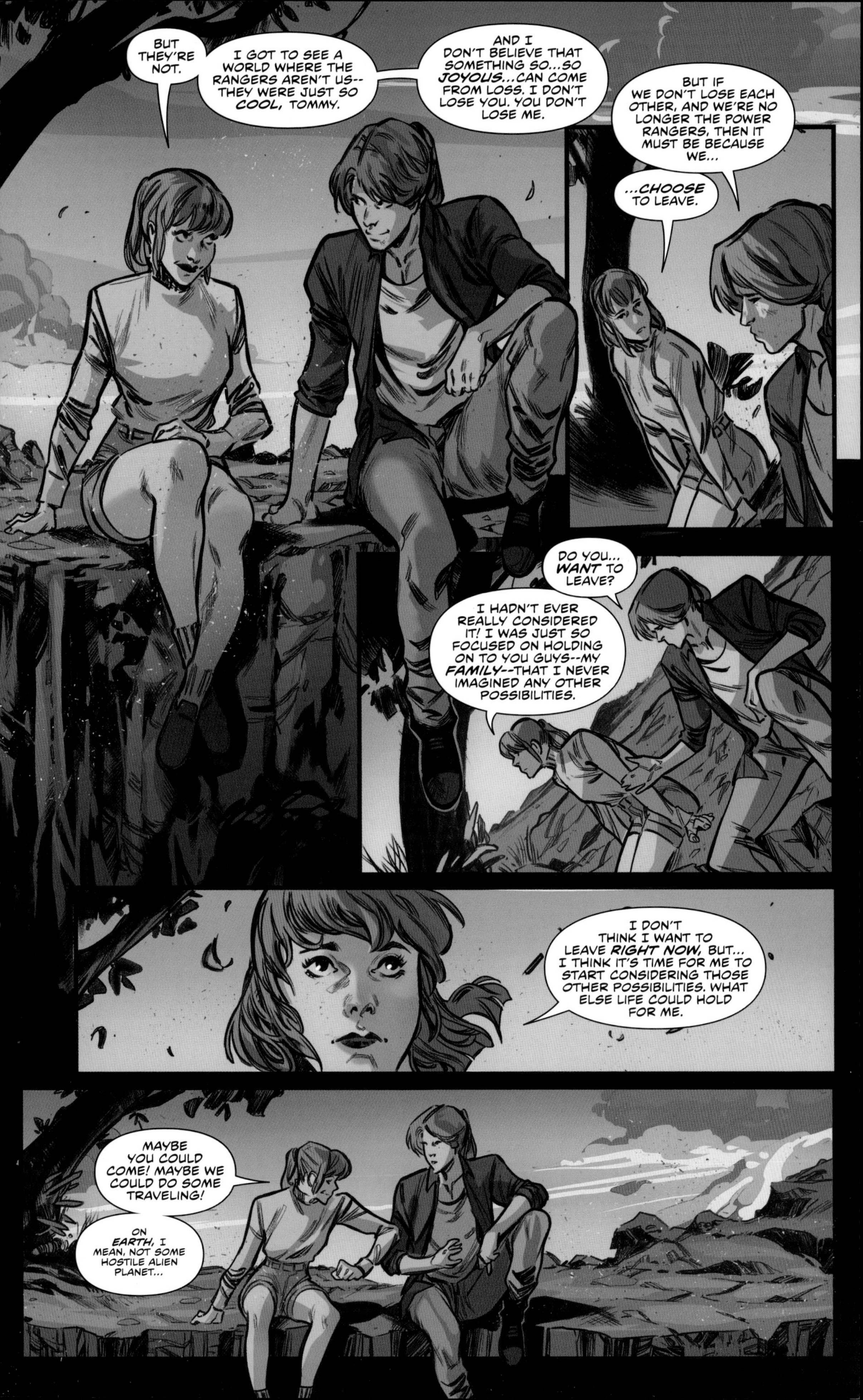

BUT THEY'RE NOT.
I GOT TO SEE A WORLD WHERE THE RANGERS AREN'T US-- THEY WERE JUST SO COOL, TOMMY.
AND I DON'T BELIEVE THAT SOMETHING SO...SO JOYOUS...CAN COME FROM LOSS. I DON'T LOSE YOU. YOU DON'T LOSE ME.
BUT IF WE DON'T LOSE EACH OTHER, AND WE'RE NO LONGER THE POWER RANGERS, THEN IT MUST BE BECAUSE WE...
...CHOOSE TO LEAVE.
DO YOU... WANT TO LEAVE?
I HADN'T EVER REALLY CONSIDERED IT! I WAS JUST SO FOCUSED ON HOLDING ON TO YOU GUYS--MY FAMILY--THAT I NEVER IMAGINED ANY OTHER POSSIBILITIES.
I DON'T THINK I WANT TO LEAVE RIGHT NOW, BUT... I THINK IT'S TIME FOR ME TO START CONSIDERING THOSE OTHER POSSIBILITIES. WHAT ELSE LIFE COULD HOLD FOR ME.
MAYBE YOU COULD COME! MAYBE WE COULD DO SOME TRAVELING!
ON EARTH, I MEAN, NOT SOME HOSTILE ALIEN PLANET...

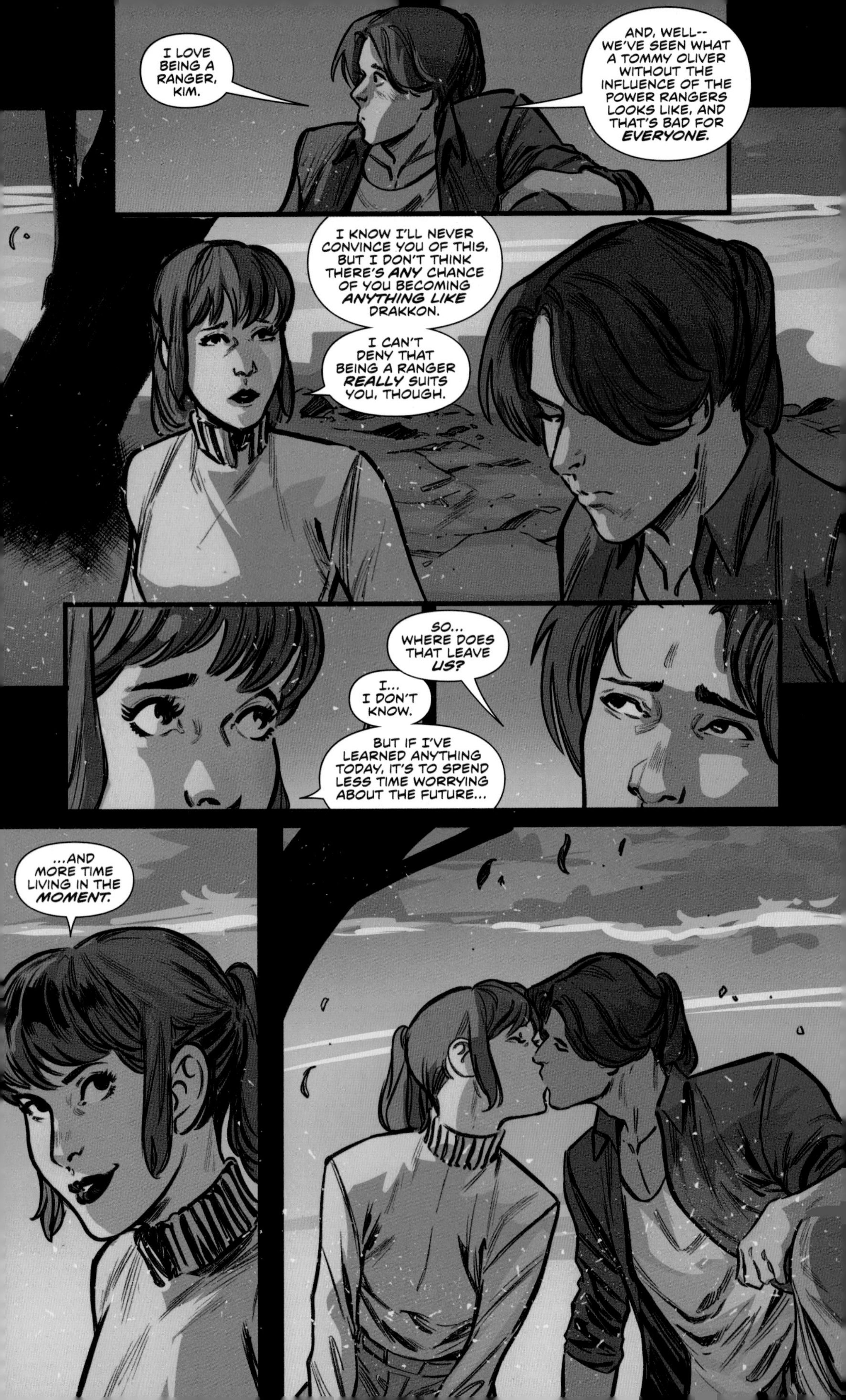
I LOVE BEING A RANGER, KIM.
AND, WELL-- WE'VE SEEN WHAT A TOMMY OLIVER WITHOUT THE INFLUENCE OF THE POWER RANGERS LOOKS LIKE, AND THAT'S BAD FOR *EVERYONE.*
I KNOW I'LL NEVER CONVINCE YOU OF THIS, BUT I DON'T THINK THERE'S *ANY* CHANCE OF YOU BECOMING *ANYTHING LIKE* DRAKKON.
I CAN'T DENY THAT BEING A RANGER *REALLY* SUITS YOU, THOUGH.
SO... WHERE DOES THAT LEAVE *US?*
I... I DON'T KNOW.
BUT IF I'VE LEARNED ANYTHING TODAY, IT'S TO SPEND LESS TIME WORRYING ABOUT THE FUTURE...
...AND MORE TIME LIVING IN THE *MOMENT.*

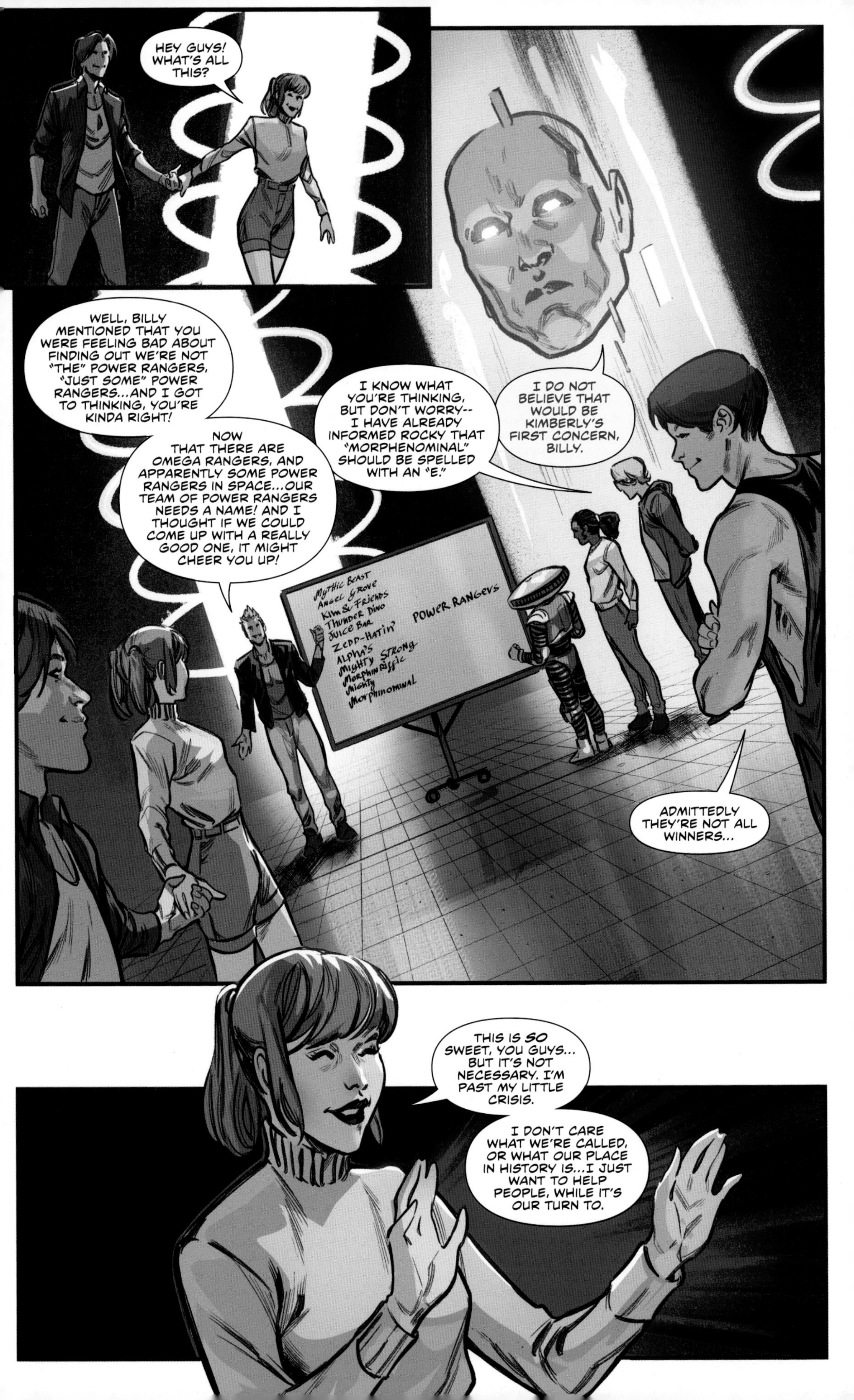
HEY GUYS! WHAT'S ALL THIS?
WELL, BILLY MENTIONED THAT YOU WERE FEELING BAD ABOUT FINDING OUT WE'RE NOT "THE" POWER RANGERS, "JUST SOME" POWER RANGERS...AND I GOT TO THINKING, YOU'RE KINDA RIGHT!
NOW THAT THERE ARE OMEGA RANGERS, AND APPARENTLY SOME POWER RANGERS IN SPACE...OUR TEAM OF POWER RANGERS NEEDS A NAME! AND I THOUGHT IF WE COULD COME UP WITH A REALLY GOOD ONE, IT MIGHT CHEER YOU UP!
I KNOW WHAT YOU'RE THINKING, BUT DON'T WORRY-- I HAVE ALREADY INFORMED ROCKY THAT "MORPHENOMINAL" SHOULD BE SPELLED WITH AN "E."
I DO NOT BELIEVE THAT WOULD BE KIMBERLY'S FIRST CONCERN, BILLY.
Mythic Beast
Angel Grove
Kim & Friends
Thunder Dino
Juice Bar
Zedd-Hatin'
Alpha's
Mighty Strong
Morphin Riffic
Mighty
Morphinominal
POWER RANGERS
ADMITTEDLY THEY'RE NOT ALL WINNERS...
THIS IS SO SWEET, YOU GUYS... BUT IT'S NOT NECESSARY. I'M PAST MY LITTLE CRISIS.
I DON'T CARE WHAT WE'RE CALLED, OR WHAT OUR PLACE IN HISTORY IS...I JUST WANT TO HELP PEOPLE, WHILE IT'S OUR TURN TO.

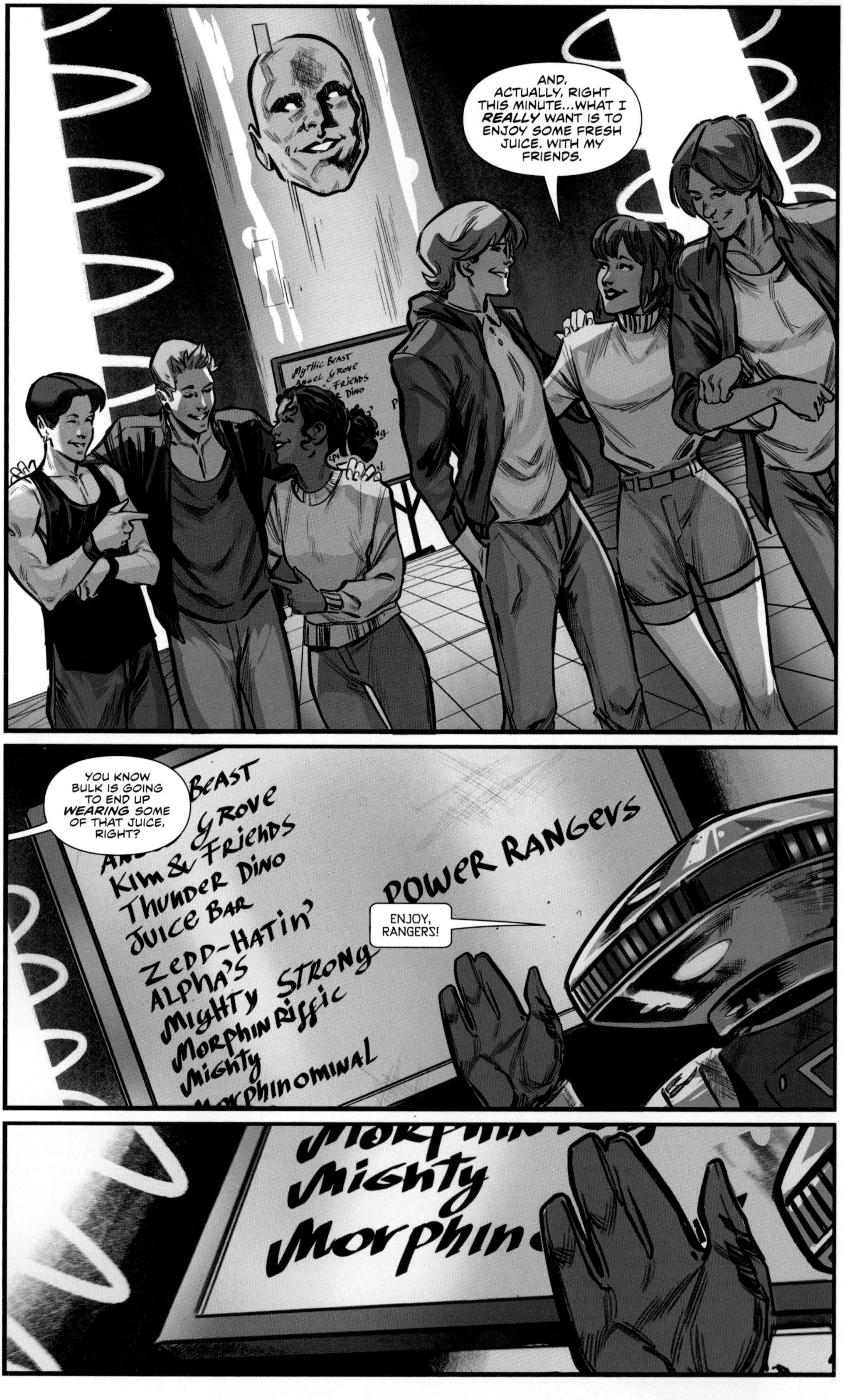
AND, ACTUALLY, RIGHT THIS MINUTE...WHAT I *REALLY* WANT IS TO ENJOY SOME FRESH JUICE. WITH MY FRIENDS.
YOU KNOW BULK IS GOING TO END UP *WEARING* SOME OF THAT JUICE, RIGHT?
Beast
Grove
Kim & Friends
Thunder Dino
Juice Bar
Zedd-Hatin'
Alpha's
Mighty Strong
Morphinriffic
Mighty
Morphinominal
POWER RANGers
ENJOY, RANGERS!
Mighty

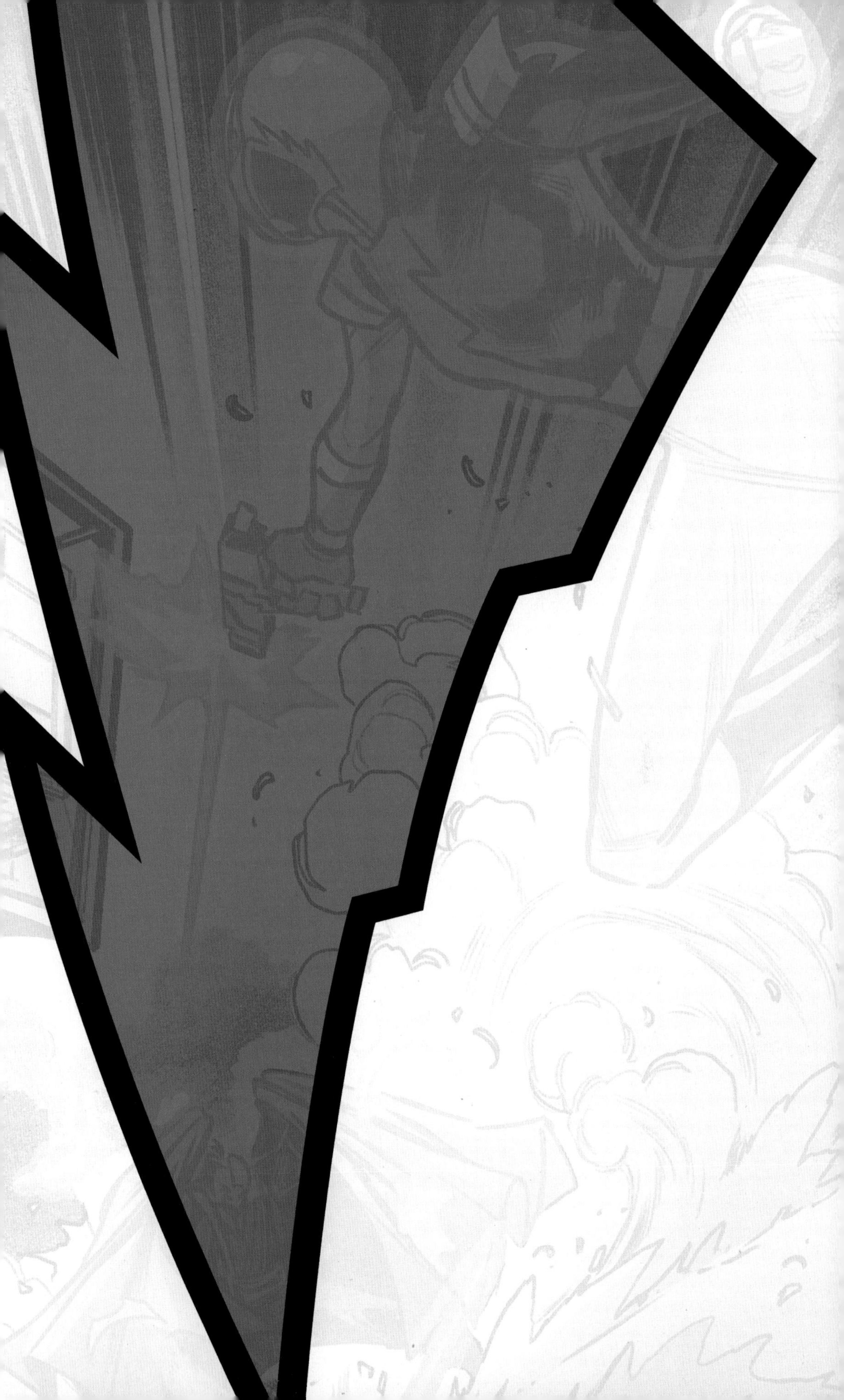

Power Rangers Unlimited

Countdown to Ruin

WRITTEN BY

MARGUERITE BENNETT

ILLUSTRATED BY

ANNA KEKOVSKY CHANDRA
& GIUSEPPE CAFARO

COLORS BY

SARA ANTONELLINI

WITH COLOR ASSISTANCE BY **SHARON MARINO**

& FABI MARQUES

LETTERS BY

ED DUKESHIRE

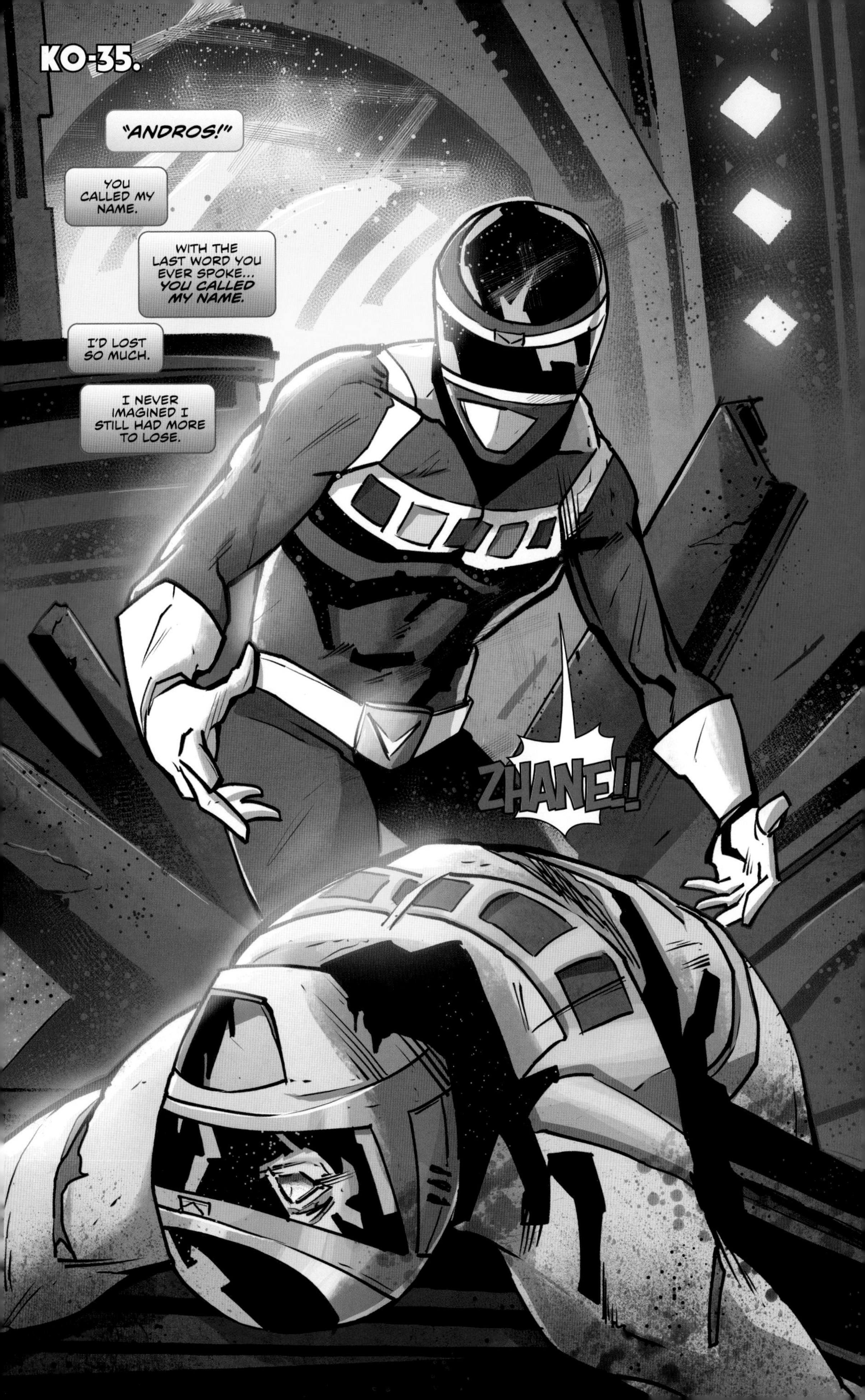
KO-35.
"ANDROS!"
YOU CALLED MY NAME.
WITH THE LAST WORD YOU EVER SPOKE... YOU CALLED MY NAME.
I'D LOST SO MUCH.
I NEVER IMAGINED I STILL HAD MORE TO LOSE.
ZHANE!!

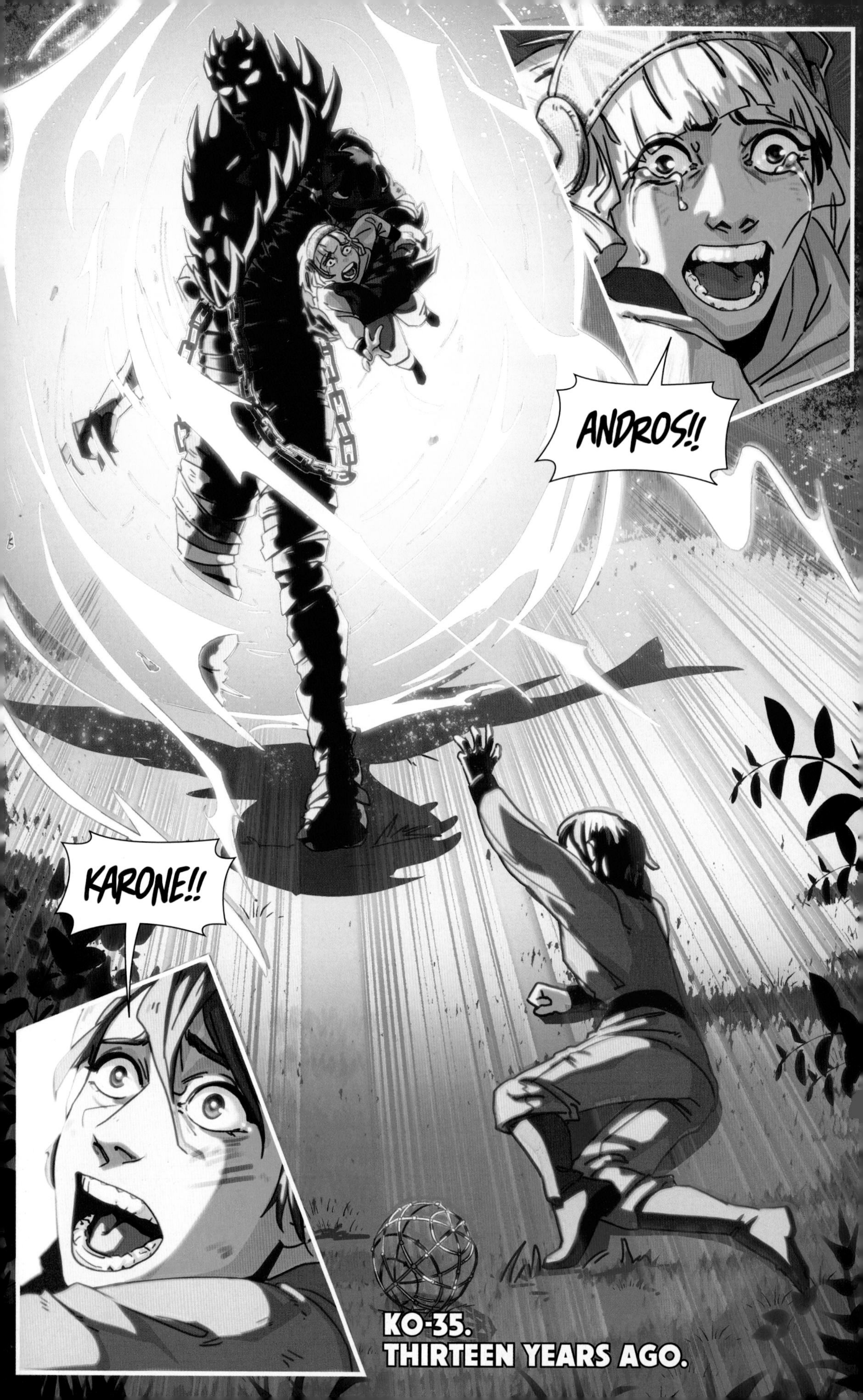
ANDROS!!
KARONE!!
KO-35.
THIRTEEN YEARS AGO.

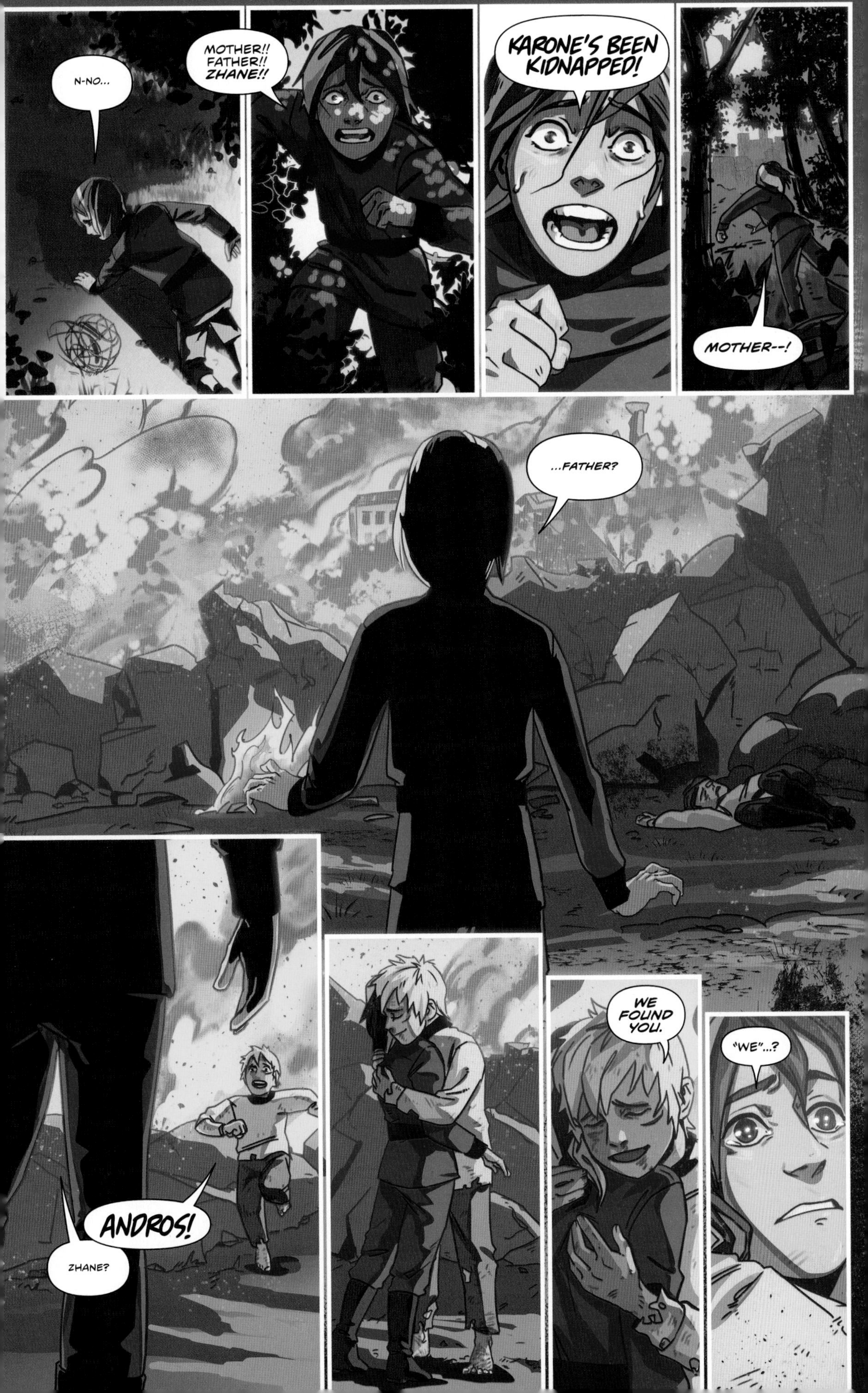
N-NO...
MOTHER!! FATHER!! ZHANE!!
KARONE'S BEEN KIDNAPPED!
MOTHER--!
...FATHER?
ANDROS!
ZHANE?
WE FOUND YOU.
"WE"...?

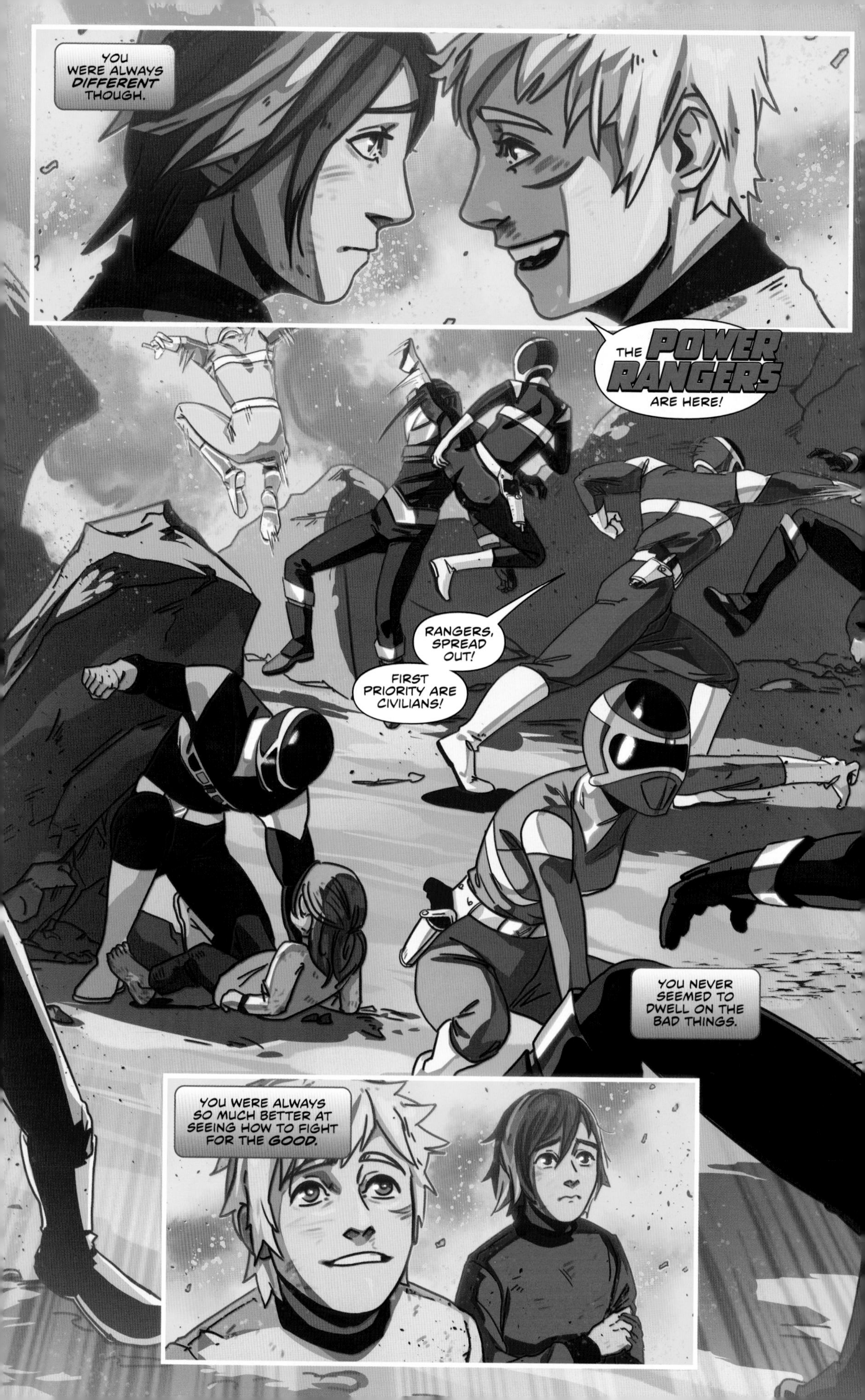
YOU WERE ALWAYS DIFFERENT THOUGH.
THE POWER RANGERS ARE HERE!
RANGERS, SPREAD OUT!
FIRST PRIORITY ARE CIVILIANS!
YOU NEVER SEEMED TO DWELL ON THE BAD THINGS.
YOU WERE ALWAYS SO MUCH BETTER AT SEEING HOW TO FIGHT FOR THE GOOD.

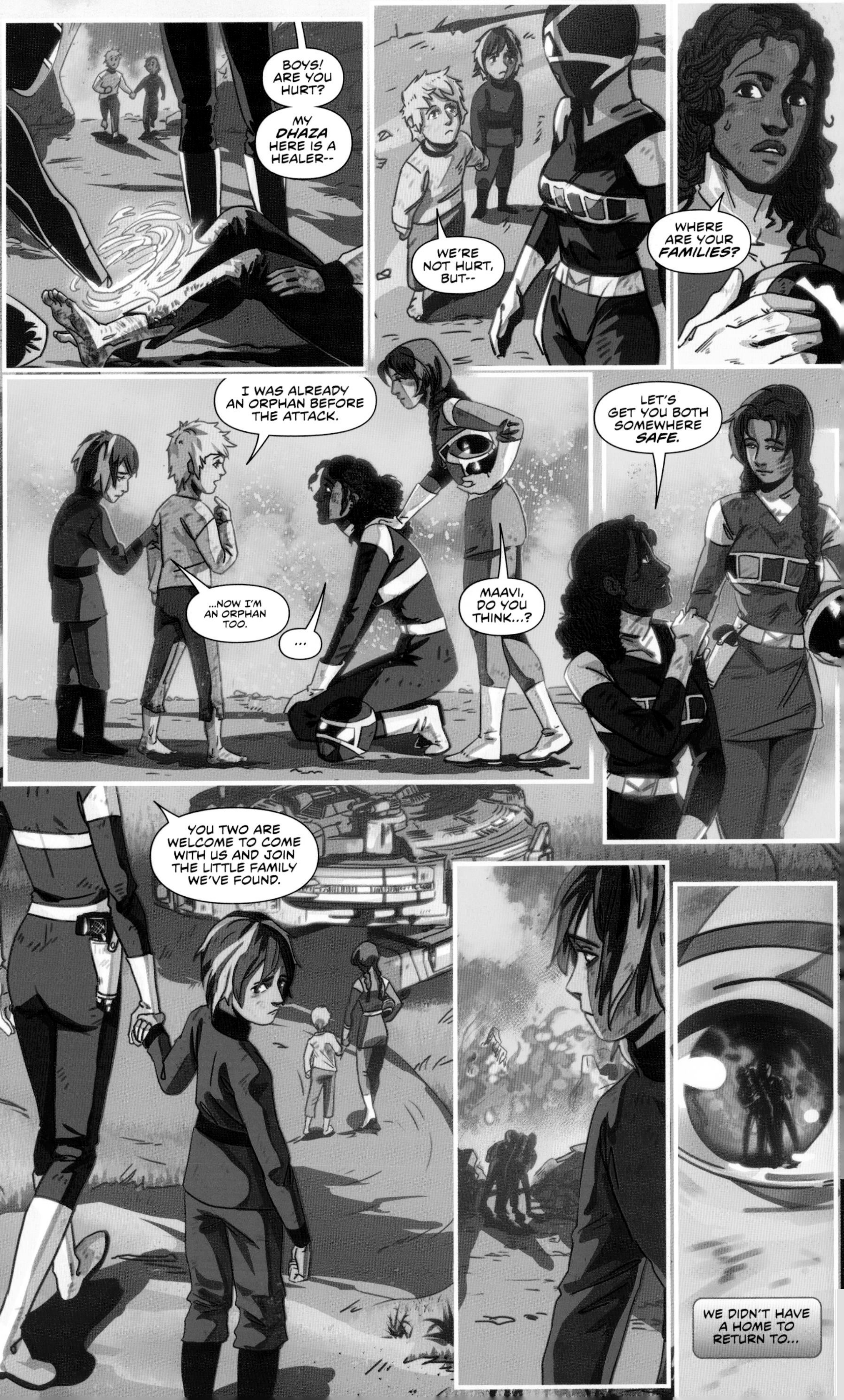
BOYS! ARE YOU HURT?
MY *DHAZA* HERE IS A HEALER--
WE'RE NOT HURT, BUT--
WHERE ARE YOUR *FAMILIES?*
I WAS ALREADY AN ORPHAN BEFORE THE ATTACK.
...NOW I'M AN ORPHAN TOO.
...
MAAVI, DO YOU THINK...?
LET'S GET YOU BOTH SOMEWHERE *SAFE.*
YOU TWO ARE WELCOME TO COME WITH US AND JOIN THE LITTLE FAMILY WE'VE FOUND.
WE DIDN'T HAVE A HOME TO RETURN TO...

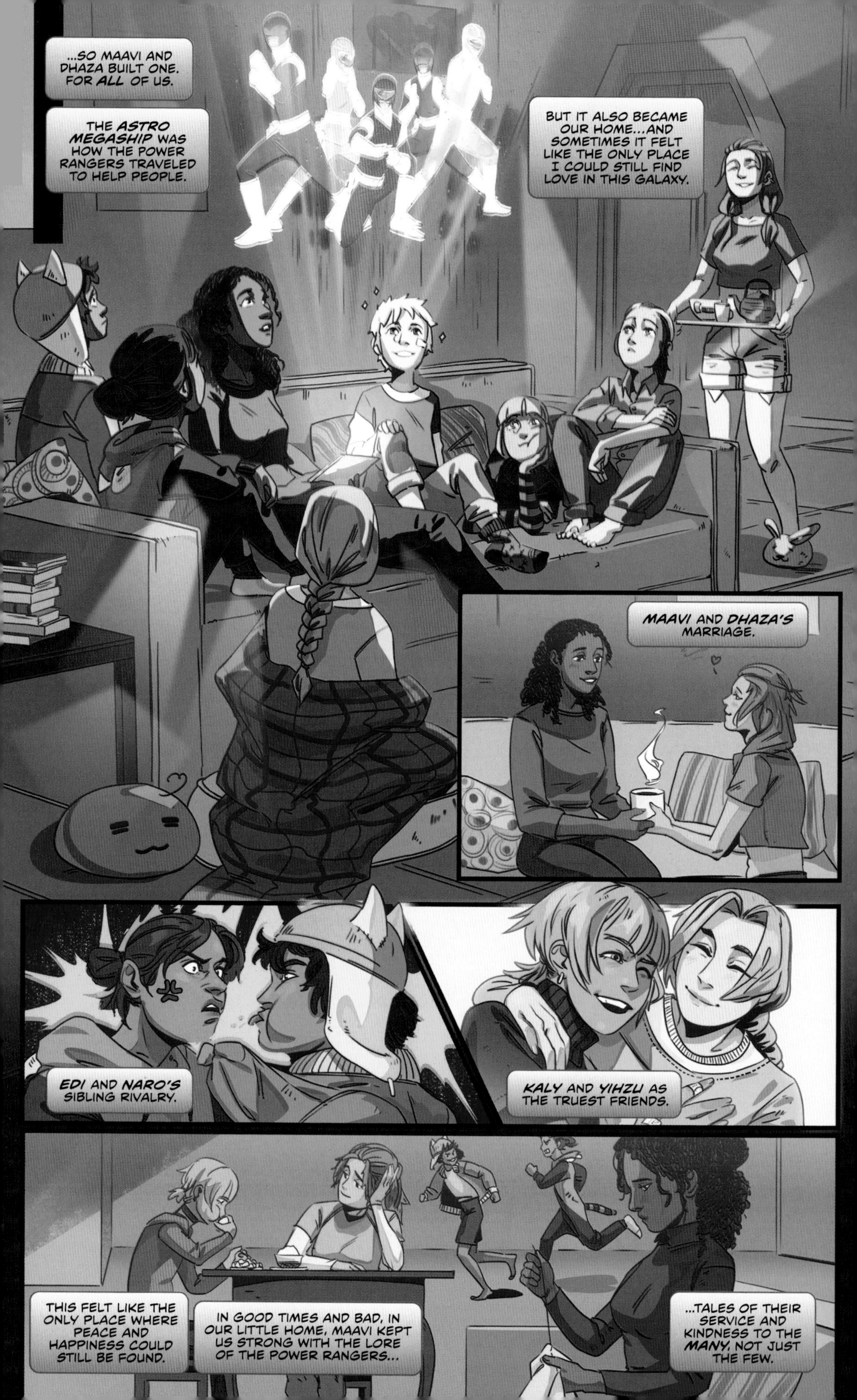
...SO MAAVI AND DHAZA BUILT ONE. FOR *ALL* OF US.
THE ***ASTRO MEGASHIP*** WAS HOW THE POWER RANGERS TRAVELED TO HELP PEOPLE.
BUT IT ALSO BECAME OUR HOME...AND SOMETIMES IT FELT LIKE THE ONLY PLACE I COULD STILL FIND LOVE IN THIS GALAXY.
MAAVI AND ***DHAZA'S*** MARRIAGE.
EDI AND ***NARO'S*** SIBLING RIVALRY.
KALY AND ***YIHZU*** AS THE TRUEST FRIENDS.
THIS FELT LIKE THE ONLY PLACE WHERE PEACE AND HAPPINESS COULD STILL BE FOUND.
IN GOOD TIMES AND BAD, IN OUR LITTLE HOME, MAAVI KEPT US STRONG WITH THE LORE OF THE POWER RANGERS...
...TALES OF THEIR SERVICE AND KINDNESS TO THE ***MANY***, NOT JUST THE FEW.

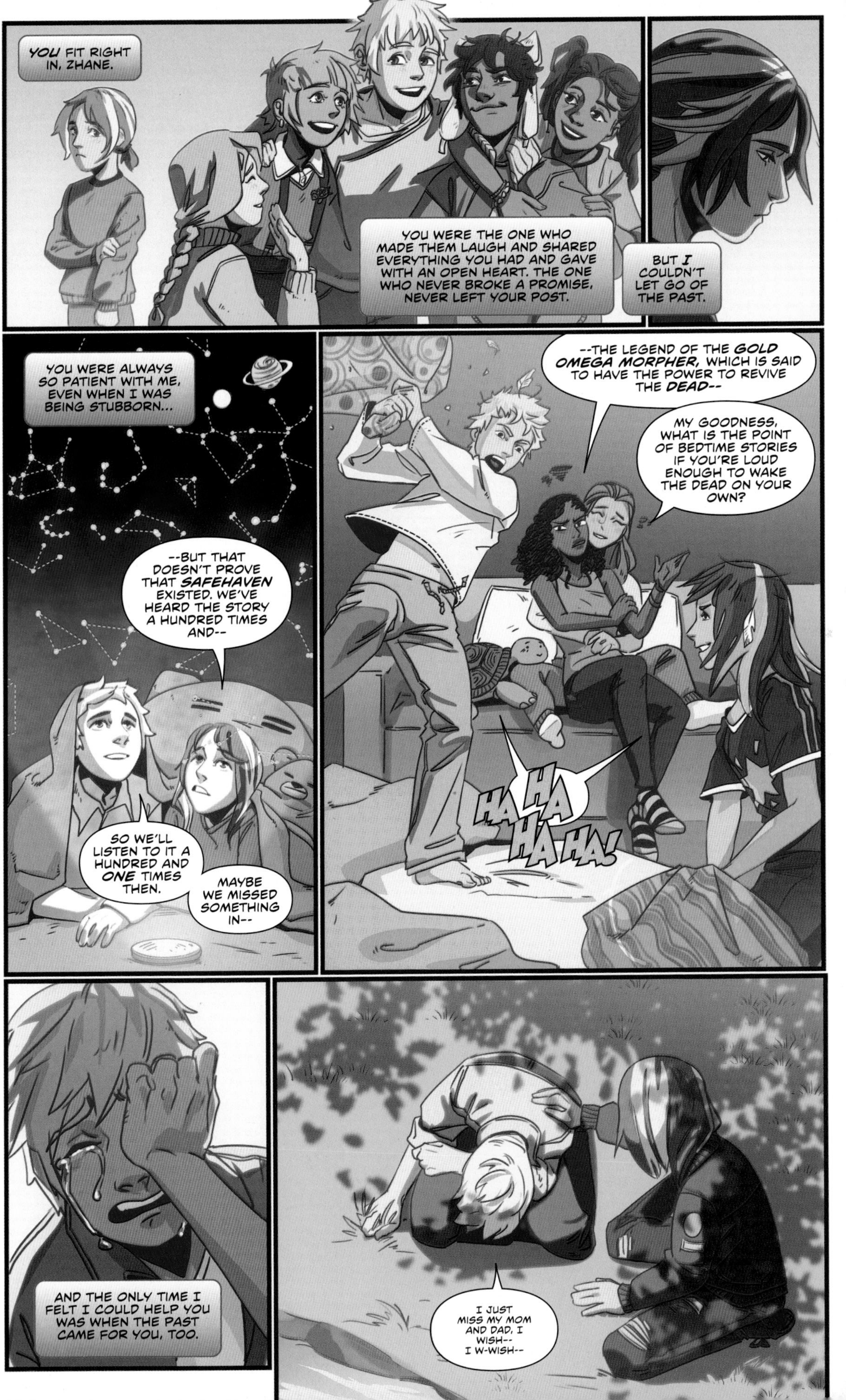

YOU FIT RIGHT IN, ZHANE.
YOU WERE THE ONE WHO MADE THEM LAUGH AND SHARED EVERYTHING YOU HAD AND GAVE WITH AN OPEN HEART. THE ONE WHO NEVER BROKE A PROMISE, NEVER LEFT YOUR POST.
BUT I COULDN'T LET GO OF THE PAST.
YOU WERE ALWAYS SO PATIENT WITH ME, EVEN WHEN I WAS BEING STUBBORN...
--BUT THAT DOESN'T PROVE THAT SAFEHAVEN EXISTED. WE'VE HEARD THE STORY A HUNDRED TIMES AND--
SO WE'LL LISTEN TO IT A HUNDRED AND ONE TIMES THEN.
MAYBE WE MISSED SOMETHING IN--
--THE LEGEND OF THE GOLD OMEGA MORPHER, WHICH IS SAID TO HAVE THE POWER TO REVIVE THE DEAD--
MY GOODNESS, WHAT IS THE POINT OF BEDTIME STORIES IF YOU'RE LOUD ENOUGH TO WAKE THE DEAD ON YOUR OWN?
HA HA HA HA!
AND THE ONLY TIME I FELT I COULD HELP YOU WAS WHEN THE PAST CAME FOR YOU, TOO.
I JUST MISS MY MOM AND DAD, I WISH-- I W-WISH--

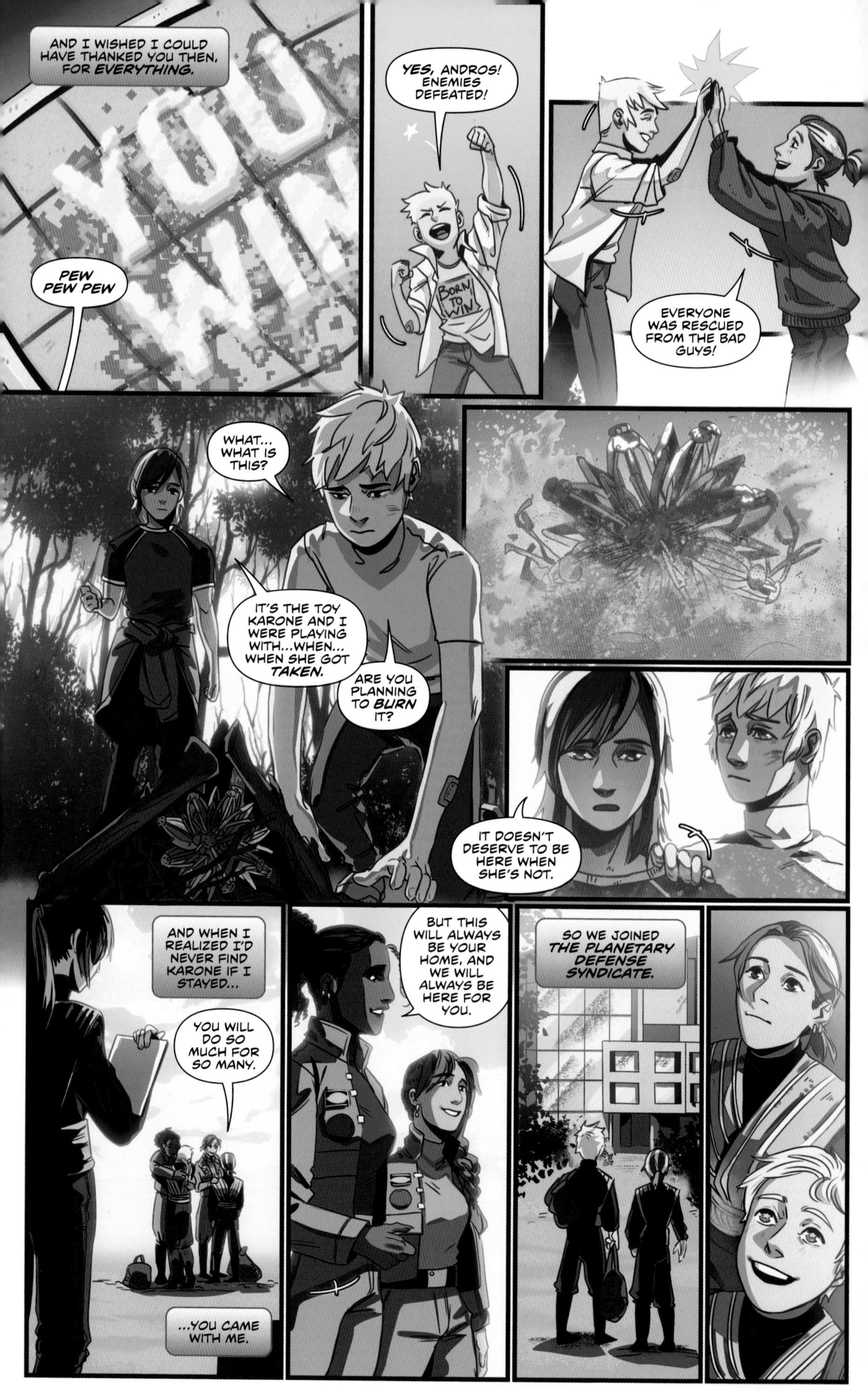
AND I WISHED I COULD HAVE THANKED YOU THEN, FOR EVERYTHING.
YOU WIN
PEW PEW PEW
YES, ANDROS! ENEMIES DEFEATED!
BORN TO WIN
EVERYONE WAS RESCUED FROM THE BAD GUYS!
WHAT... WHAT IS THIS?
IT'S THE TOY KARONE AND I WERE PLAYING WITH...WHEN... WHEN SHE GOT TAKEN.
ARE YOU PLANNING TO BURN IT?
IT DOESN'T DESERVE TO BE HERE WHEN SHE'S NOT.
AND WHEN I REALIZED I'D NEVER FIND KARONE IF I STAYED...
YOU WILL DO SO MUCH FOR SO MANY.
...YOU CAME WITH ME.
BUT THIS WILL ALWAYS BE YOUR HOME, AND WE WILL ALWAYS BE HERE FOR YOU.
SO WE JOINED THE PLANETARY DEFENSE SYNDICATE.

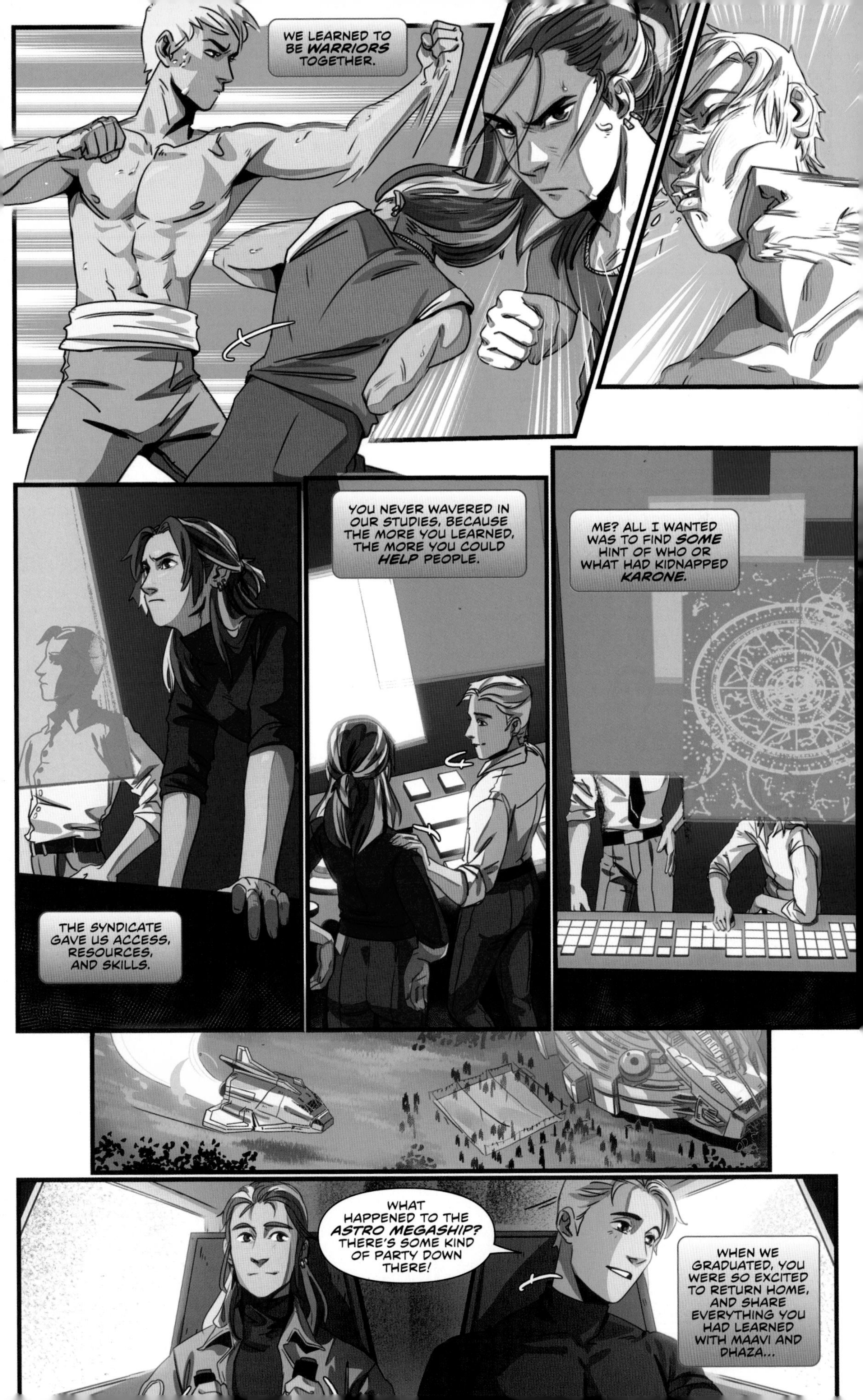
WE LEARNED TO BE WARRIORS TOGETHER.
YOU NEVER WAVERED IN OUR STUDIES, BECAUSE THE MORE YOU LEARNED, THE MORE YOU COULD HELP PEOPLE.
ME? ALL I WANTED WAS TO FIND SOME HINT OF WHO OR WHAT HAD KIDNAPPED KARONE.
THE SYNDICATE GAVE US ACCESS, RESOURCES, AND SKILLS.
WHAT HAPPENED TO THE ASTRO MEGASHIP? THERE'S SOME KIND OF PARTY DOWN THERE!
WHEN WE GRADUATED, YOU WERE SO EXCITED TO RETURN HOME, AND SHARE EVERYTHING YOU HAD LEARNED WITH MAAVI AND DHAZA...

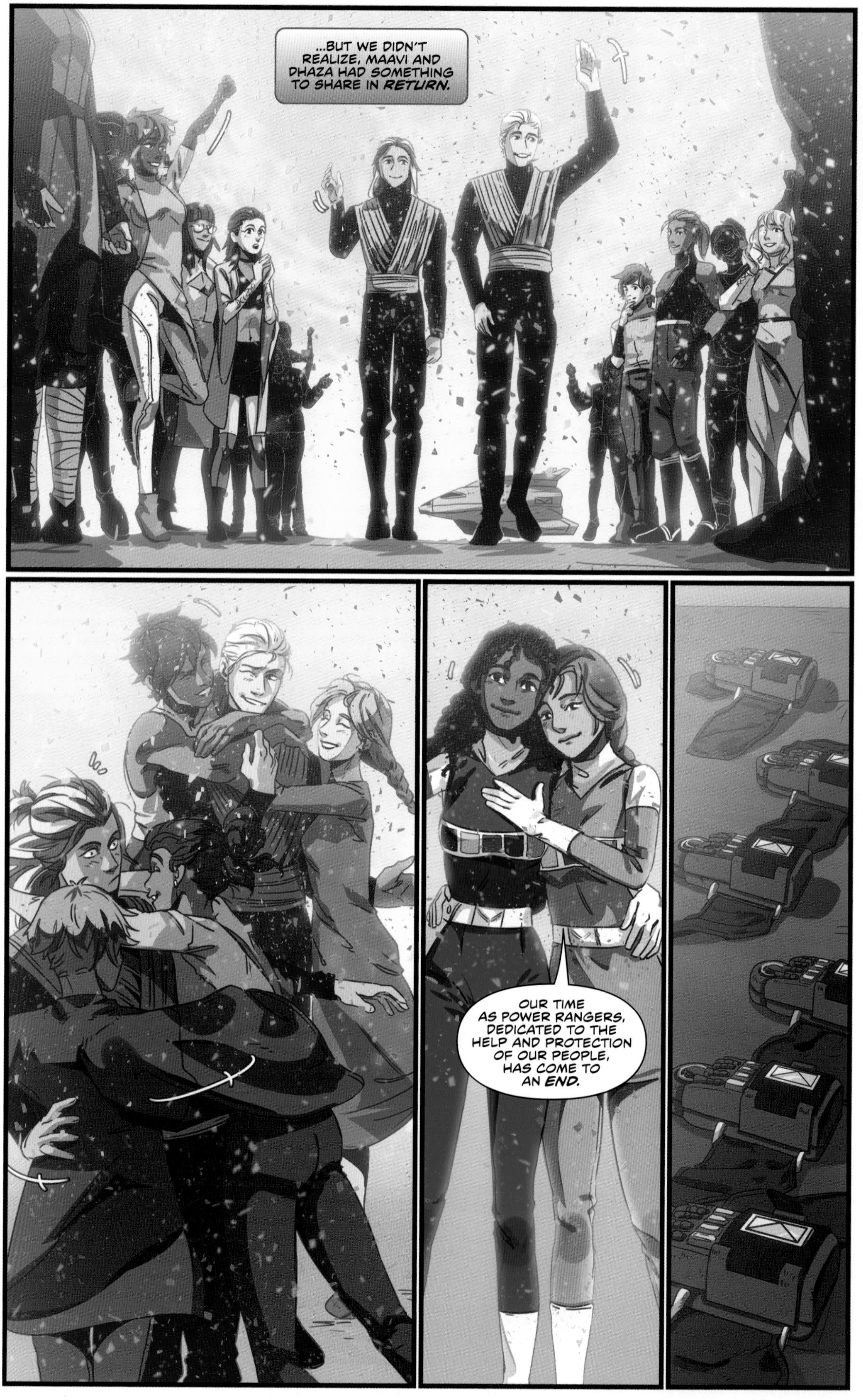
...BUT WE DIDN'T REALIZE, MAAVI AND DHAZA HAD SOMETHING TO SHARE IN *RETURN*.
OUR TIME AS POWER RANGERS, DEDICATED TO THE HELP AND PROTECTION OF OUR PEOPLE, HAS COME TO AN *END*.

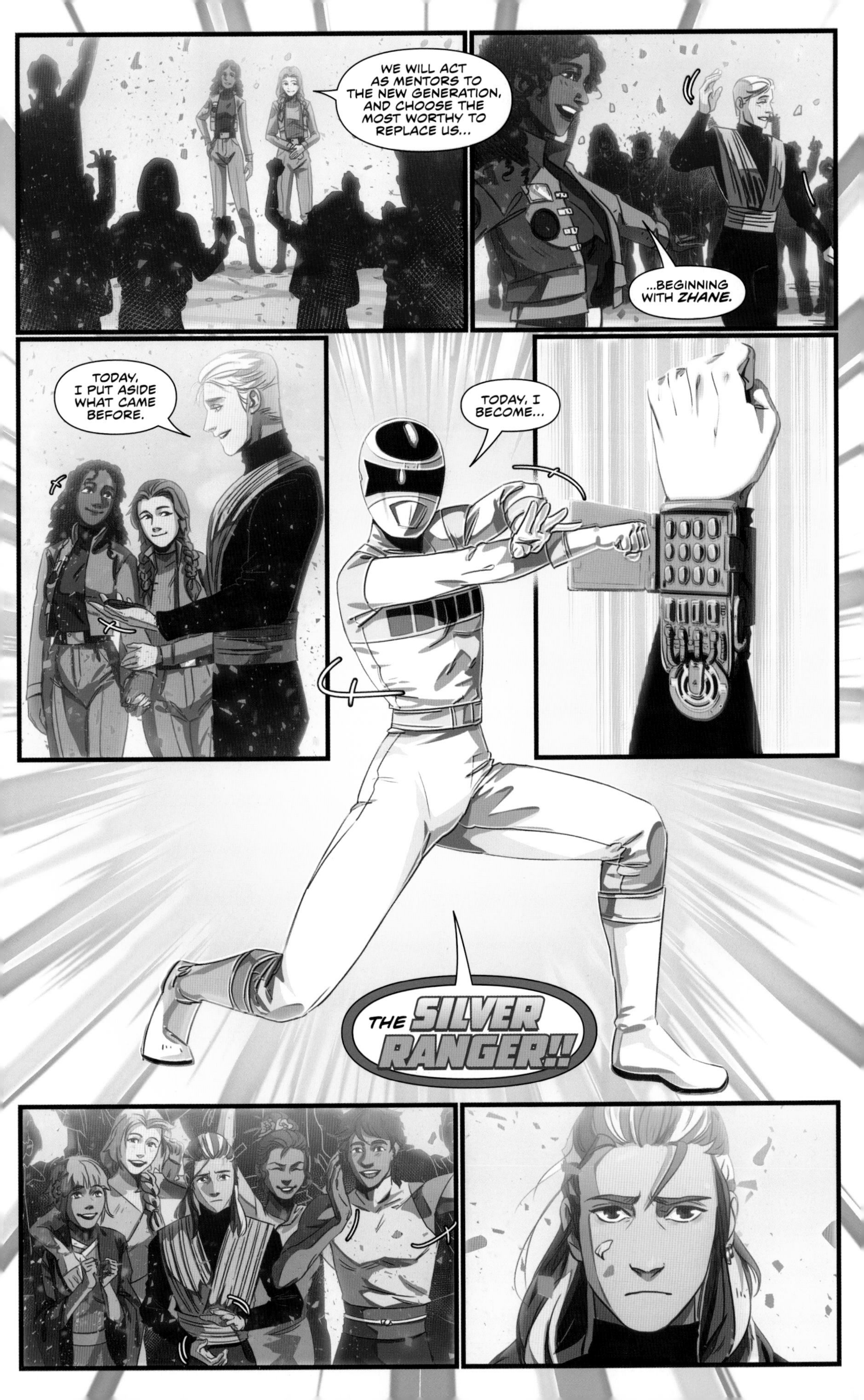
WE WILL ACT AS MENTORS TO THE NEW GENERATION, AND CHOOSE THE MOST WORTHY TO REPLACE US...
...BEGINNING WITH ZHANE.
TODAY, I PUT ASIDE WHAT CAME BEFORE.
TODAY, I BECOME...
THE SILVER RANGER!!

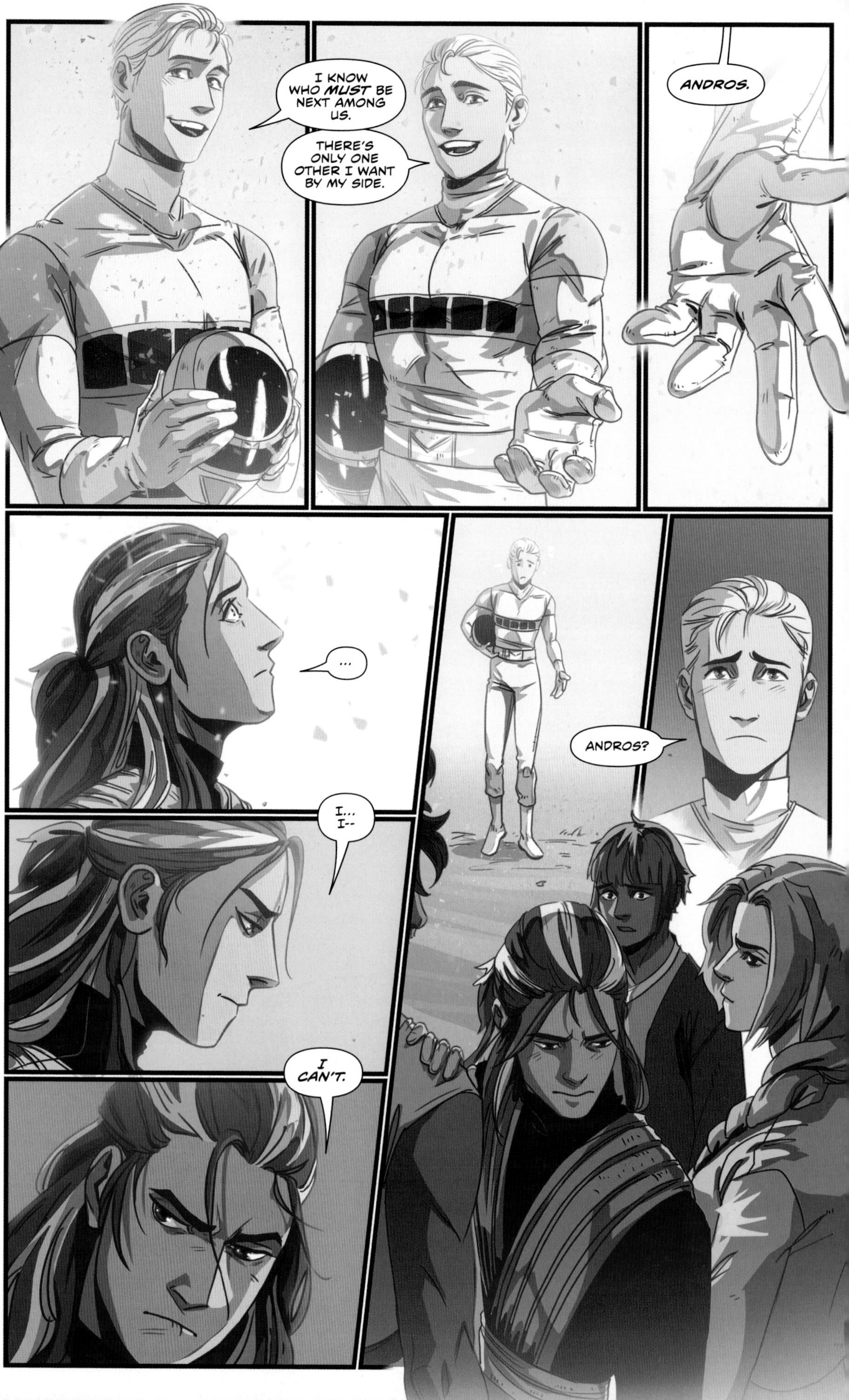
I KNOW WHO MUST BE NEXT AMONG US.
THERE'S ONLY ONE OTHER I WANT BY MY SIDE.
ANDROS.
...
ANDROS?
I... I--
I CAN'T.

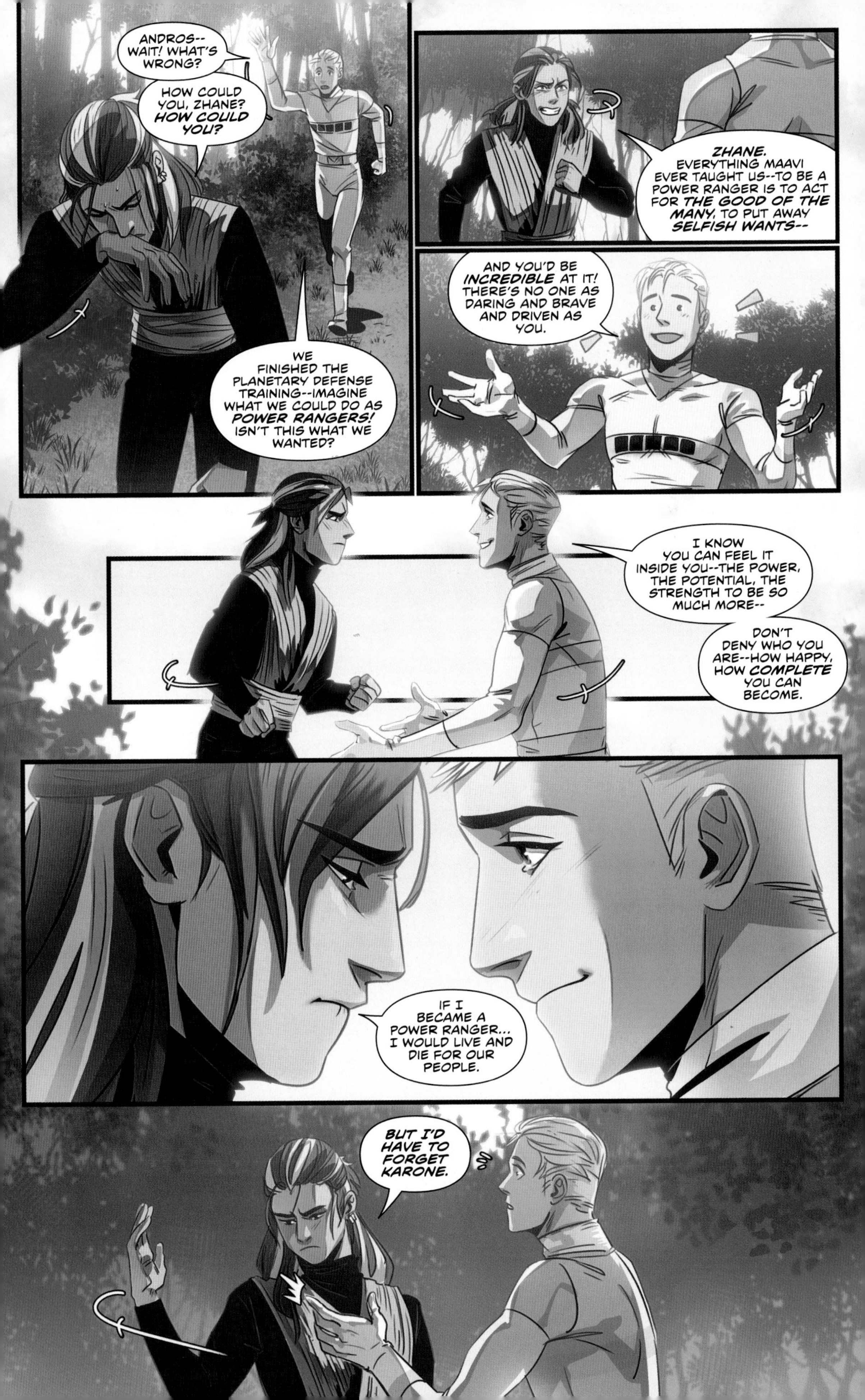
ANDROS-- WAIT! WHAT'S WRONG?
HOW COULD YOU, ZHANE? HOW COULD YOU?
WE FINISHED THE PLANETARY DEFENSE TRAINING--IMAGINE WHAT WE COULD DO AS POWER RANGERS! ISN'T THIS WHAT WE WANTED?
ZHANE. EVERYTHING MAAVI EVER TAUGHT US--TO BE A POWER RANGER IS TO ACT FOR THE GOOD OF THE MANY, TO PUT AWAY SELFISH WANTS--
AND YOU'D BE INCREDIBLE AT IT! THERE'S NO ONE AS DARING AND BRAVE AND DRIVEN AS YOU.
I KNOW YOU CAN FEEL IT INSIDE YOU--THE POWER, THE POTENTIAL, THE STRENGTH TO BE SO MUCH MORE--
DON'T DENY WHO YOU ARE--HOW HAPPY, HOW COMPLETE YOU CAN BECOME.
IF I BECAME A POWER RANGER... I WOULD LIVE AND DIE FOR OUR PEOPLE.
BUT I'D HAVE TO FORGET KARONE.

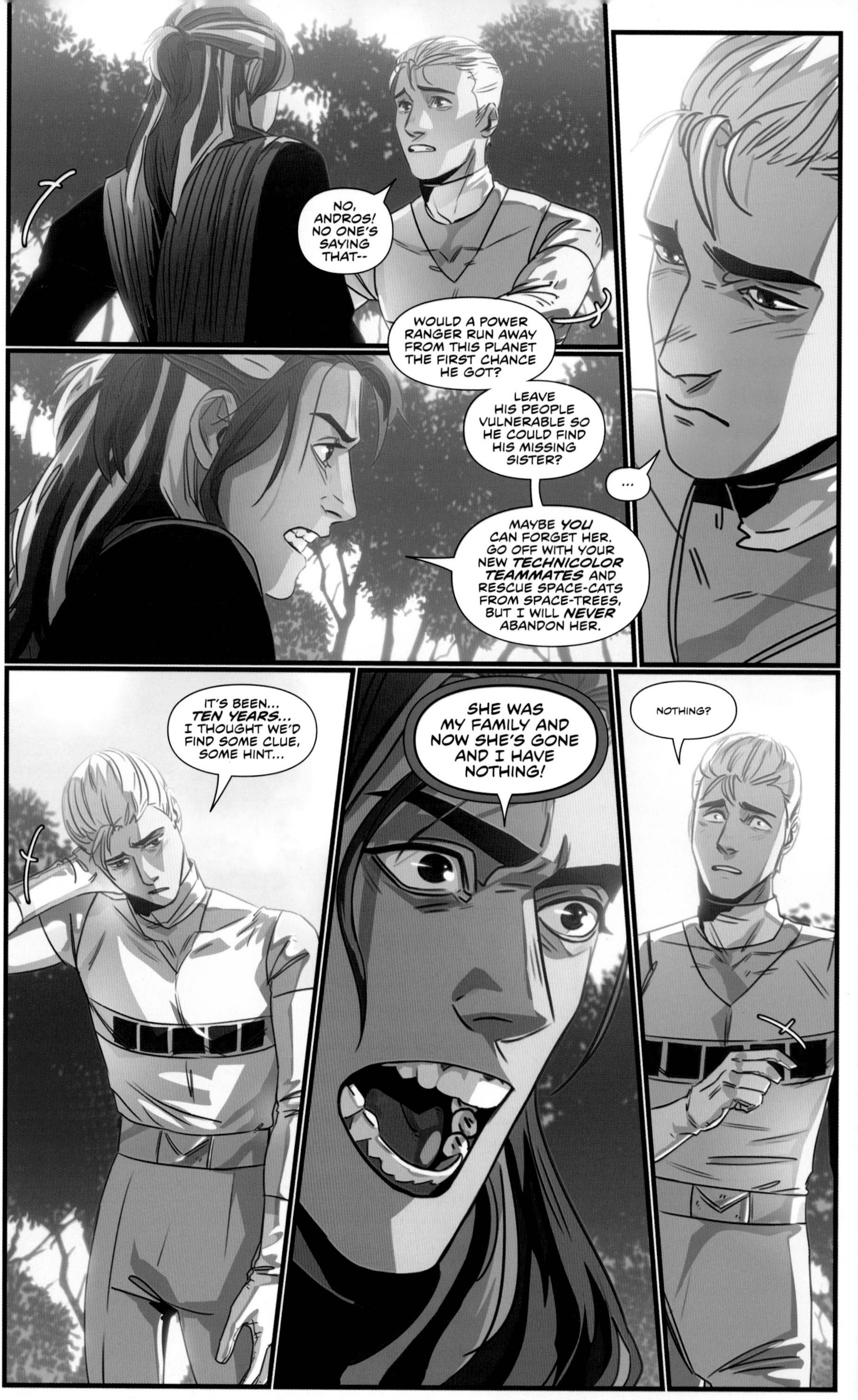
NO, ANDROS! NO ONE'S SAYING THAT--
WOULD A POWER RANGER RUN AWAY FROM THIS PLANET THE FIRST CHANCE HE GOT?
LEAVE HIS PEOPLE VULNERABLE SO HE COULD FIND HIS MISSING SISTER?
MAYBE YOU CAN FORGET HER. GO OFF WITH YOUR NEW TECHNICOLOR TEAMMATES AND RESCUE SPACE-CATS FROM SPACE-TREES, BUT I WILL NEVER ABANDON HER.
...
IT'S BEEN... TEN YEARS... I THOUGHT WE'D FIND SOME CLUE, SOME HINT...
SHE WAS MY FAMILY AND NOW SHE'S GONE AND I HAVE NOTHING!
NOTHING?

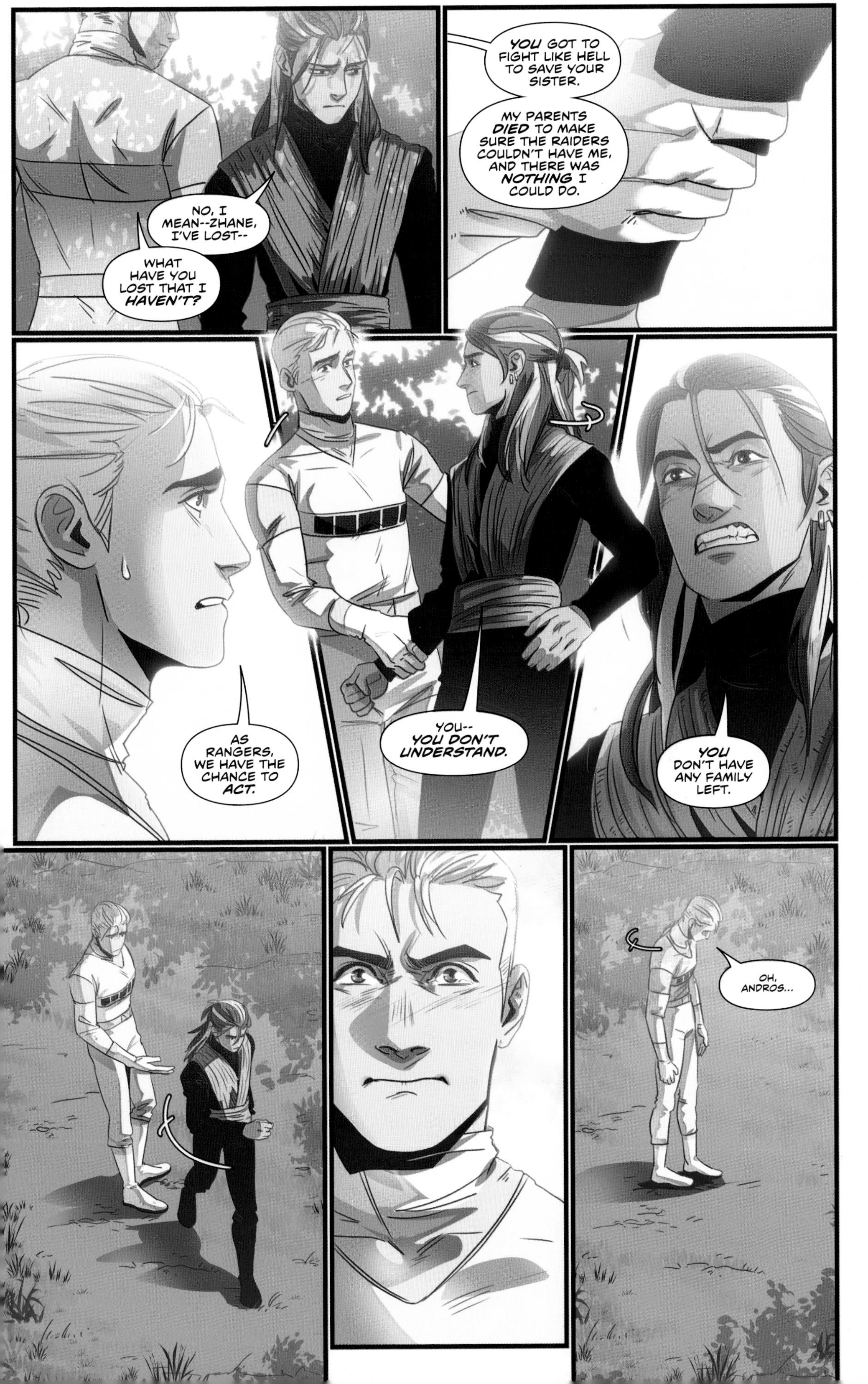
NO, I MEAN--ZHANE, I'VE LOST--
WHAT HAVE YOU LOST THAT I HAVEN'T?
YOU GOT TO FIGHT LIKE HELL TO SAVE YOUR SISTER.
MY PARENTS DIED TO MAKE SURE THE RAIDERS COULDN'T HAVE ME, AND THERE WAS NOTHING I COULD DO.
AS RANGERS, WE HAVE THE CHANCE TO ACT.
YOU-- YOU DON'T UNDERSTAND.
YOU DON'T HAVE ANY FAMILY LEFT.
OH, ANDROS...

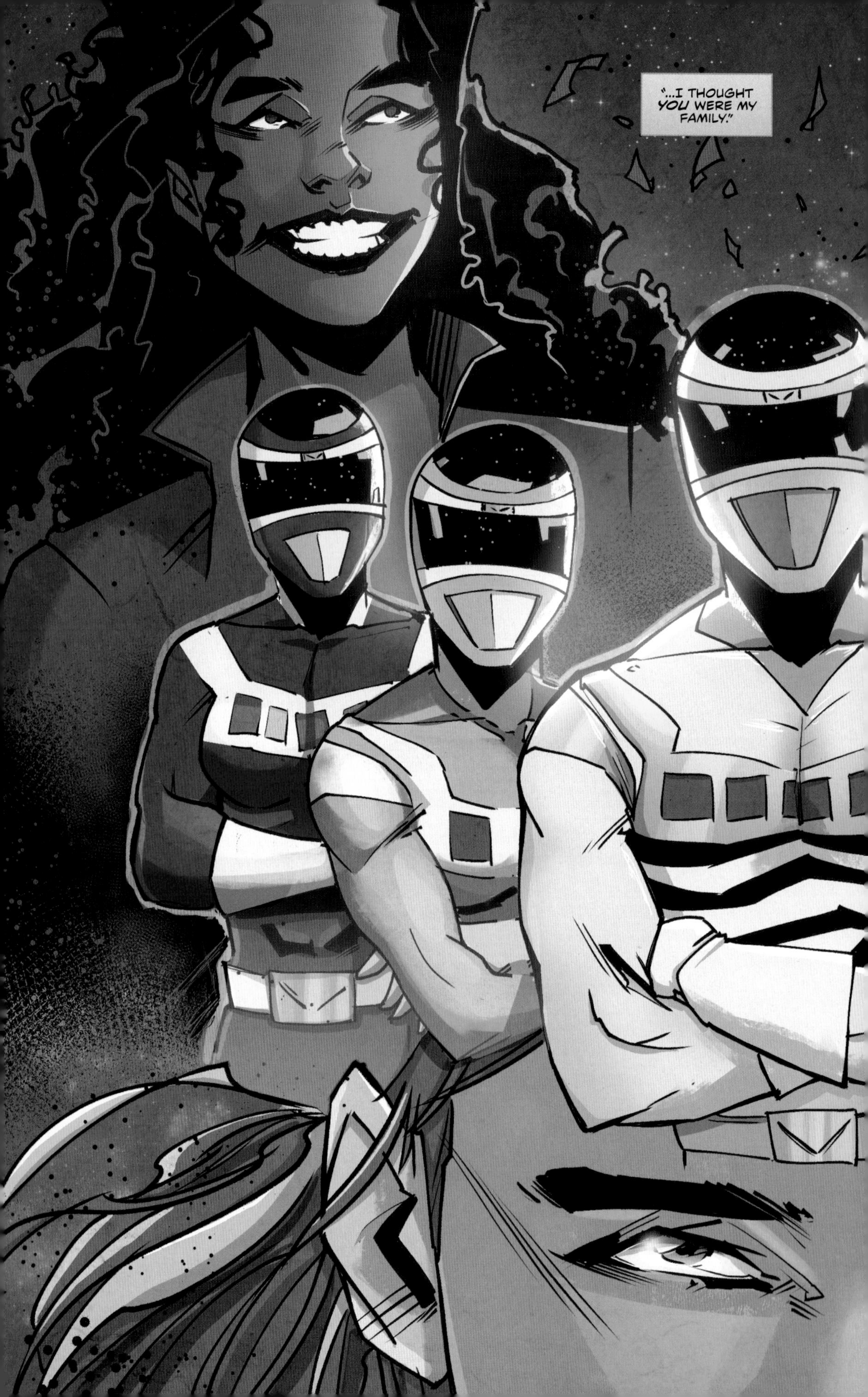
"...I THOUGHT *YOU* WERE MY FAMILY."

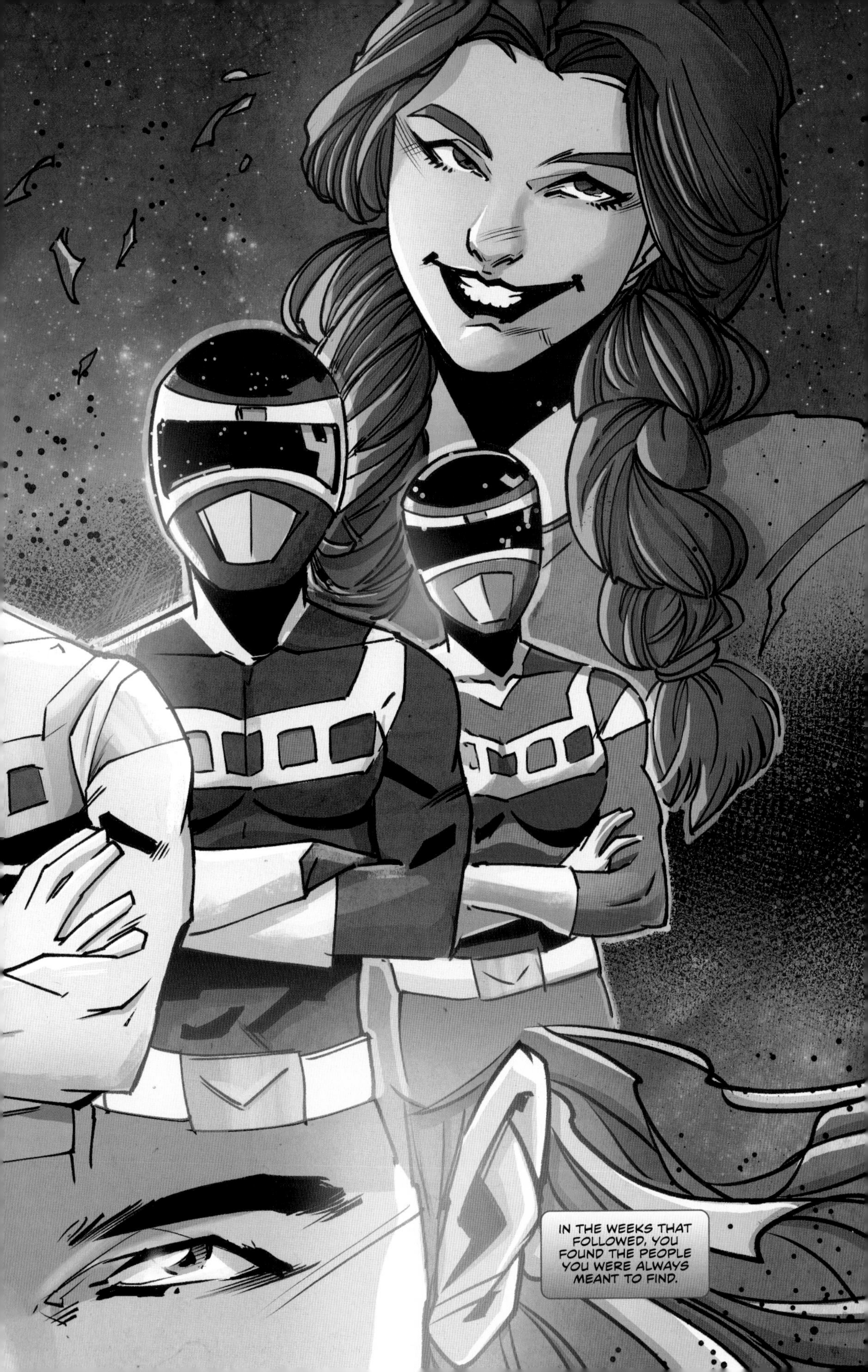
IN THE WEEKS THAT FOLLOWED, YOU FOUND THE PEOPLE YOU WERE ALWAYS MEANT TO FIND.

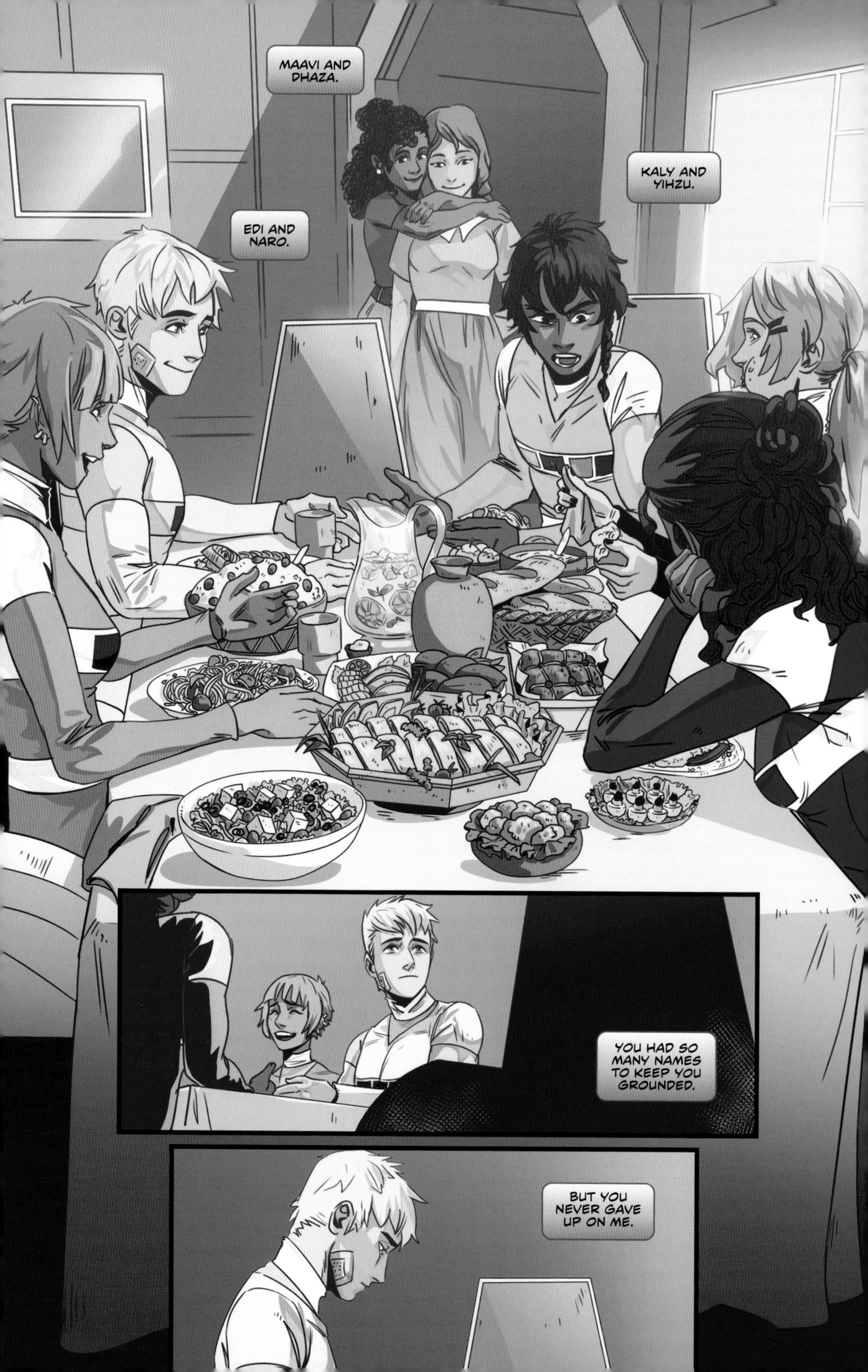
MAAVI AND DHAZA.
EDI AND NARO.
KALY AND YIHZU.
YOU HAD SO MANY NAMES TO KEEP YOU GROUNDED.
BUT YOU NEVER GAVE UP ON ME.

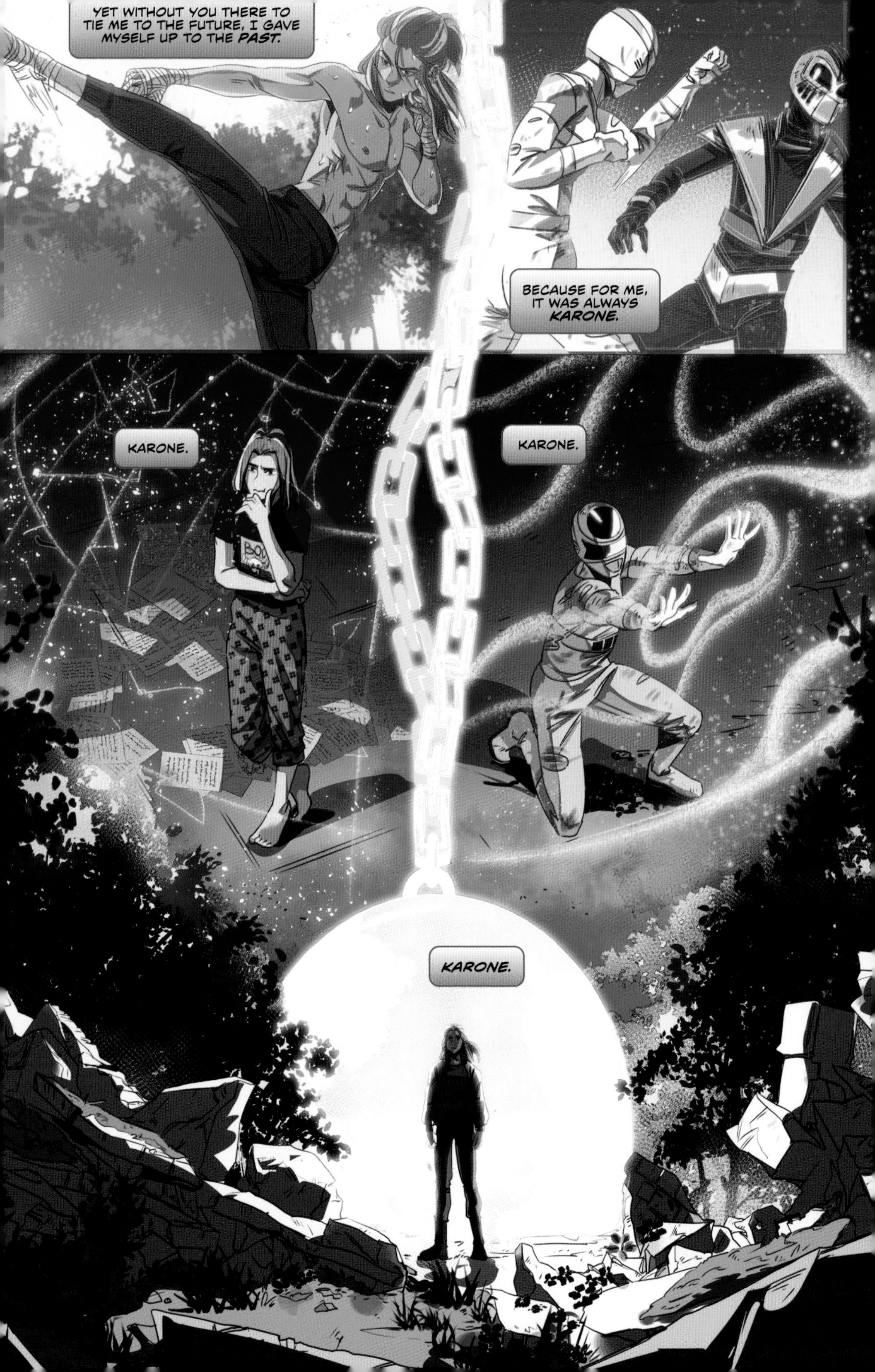
YET WITHOUT YOU THERE TO TIE ME TO THE FUTURE, I GAVE MYSELF UP TO THE *PAST.*
BECAUSE FOR ME, IT WAS ALWAYS *KARONE.*
KARONE.
KARONE.
KARONE.

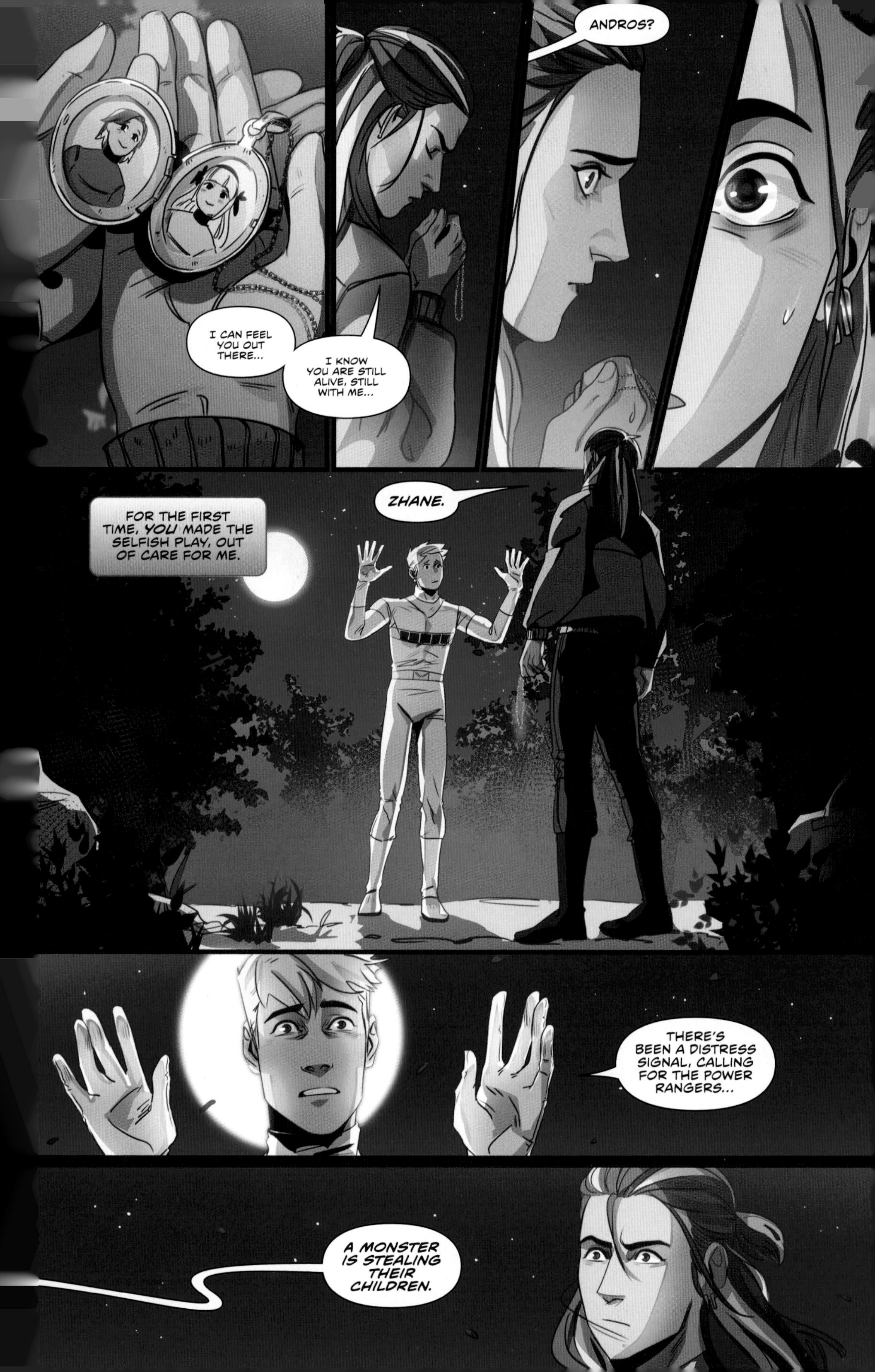
I CAN FEEL YOU OUT THERE...
I KNOW YOU ARE STILL ALIVE, STILL WITH ME...
ANDROS?
FOR THE FIRST TIME, *YOU* MADE THE SELFISH PLAY, OUT OF CARE FOR ME.
ZHANE.
THERE'S BEEN A DISTRESS SIGNAL, CALLING FOR THE POWER RANGERS...
A MONSTER IS STEALING THEIR CHILDREN.

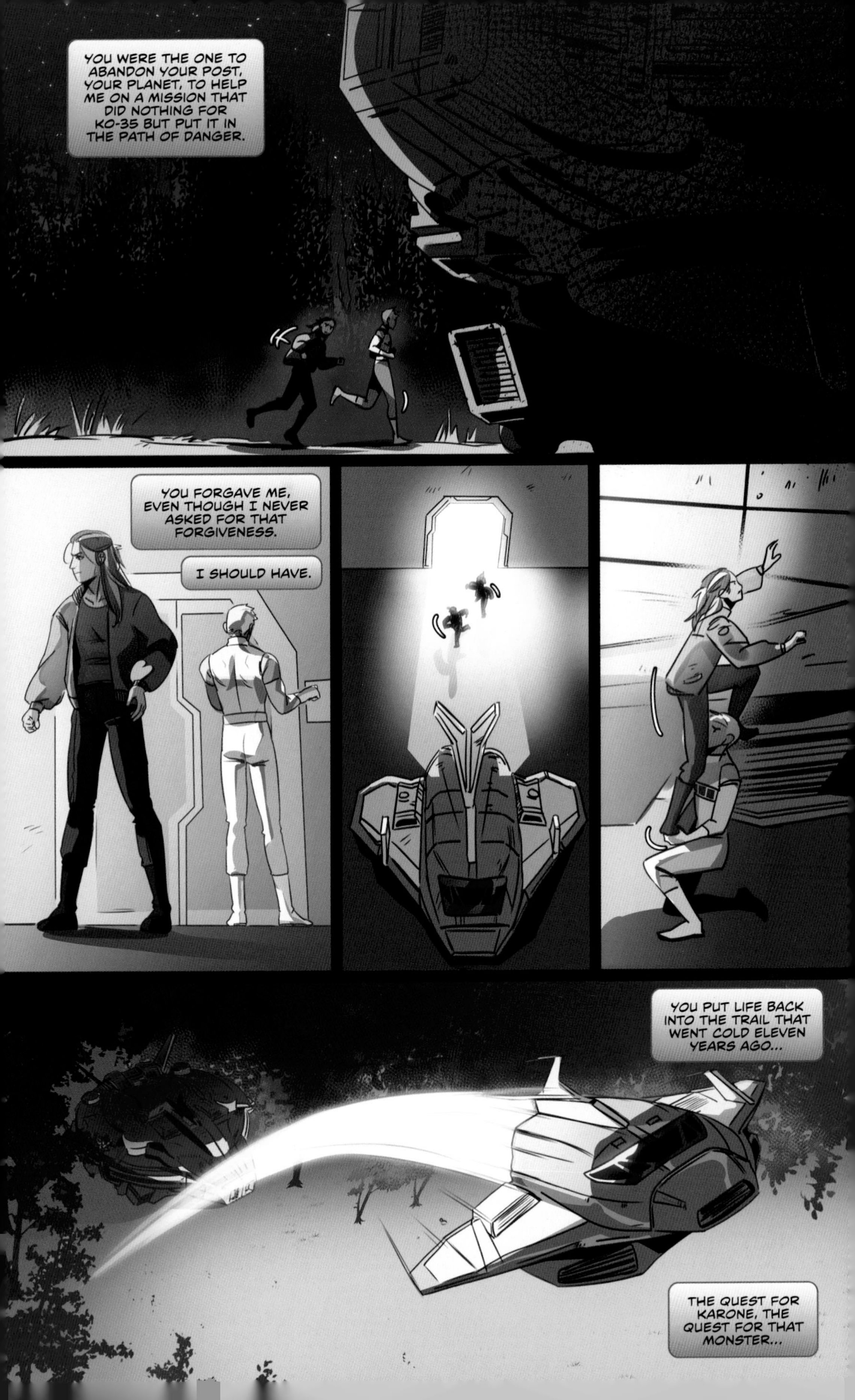
YOU WERE THE ONE TO ABANDON YOUR POST, YOUR PLANET, TO HELP ME ON A MISSION THAT DID NOTHING FOR KO-35 BUT PUT IT IN THE PATH OF DANGER.
YOU FORGAVE ME, EVEN THOUGH I NEVER ASKED FOR THAT FORGIVENESS.
I SHOULD HAVE.
YOU PUT LIFE BACK INTO THE TRAIL THAT WENT COLD ELEVEN YEARS AGO...
THE QUEST FOR KARONE, THE QUEST FOR THAT MONSTER...

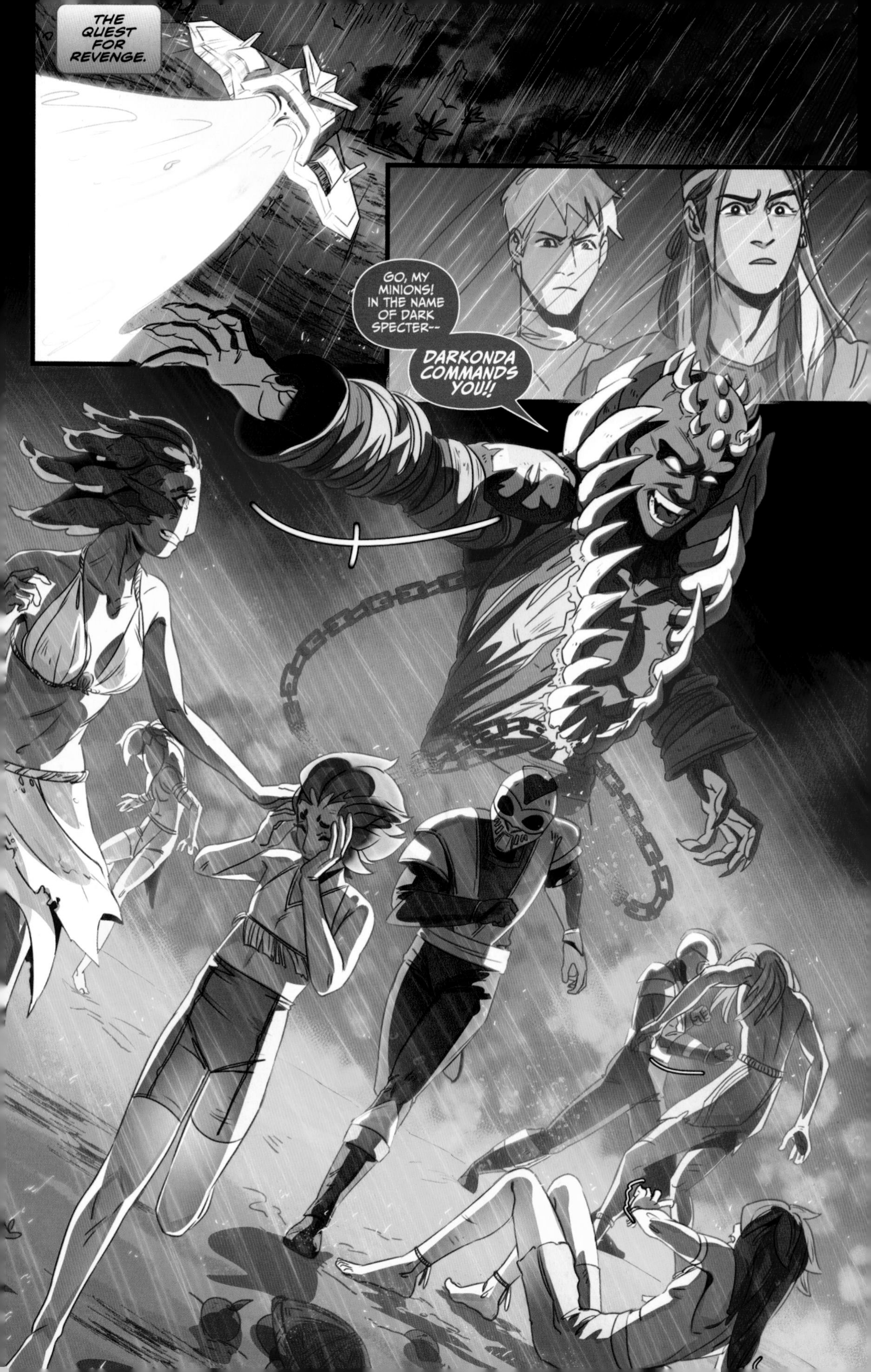
THE QUEST FOR REVENGE.
GO, MY MINIONS! IN THE NAME OF DARK SPECTER--
DARKONDA COMMANDS YOU!!

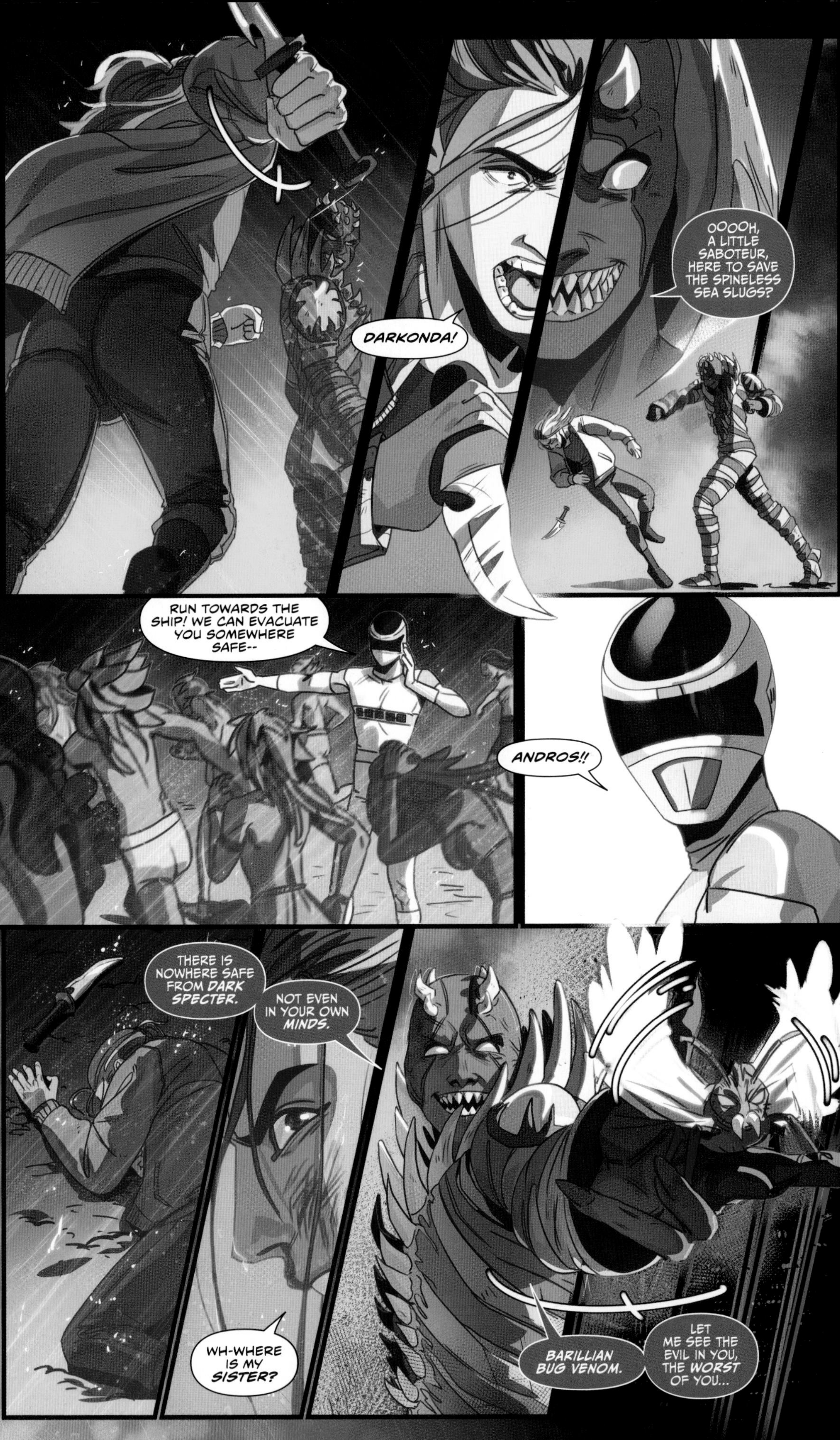
DARKONDA!
OOOOH, A LITTLE SABOTEUR, HERE TO SAVE THE SPINELESS SEA SLUGS?
RUN TOWARDS THE SHIP! WE CAN EVACUATE YOU SOMEWHERE SAFE--
ANDROS!!
THERE IS NOWHERE SAFE FROM DARK SPECTER.
NOT EVEN IN YOUR OWN MINDS.
WH-WHERE IS MY SISTER?
BARILLIAN BUG VENOM.
LET ME SEE THE EVIL IN YOU, THE WORST OF YOU...

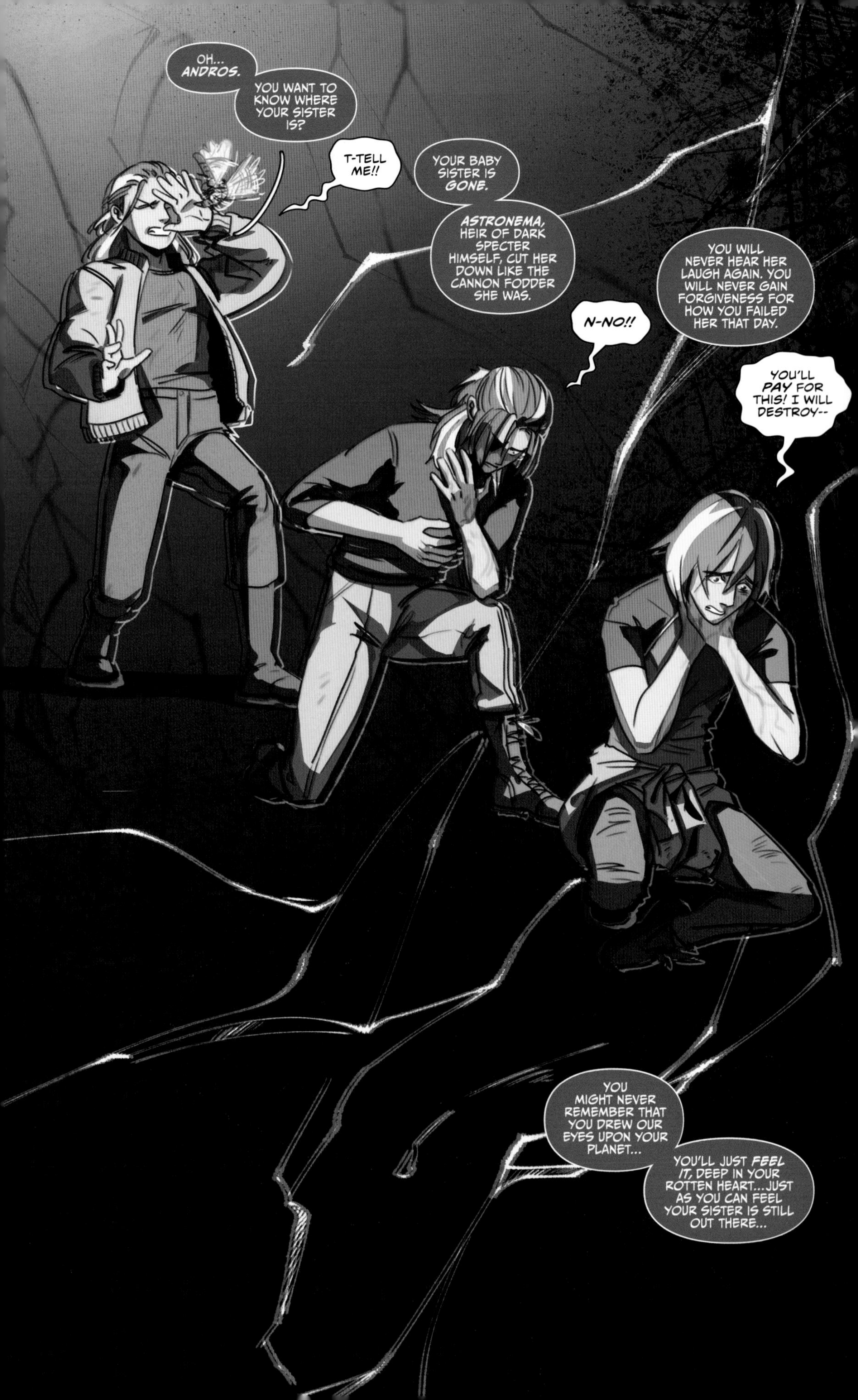
OH... ANDROS.
YOU WANT TO KNOW WHERE YOUR SISTER IS?
T-TELL ME!!
YOUR BABY SISTER IS GONE.
ASTRONEMA, HEIR OF DARK SPECTER HIMSELF, CUT HER DOWN LIKE THE CANNON FODDER SHE WAS.
N-NO!!
YOU WILL NEVER HEAR HER LAUGH AGAIN. YOU WILL NEVER GAIN FORGIVENESS FOR HOW YOU FAILED HER THAT DAY.
YOU'LL PAY FOR THIS! I WILL DESTROY--
YOU MIGHT NEVER REMEMBER THAT YOU DREW OUR EYES UPON YOUR PLANET...
YOU'LL JUST FEEL IT, DEEP IN YOUR ROTTEN HEART...JUST AS YOU CAN FEEL YOUR SISTER IS STILL OUT THERE...

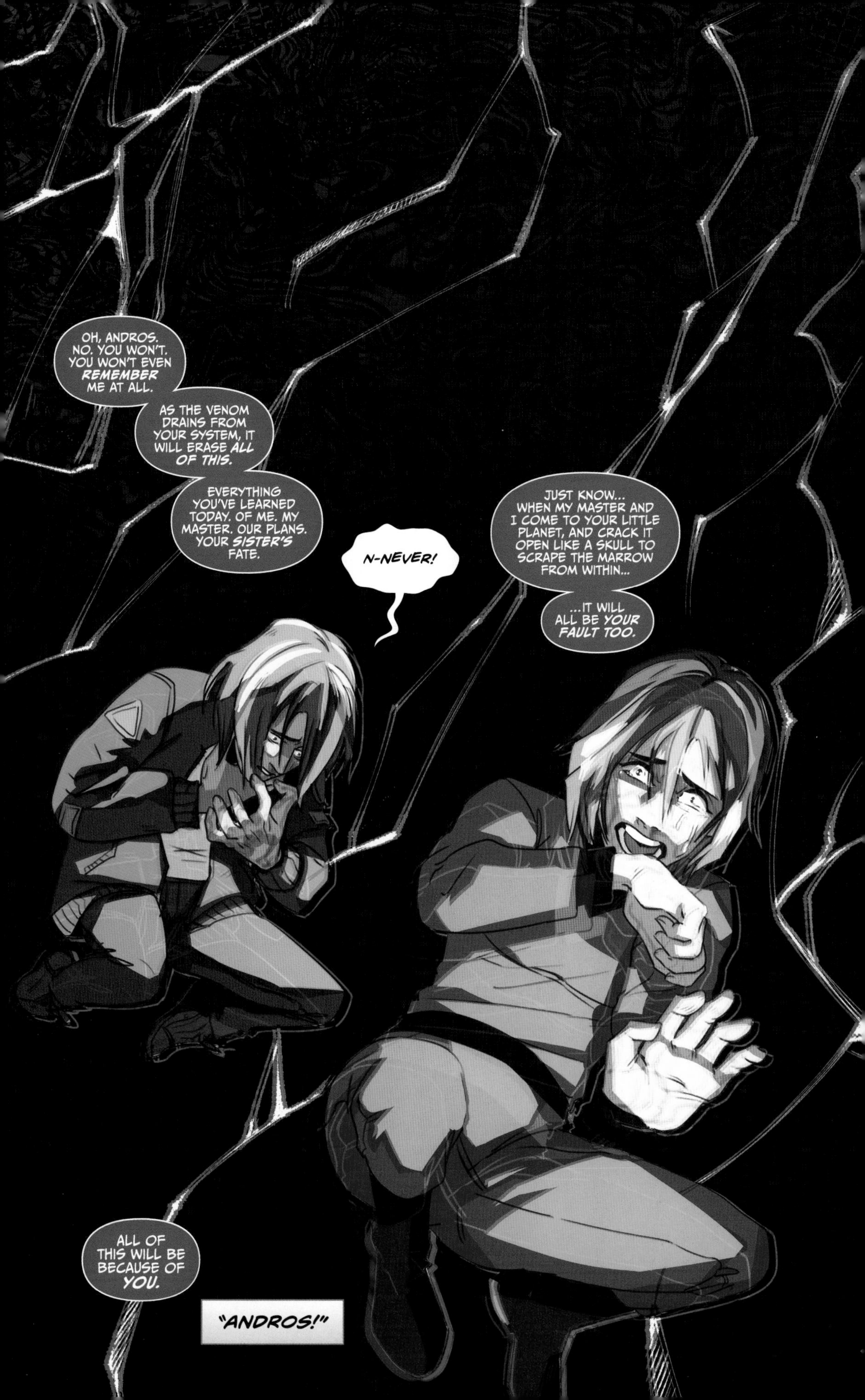
OH, ANDROS. NO. YOU WON'T. YOU WON'T EVEN *REMEMBER* ME AT ALL.
AS THE VENOM DRAINS FROM YOUR SYSTEM, IT WILL ERASE *ALL OF THIS.*
EVERYTHING YOU'VE LEARNED TODAY. OF ME. MY MASTER. OUR PLANS. YOUR *SISTER'S* FATE.
N-NEVER!
JUST KNOW... WHEN MY MASTER AND I COME TO YOUR LITTLE PLANET, AND CRACK IT OPEN LIKE A SKULL TO SCRAPE THE MARROW FROM WITHIN...
...IT WILL ALL BE *YOUR FAULT TOO.*
ALL OF THIS WILL BE BECAUSE OF *YOU.*
"ANDROS!"

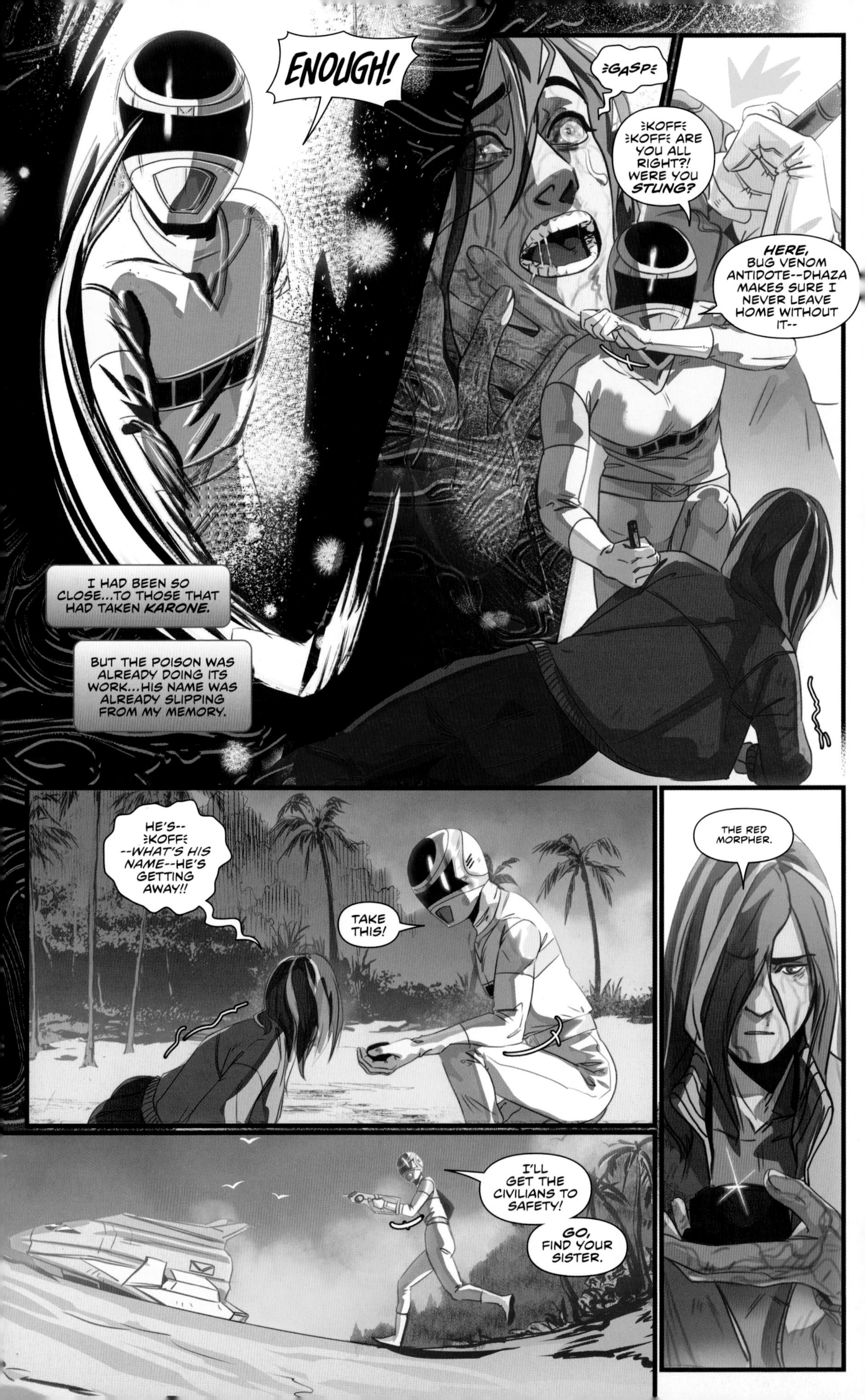
ENOUGH!
GASP
KOFF KOFF ARE YOU ALL RIGHT?! WERE YOU STUNG?
HERE, BUG VENOM ANTIDOTE--DHAZA MAKES SURE I NEVER LEAVE HOME WITHOUT IT--
I HAD BEEN SO CLOSE...TO THOSE THAT HAD TAKEN KARONE.
BUT THE POISON WAS ALREADY DOING ITS WORK...HIS NAME WAS ALREADY SLIPPING FROM MY MEMORY.
HE'S-- KOFF --WHAT'S HIS NAME--HE'S GETTING AWAY!!
TAKE THIS!
THE RED MORPHER.
I'LL GET THE CIVILIANS TO SAFETY!
GO, FIND YOUR SISTER.

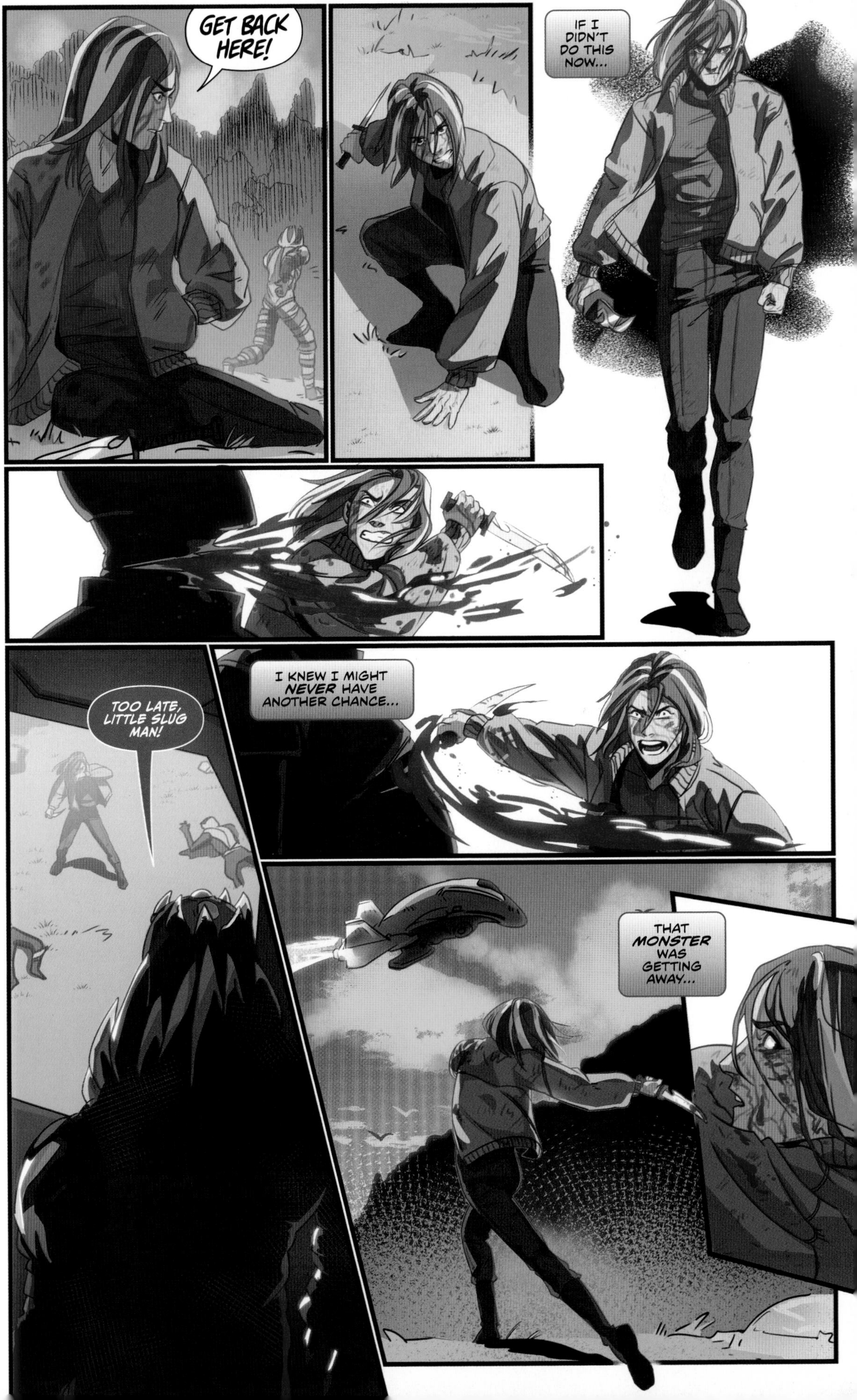
GET BACK HERE!
IF I DIDN'T DO THIS NOW...
TOO LATE, LITTLE SLUG MAN!
I KNEW I MIGHT NEVER HAVE ANOTHER CHANCE...
THAT MONSTER WAS GETTING AWAY...

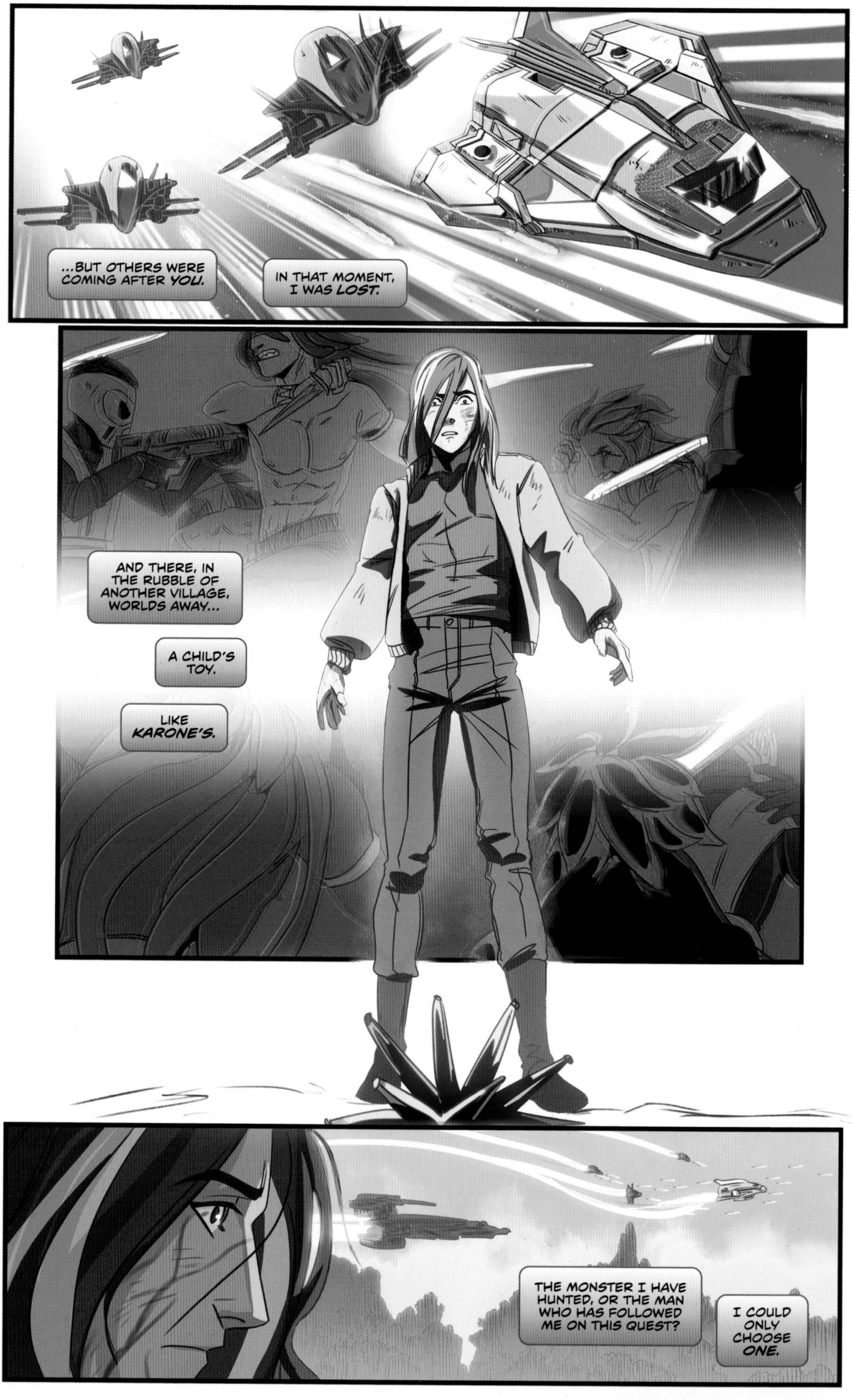
...BUT OTHERS WERE COMING AFTER YOU.
IN THAT MOMENT, I WAS LOST.
AND THERE, IN THE RUBBLE OF ANOTHER VILLAGE, WORLDS AWAY...
A CHILD'S TOY.
LIKE KARONE'S.
THE MONSTER I HAVE HUNTED, OR THE MAN WHO HAS FOLLOWED ME ON THIS QUEST?
I COULD ONLY CHOOSE ONE.

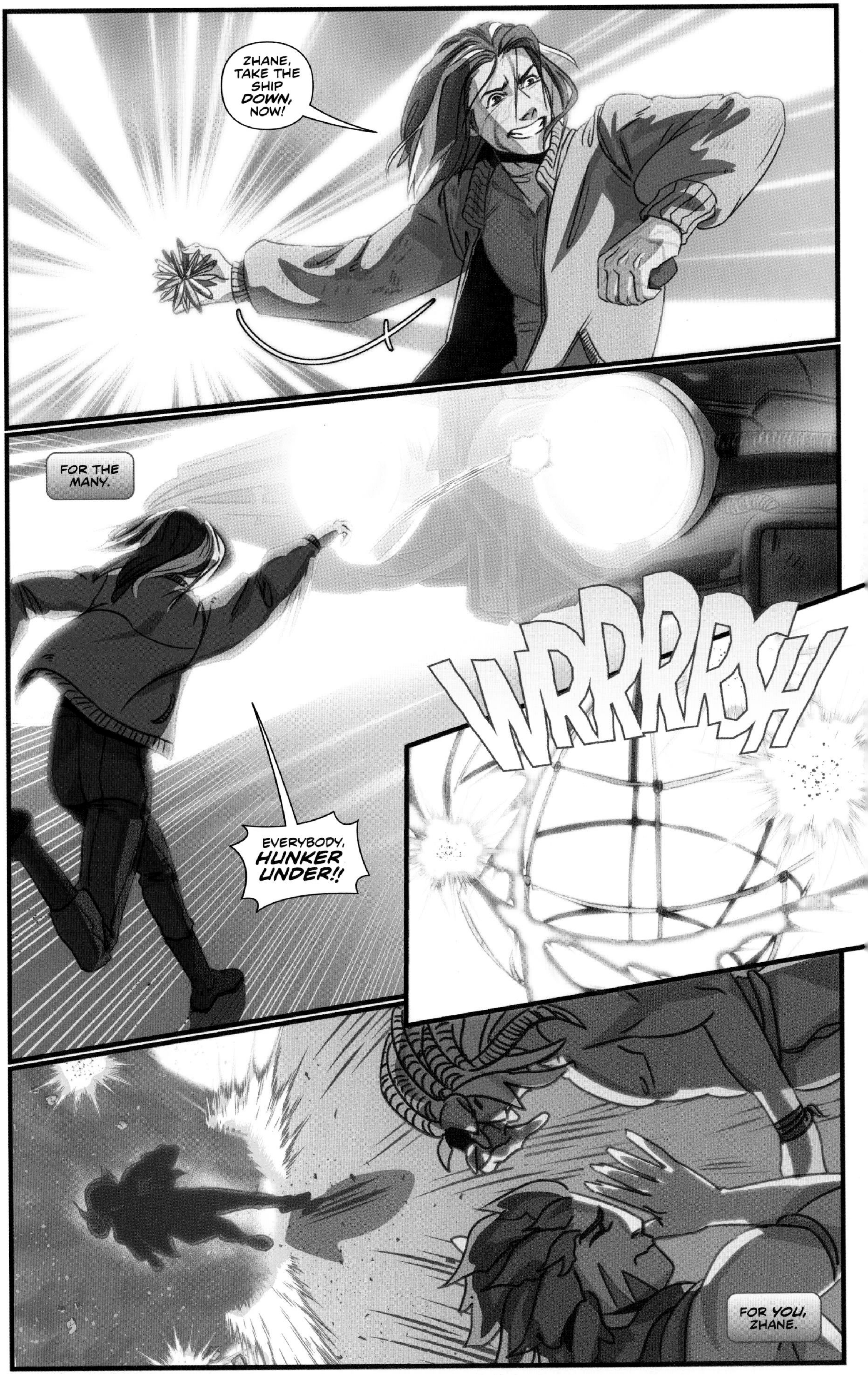
ZHANE, TAKE THE SHIP DOWN, NOW!
FOR THE MANY.
EVERYBODY, HUNKER UNDER!!
WRRRRSH
FOR YOU, ZHANE.

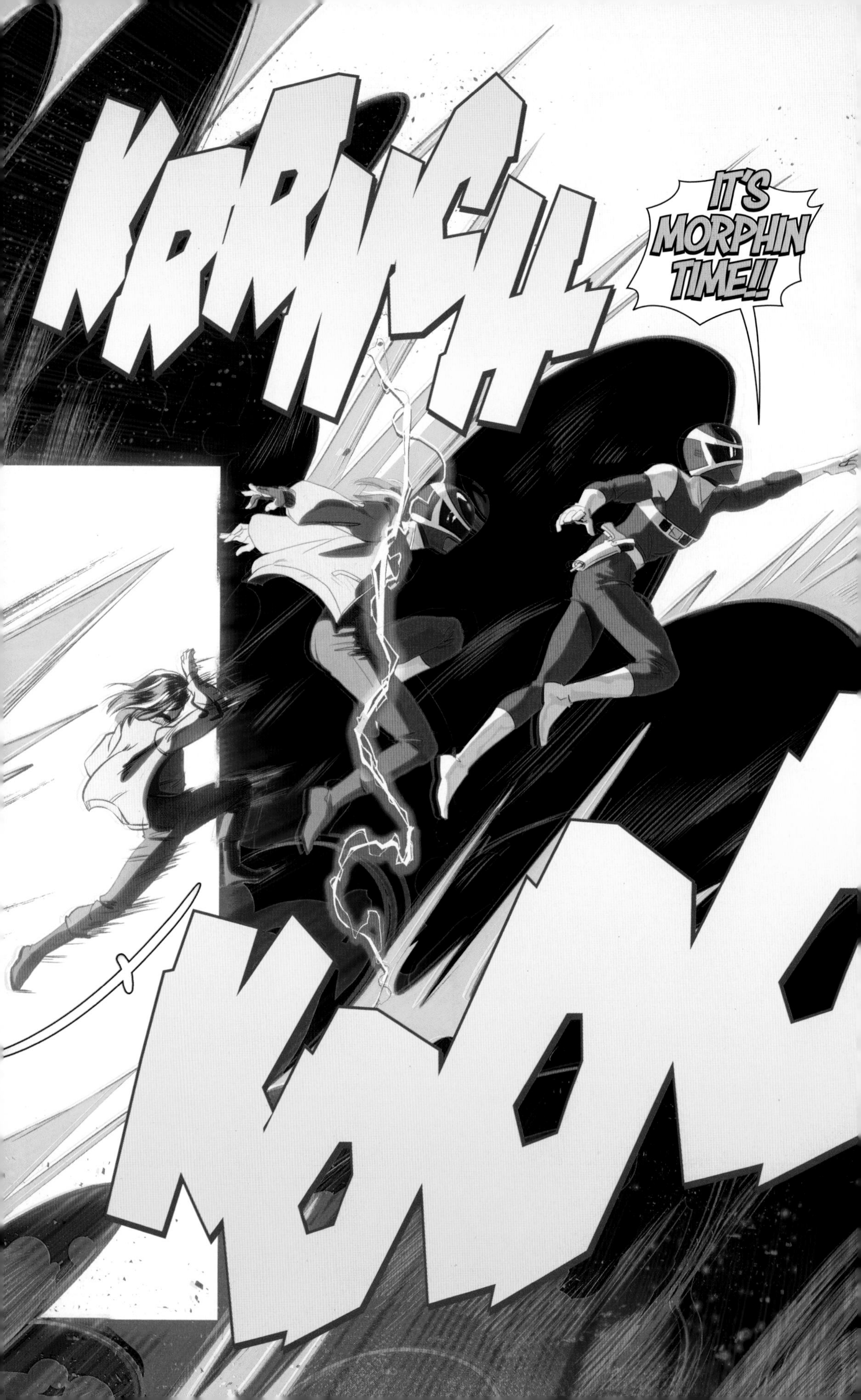
IT'S MORPHIN TIME!!

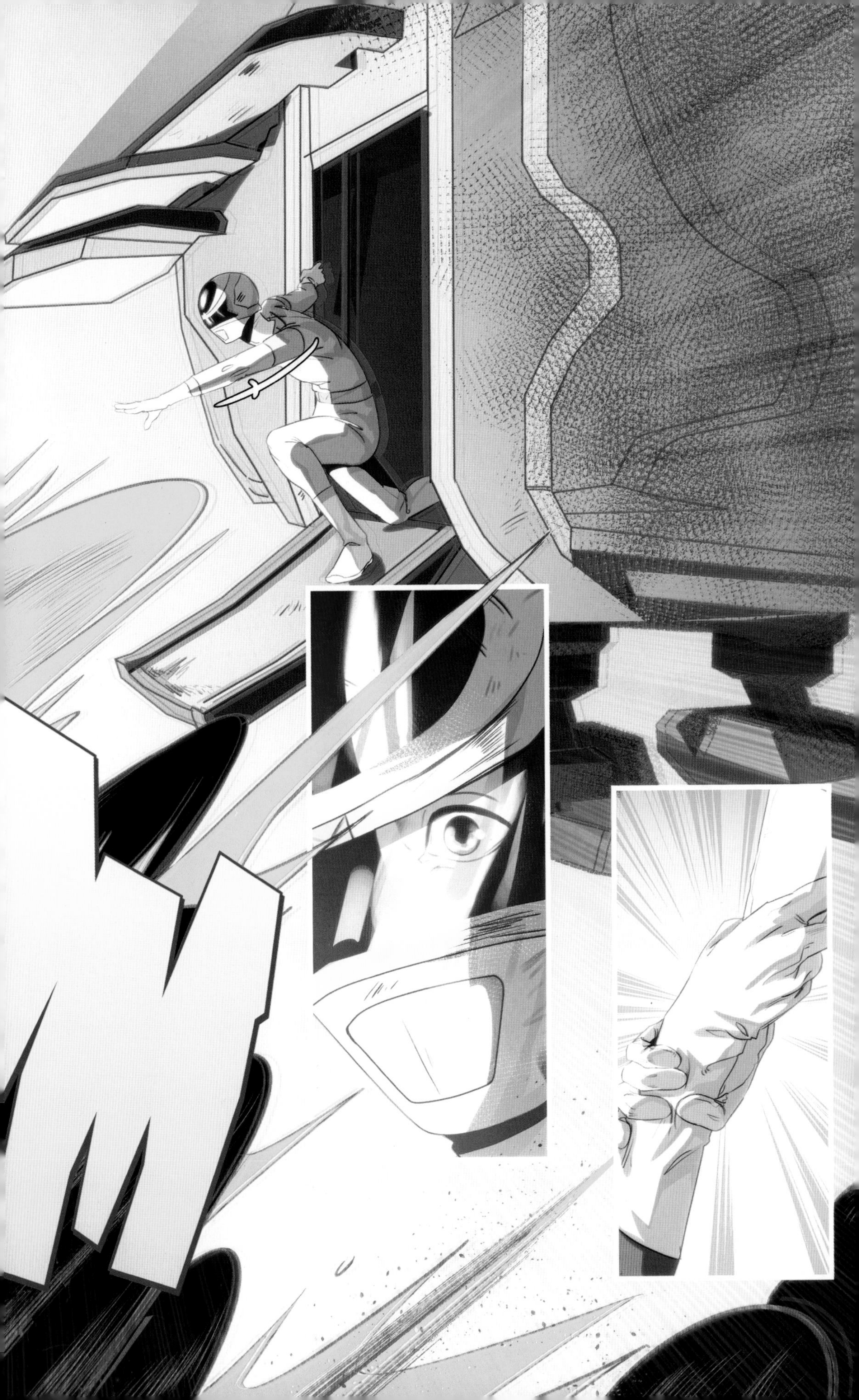
M

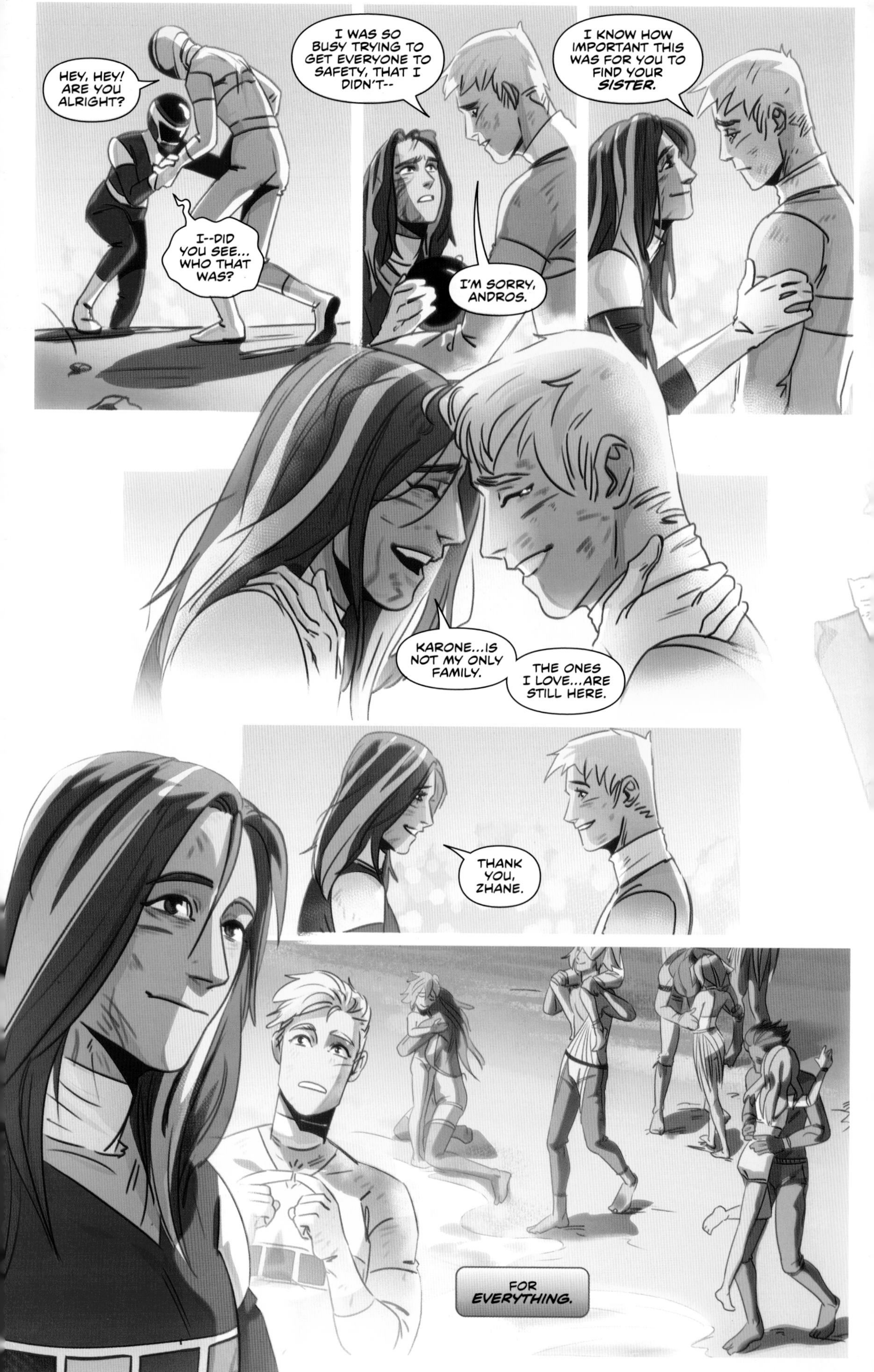
HEY, HEY! ARE YOU ALRIGHT?
I--DID YOU SEE... WHO THAT WAS?
I WAS SO BUSY TRYING TO GET EVERYONE TO SAFETY, THAT I DIDN'T--
I'M SORRY, ANDROS.
I KNOW HOW IMPORTANT THIS WAS FOR YOU TO FIND YOUR SISTER.
KARONE...IS NOT MY ONLY FAMILY.
THE ONES I LOVE...ARE STILL HERE.
THANK YOU, ZHANE.
FOR EVERYTHING.

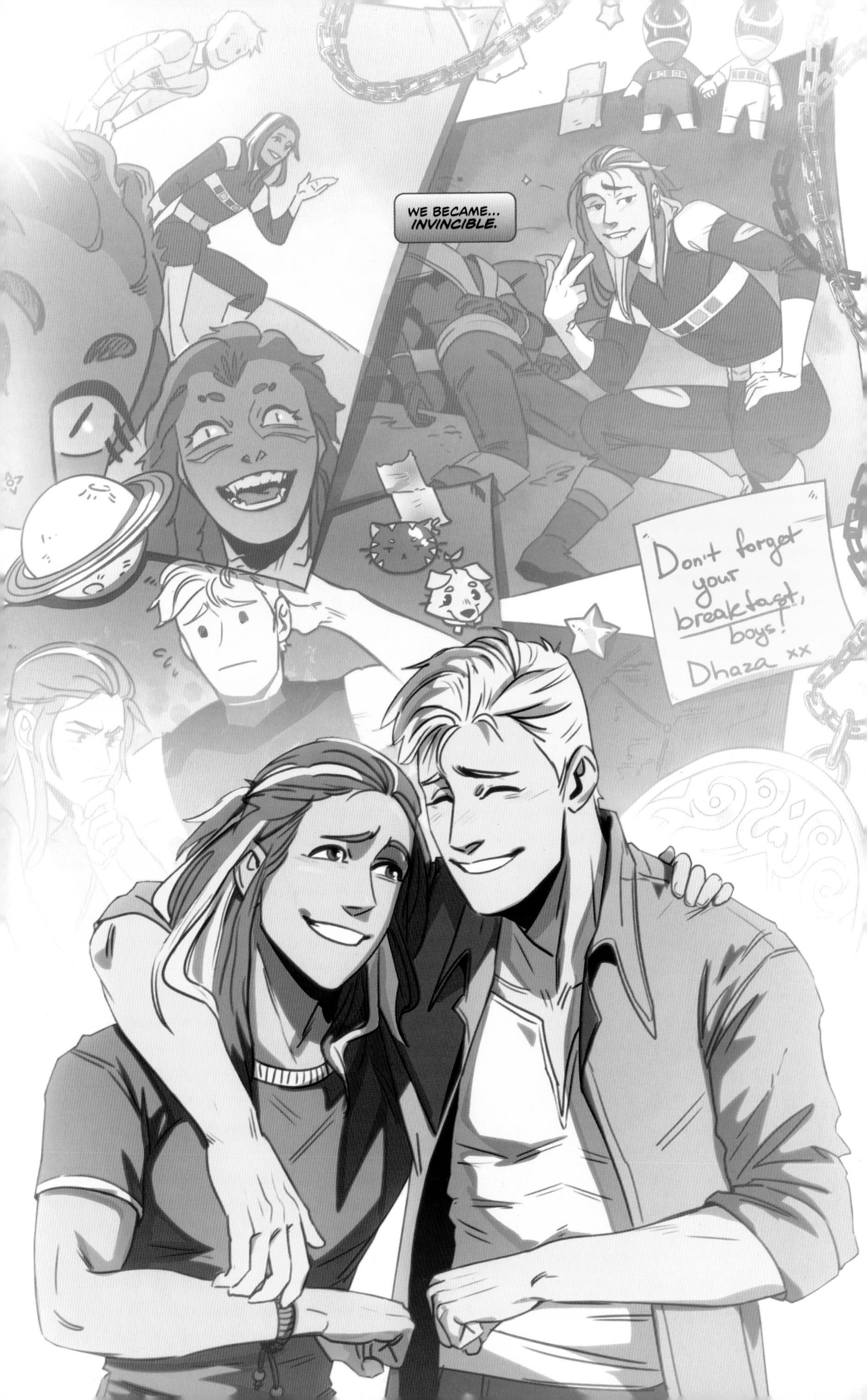
WE BECAME...
INVINCIBLE.
Don't forget your breakfast, boys!
Dhaza xx

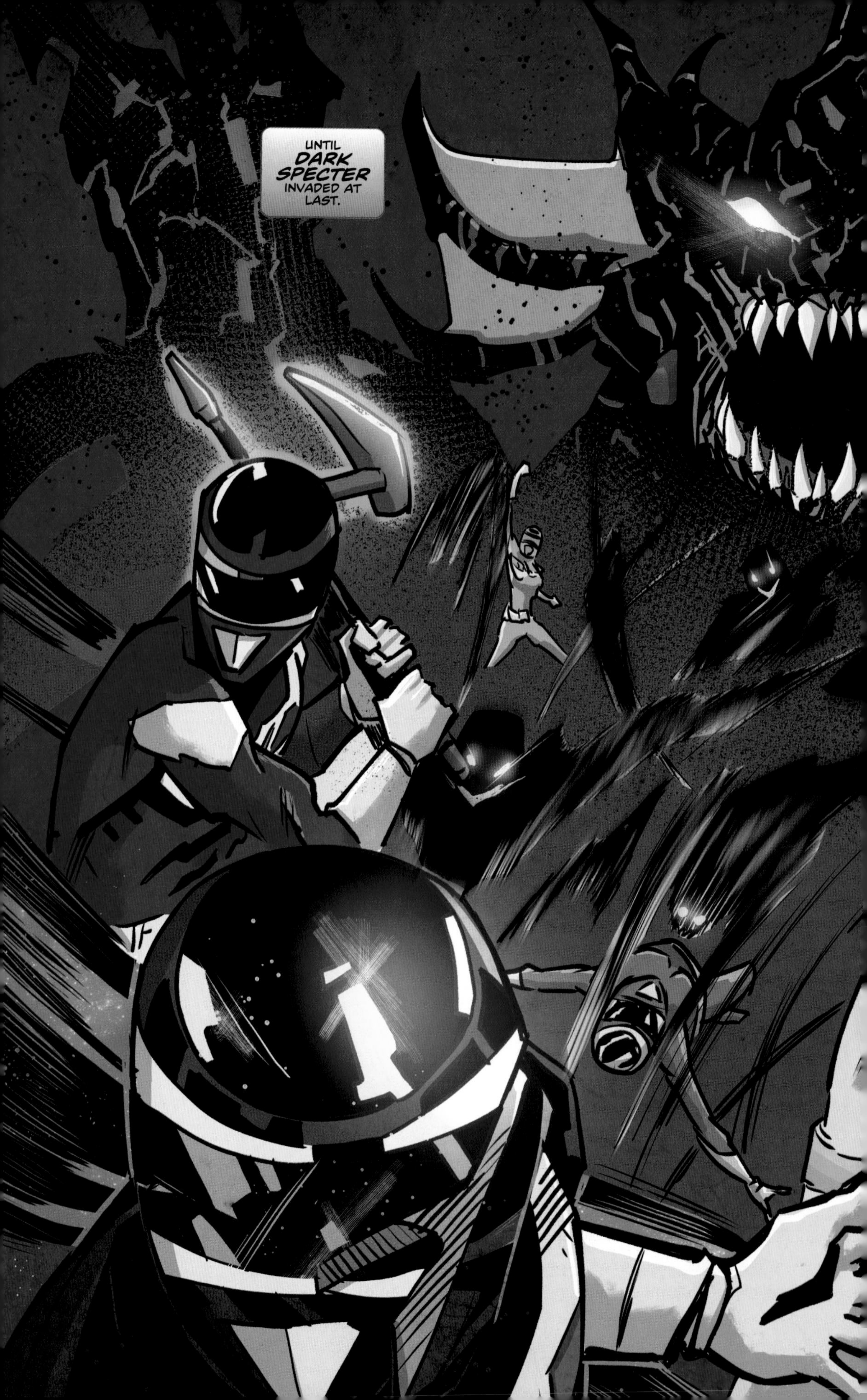
UNTIL DARK SPECTER INVADED AT LAST.

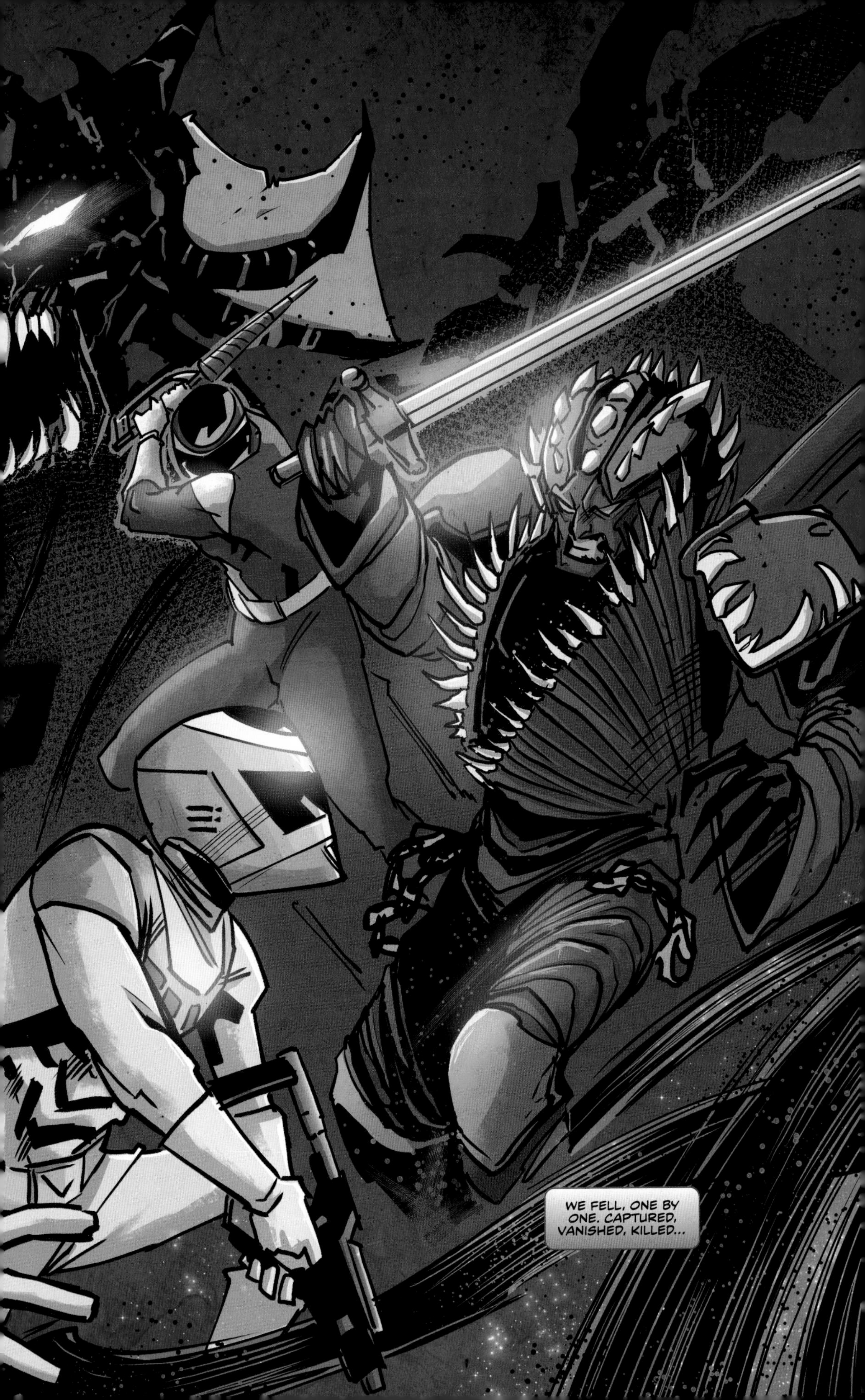
WE FELL, ONE BY ONE. CAPTURED, VANISHED, KILLED...

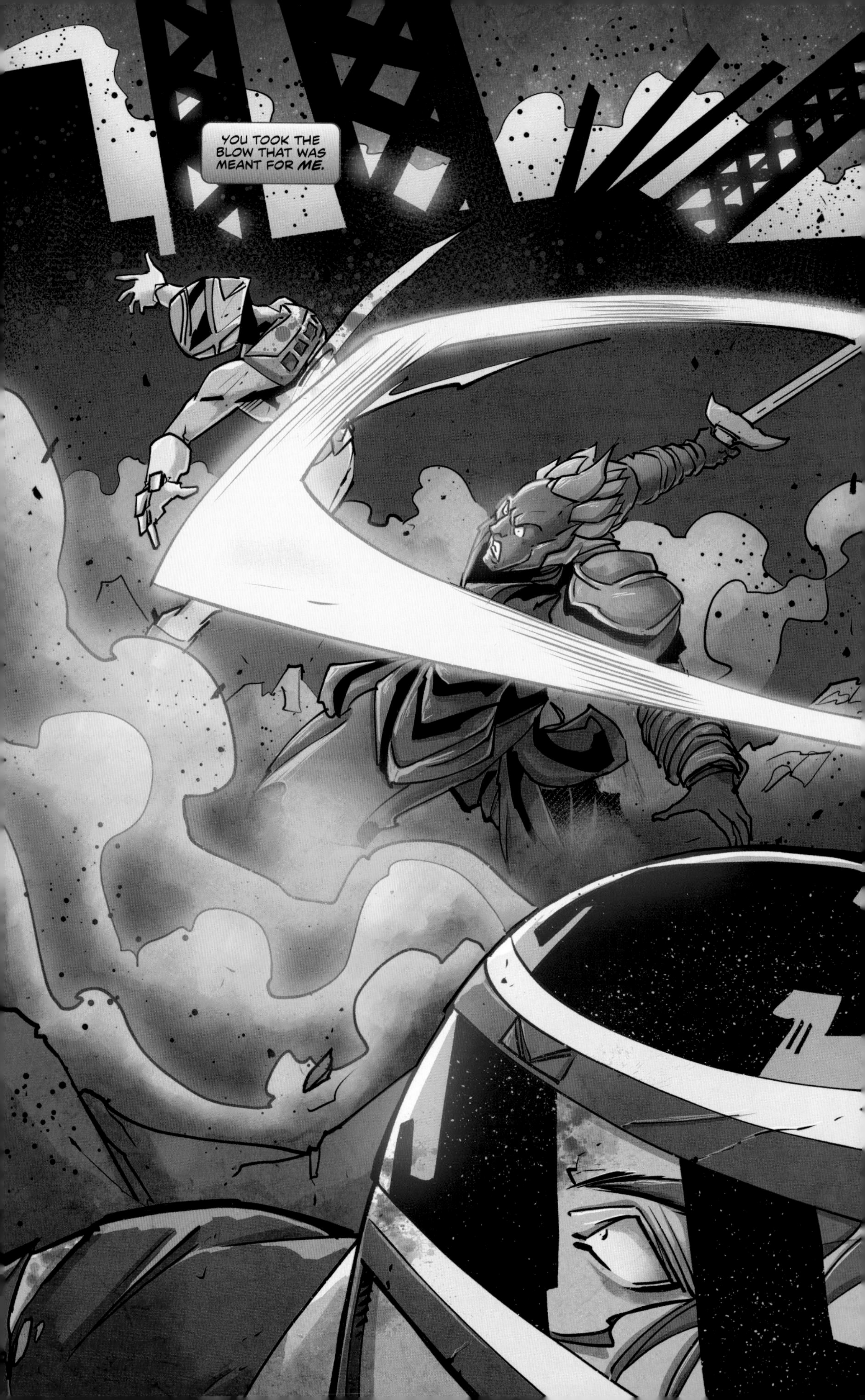
YOU TOOK THE BLOW THAT WAS MEANT FOR *ME*.

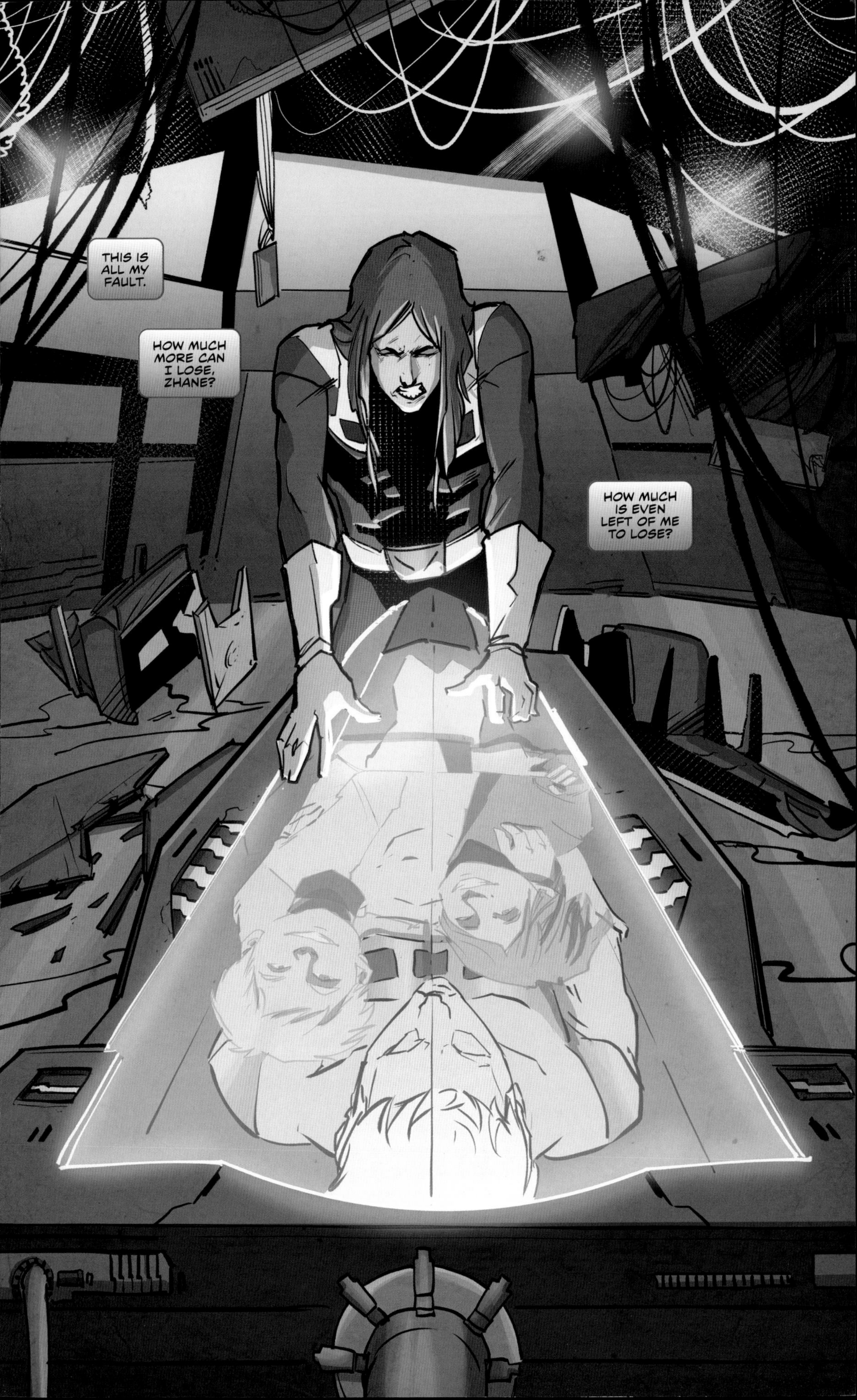
THIS IS ALL MY FAULT.
HOW MUCH MORE CAN I LOSE, ZHANE?
HOW MUCH IS EVEN LEFT OF ME TO LOSE?

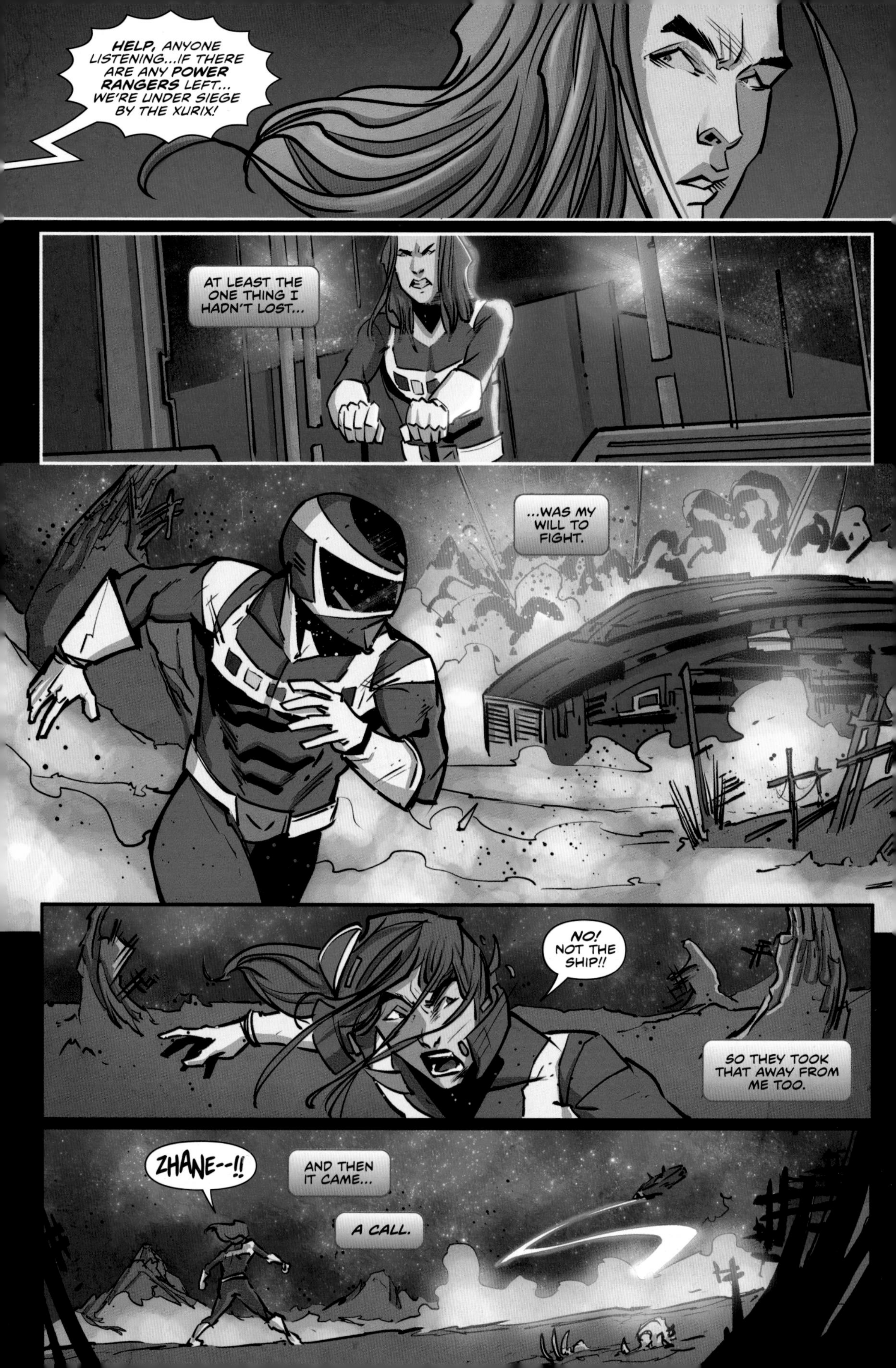
HELP, ANYONE LISTENING...IF THERE ARE ANY POWER RANGERS LEFT... WE'RE UNDER SIEGE BY THE XURIX!
AT LEAST THE ONE THING I HADN'T LOST...
...WAS MY WILL TO FIGHT.
NO! NOT THE SHIP!!
SO THEY TOOK THAT AWAY FROM ME TOO.
ZHANE--!!
AND THEN IT CAME...
A CALL.

THE RUINS OF KO-35.
TO ALL THOSE WHO HEAR THESE WORDS...YOU ARE NOT ALONE.
A CALL LIKE THE FIRST--YOU, CRYING OUT MY NAME, ASKING ME TO COME WITH YOU, TO JOIN YOUR LITTLE FOUND FAMILY.
LIKE YOU NAMING ME BEFORE THE VILLAGE, SHOUTING ALOUD FOR ALL TO HEAR, THAT I WAS WORTHY--THAT I WAS WANTED.
LIKE YOU CALLING MY NAME IN THE RUINS, THE NIGHT THAT WE HAD OUR FIRST CLUE TO KARONE'S WHEREABOUTS IN MORE THAN TEN YEARS.
LIKE YOU CALLING MY NAME IN BATTLE, THE MOMENT BEFORE YOU FELL.
YOUR LAST WORDS.
YOUR LAST WORDS WERE MY NAME.
AND THIS CALL I HEAR NOW, FROM A DISTANT RED RANGER ON A DISTANT PLANET, REMINDS ME SO MUCH OF YOUR VOICE...
IT SOUNDS LIKE HELP, AT LAST.

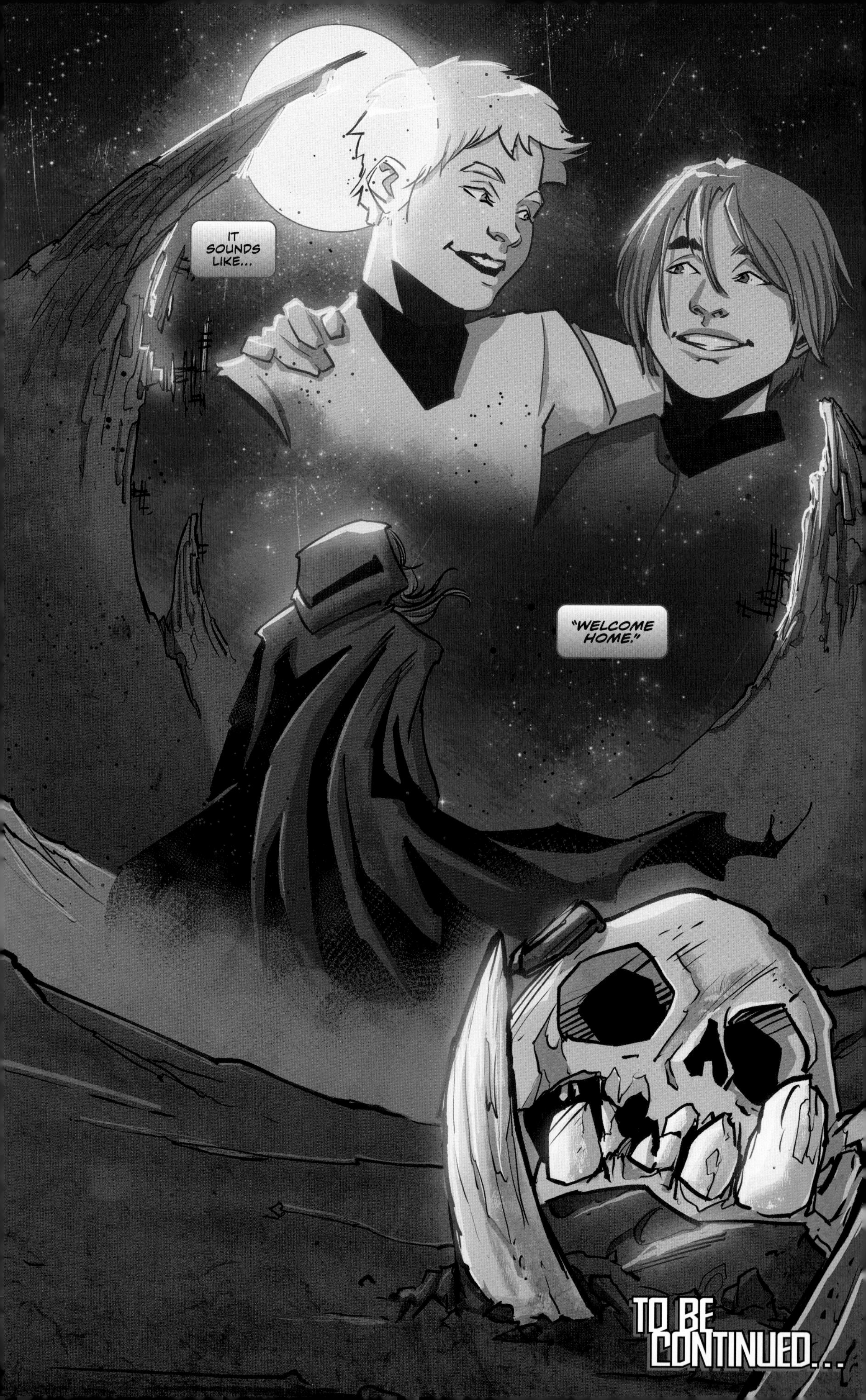
IT SOUNDS LIKE...
"WELCOME HOME."
TO BE CONTINUED...

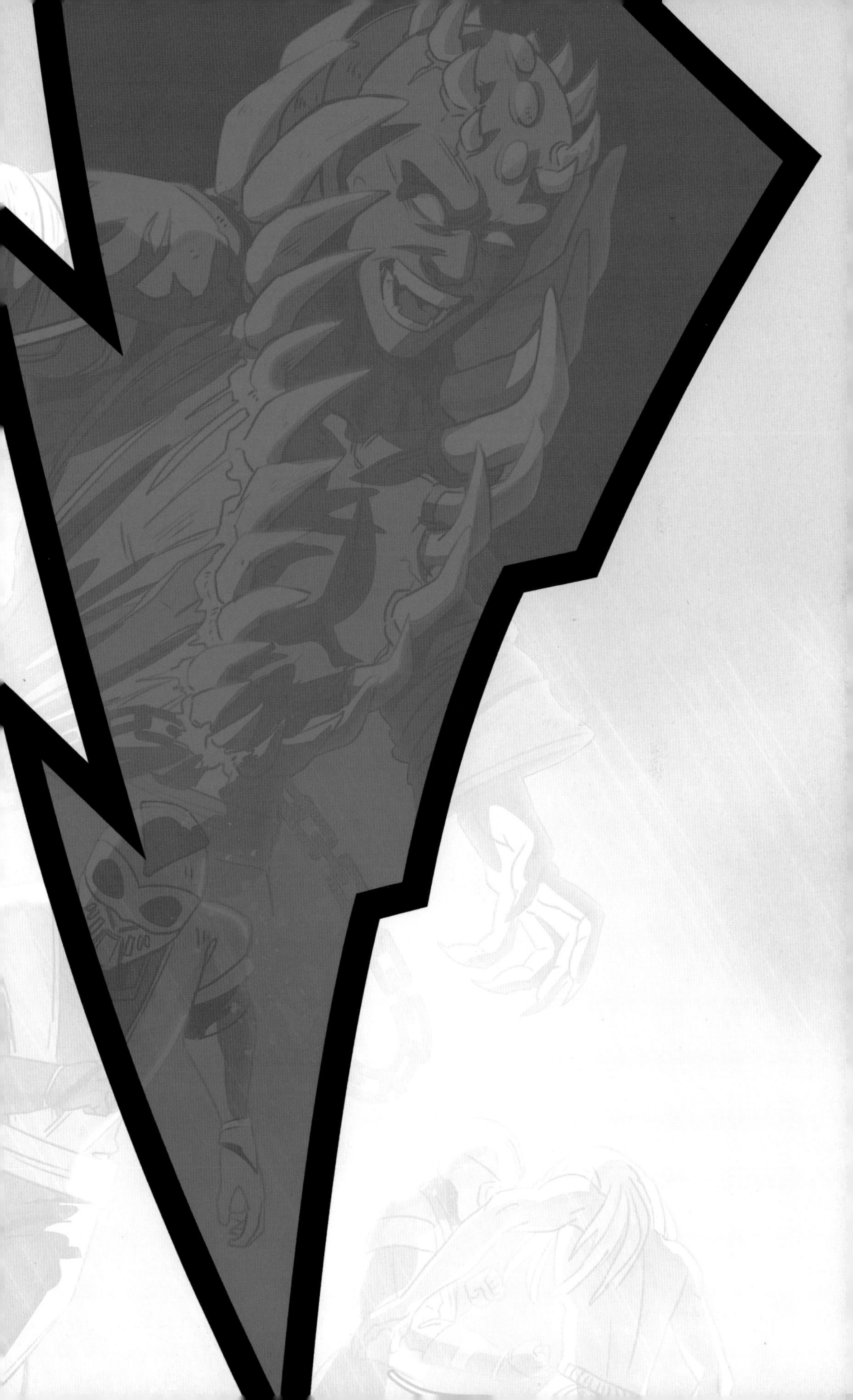

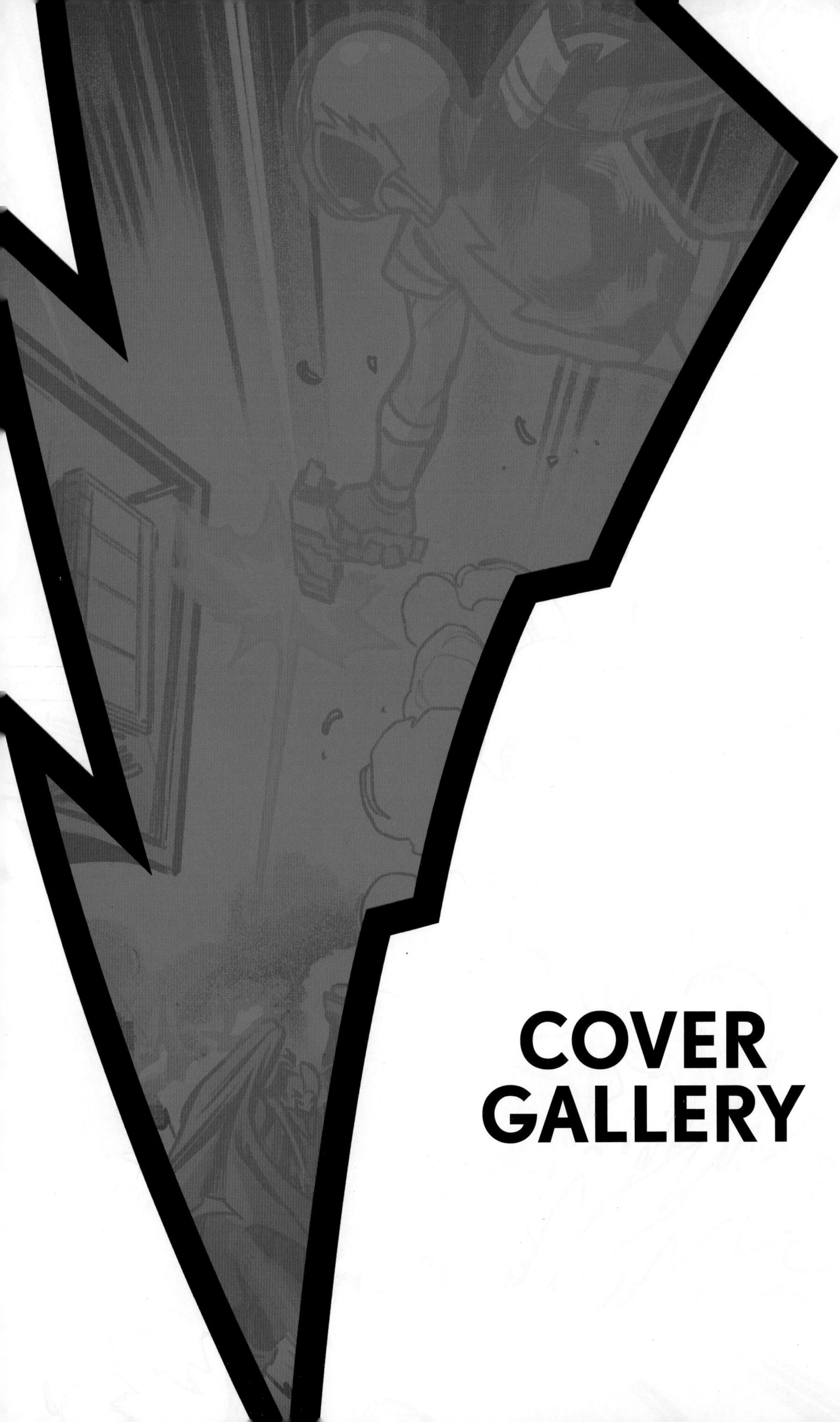

COVER GALLERY

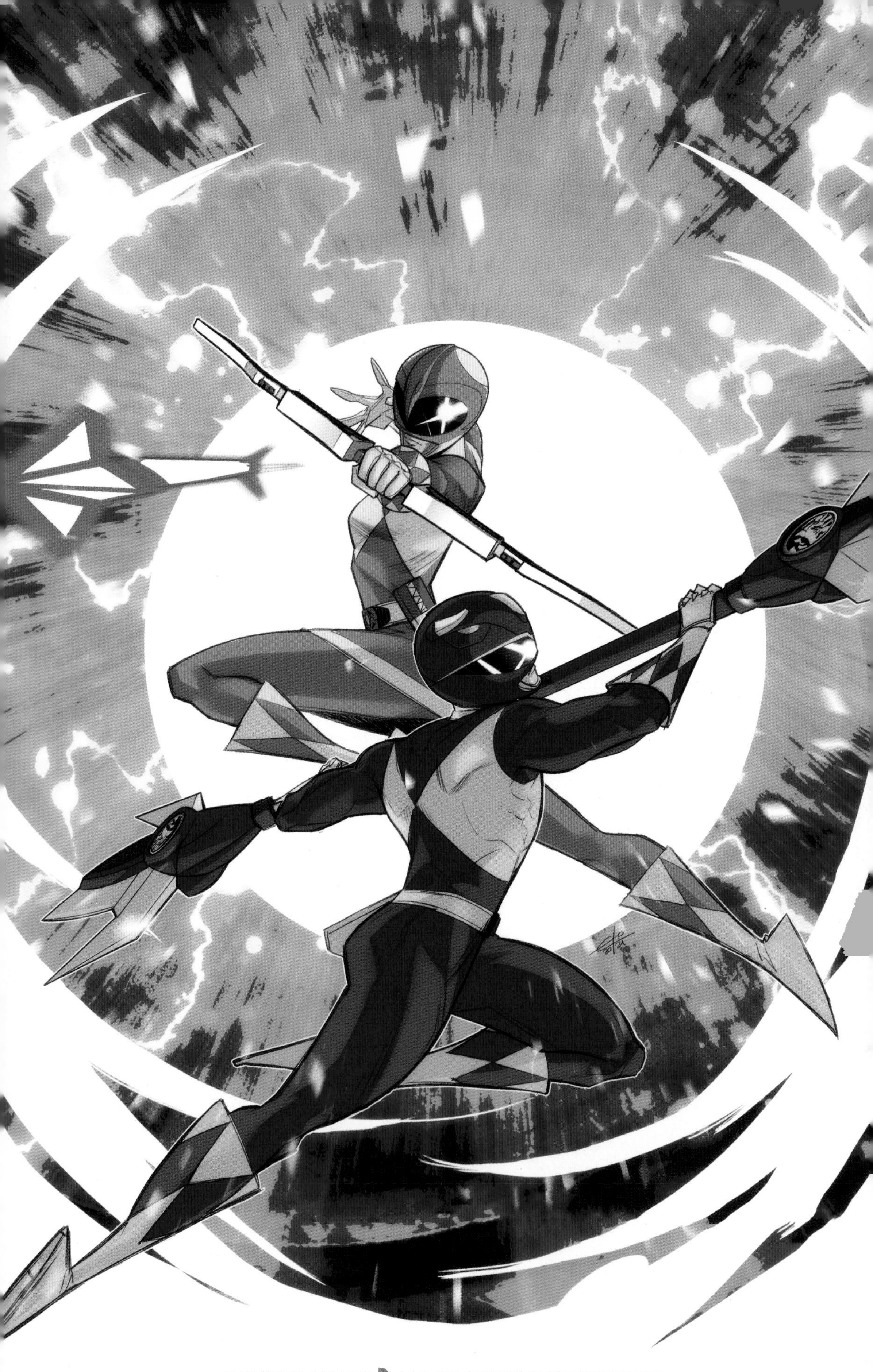

ELEONORA CARLINI MIGHTY MORPHIN #21 VARIANT COVER

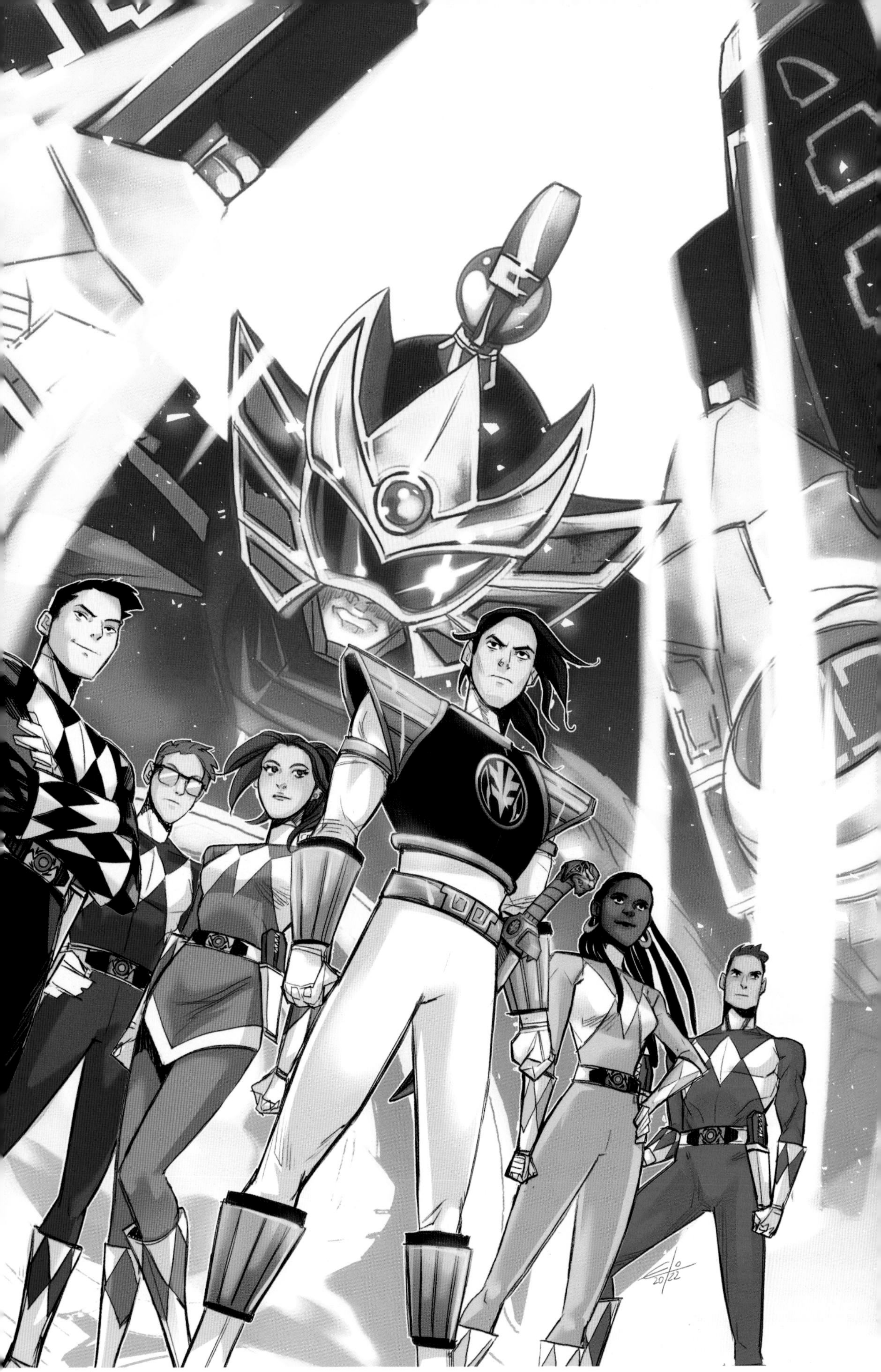

ELEONORA CARLINI MIGHTY MORPHIN #22 VARIANT COVER

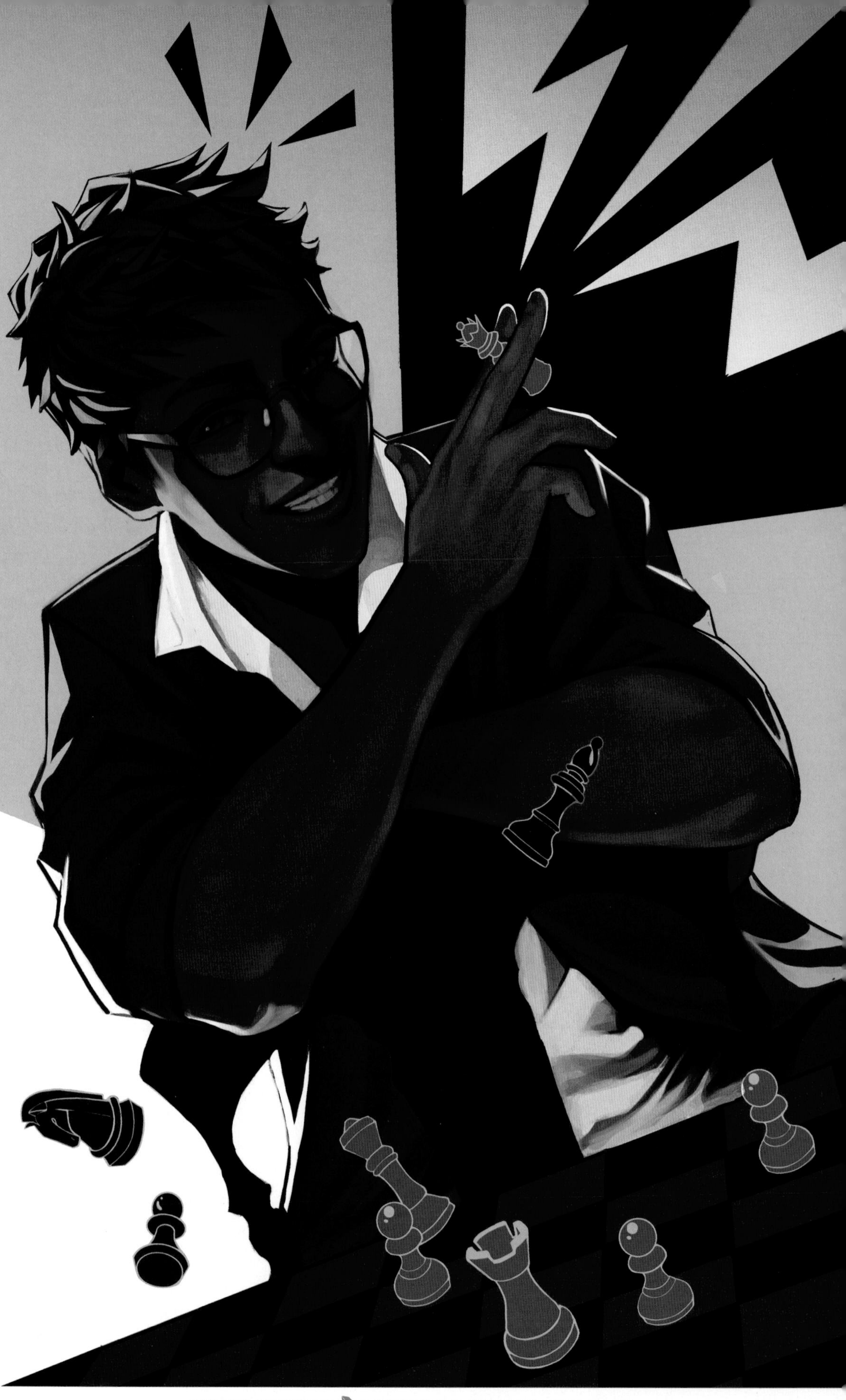

QISTINA KHALIDAH MIGHTY MORPHIN #21 VARIANT COVER

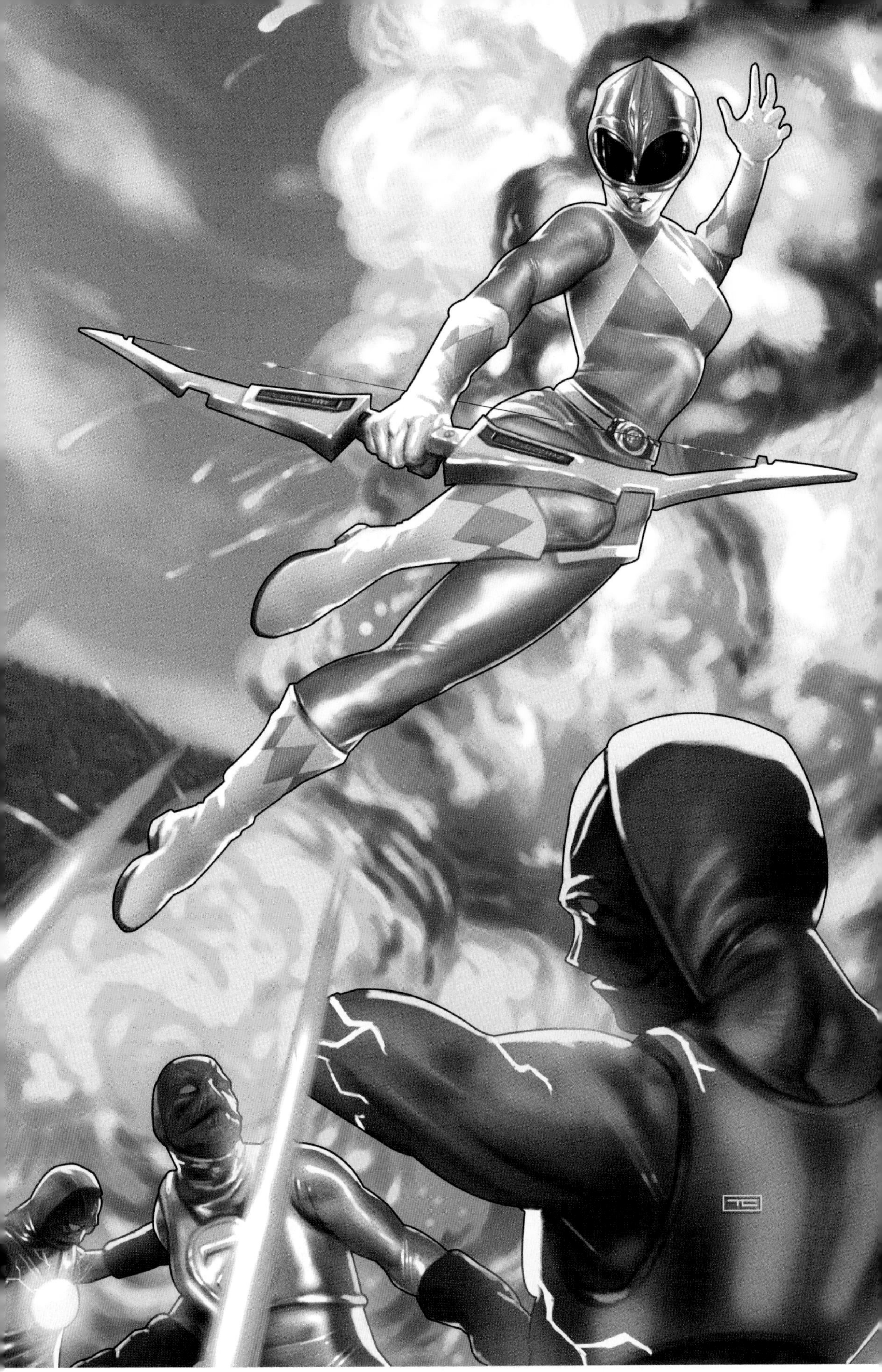

TAURIN CLARKE MIGHTY MORPHIN #20 VARIANT COVER

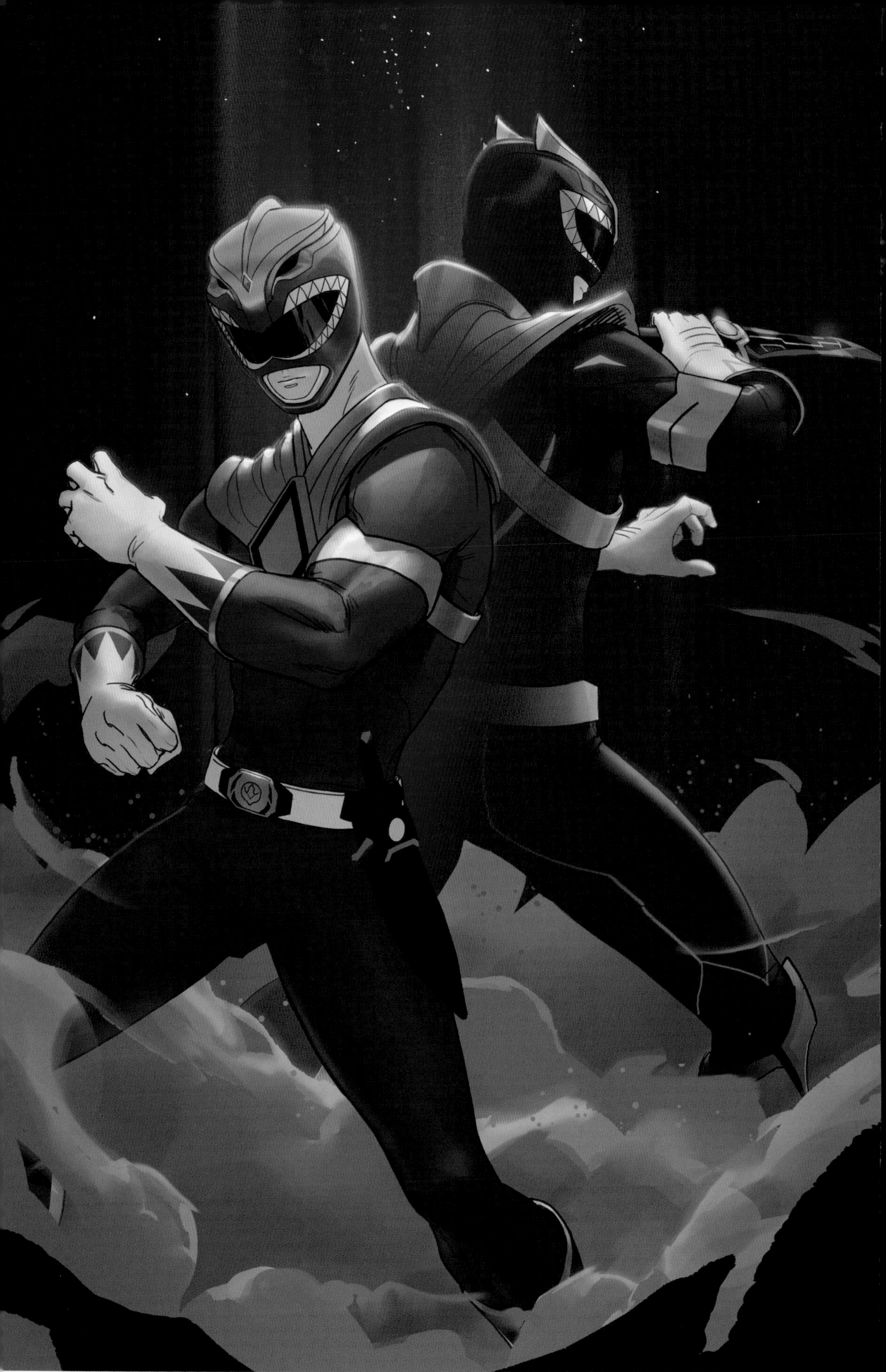

MONIKA PALOSZ MIGHTY MORPHIN #22 VARIANT COVER

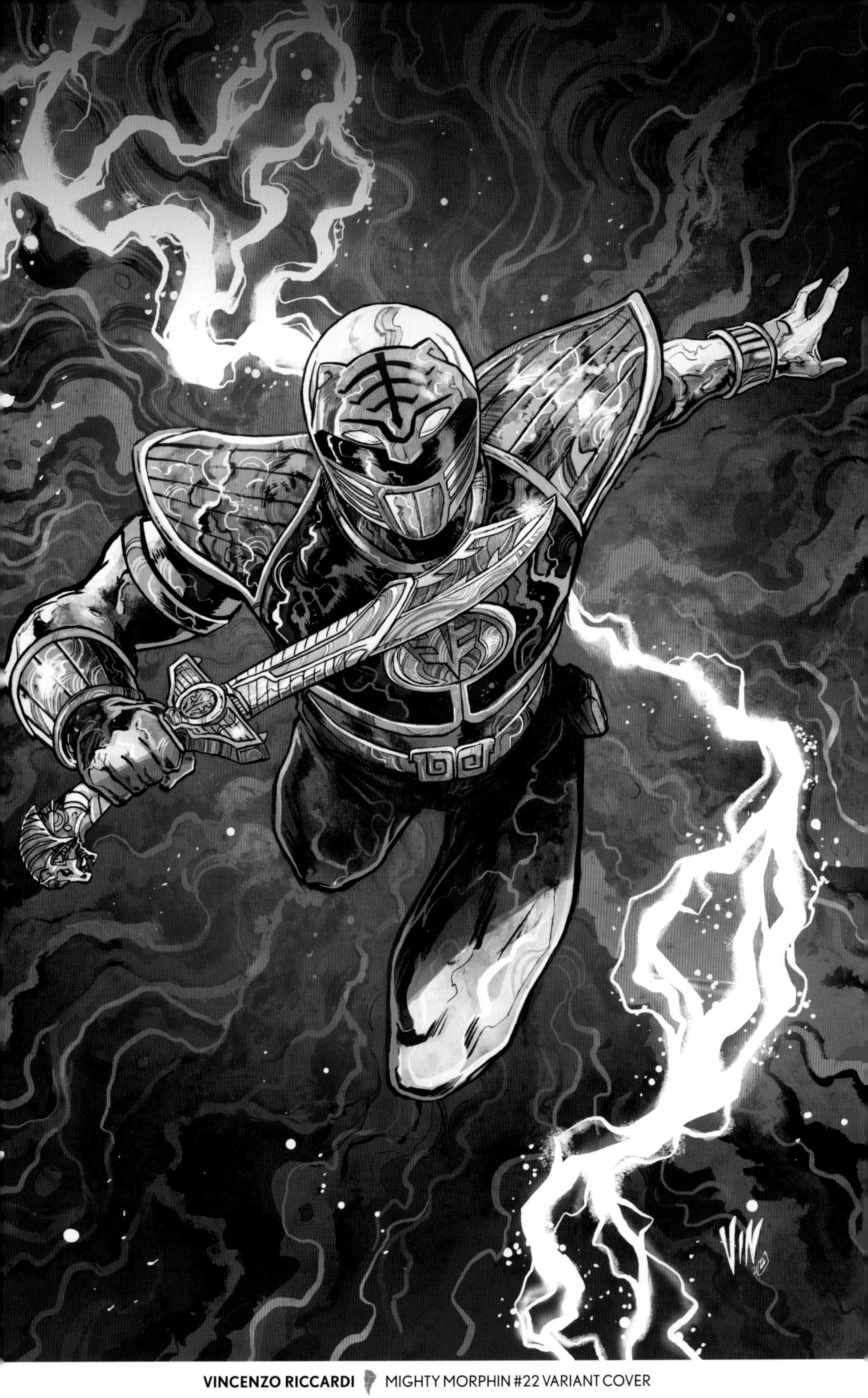
VIN

VINCENZO RICCARDI MIGHTY MORPHIN #22 VARIANT COVER

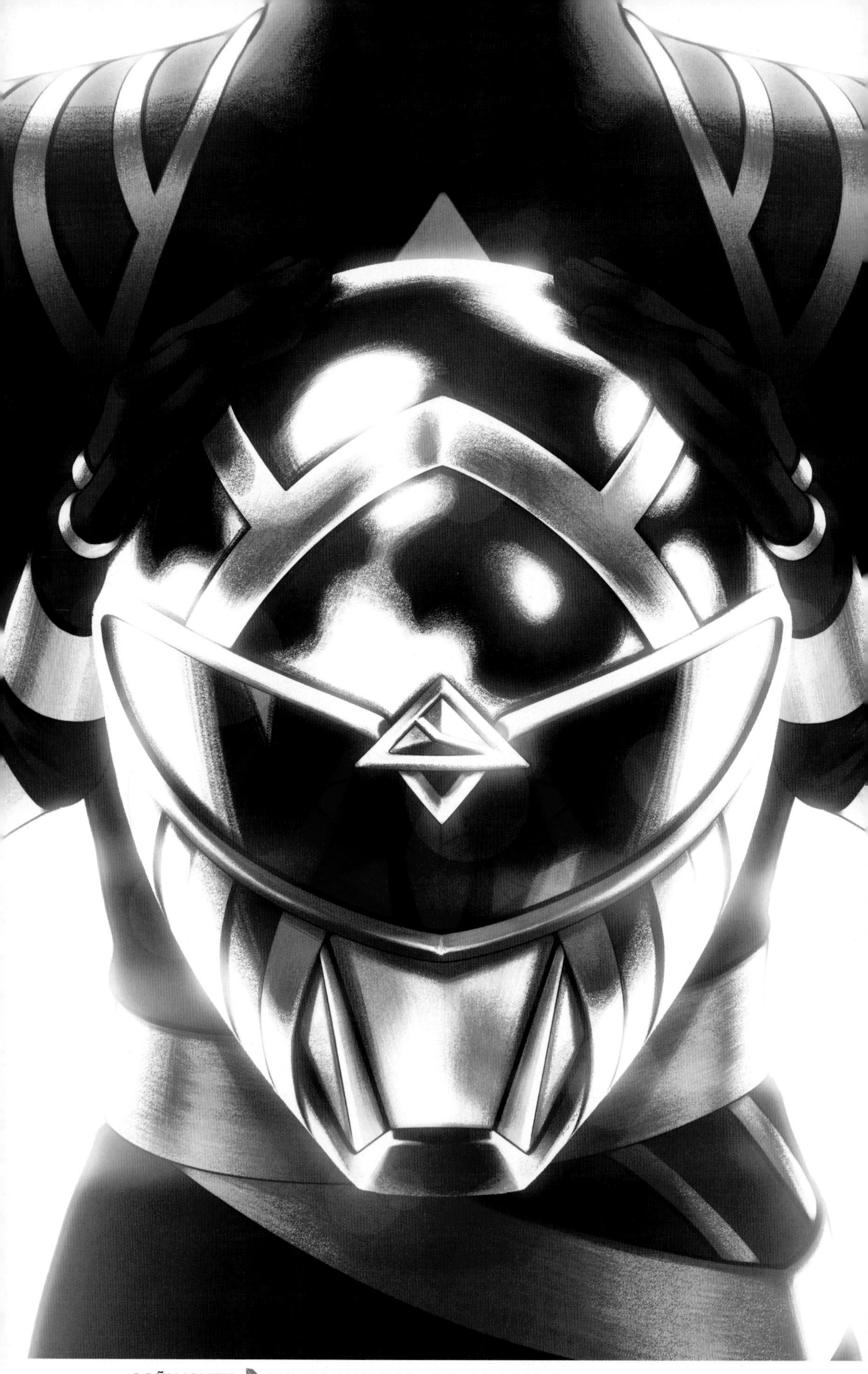

GOÑI MONTES POWER RANGERS UNLIMITED: COUNTDOWN TO RUIN #1 VARIANT COVER

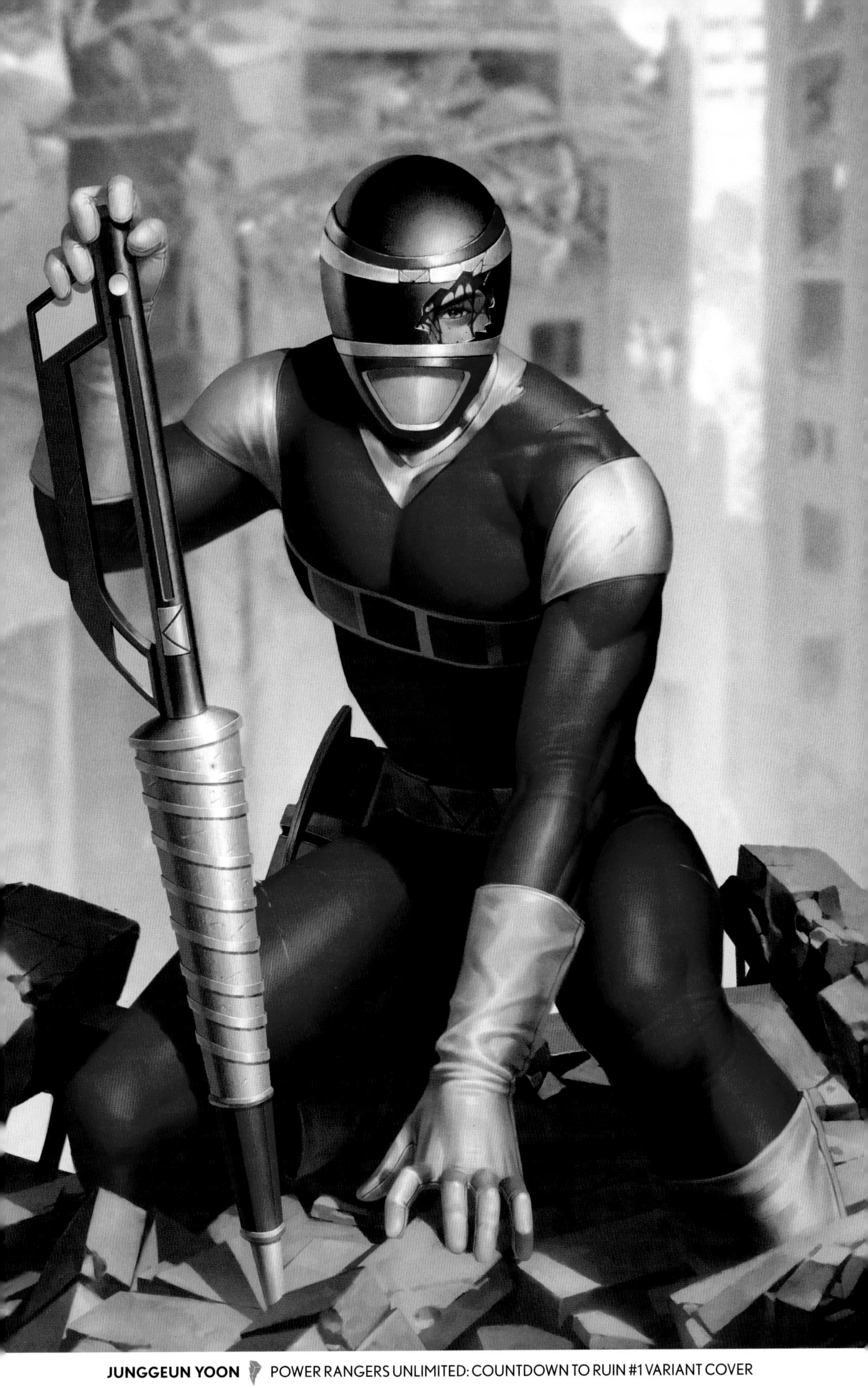

JUNGGEUN YOON POWER RANGERS UNLIMITED: COUNTDOWN TO RUIN #1 VARIANT COVER

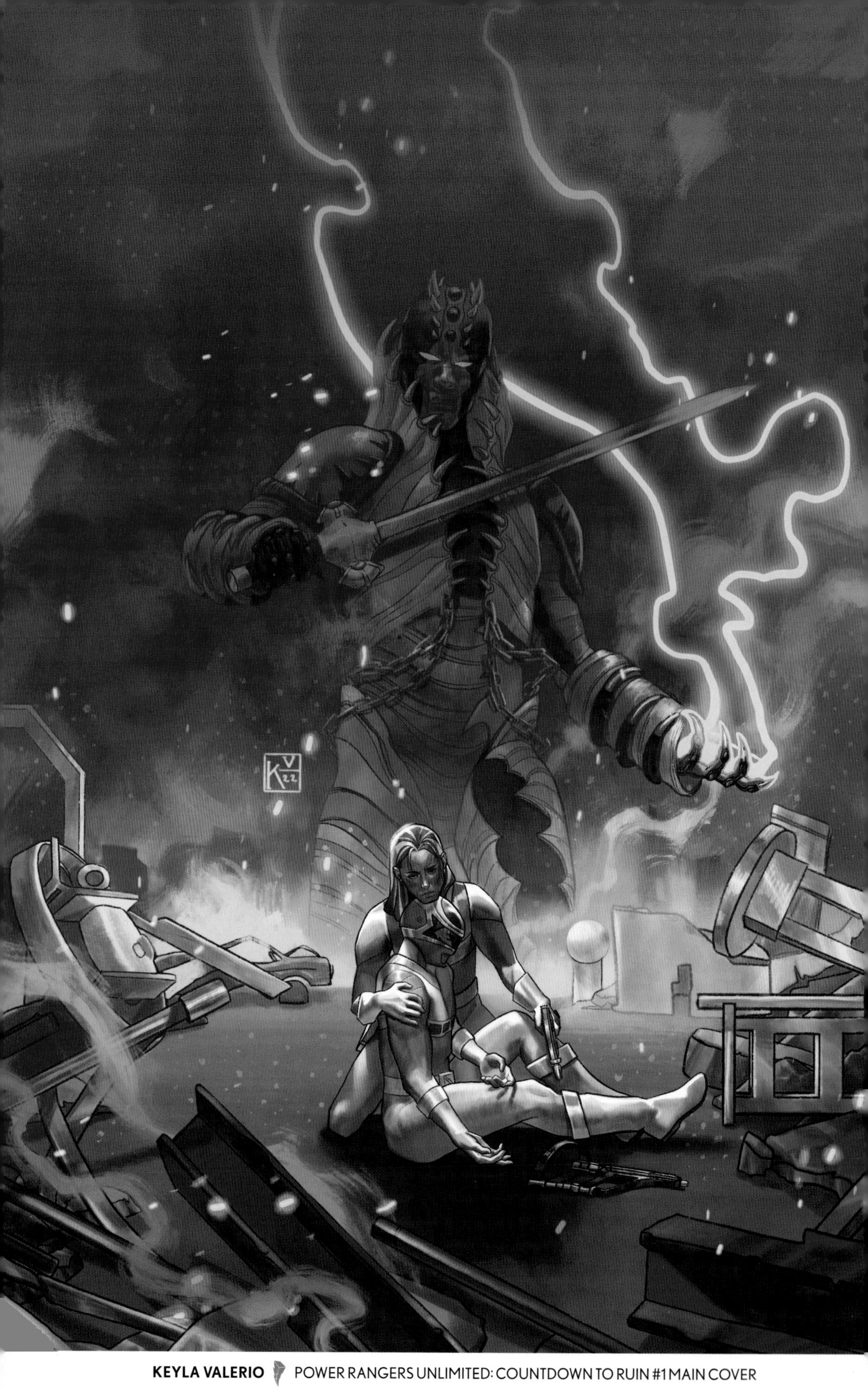

KEYLA VALERIO POWER RANGERS UNLIMITED: COUNTDOWN TO RUIN #1 MAIN COVER

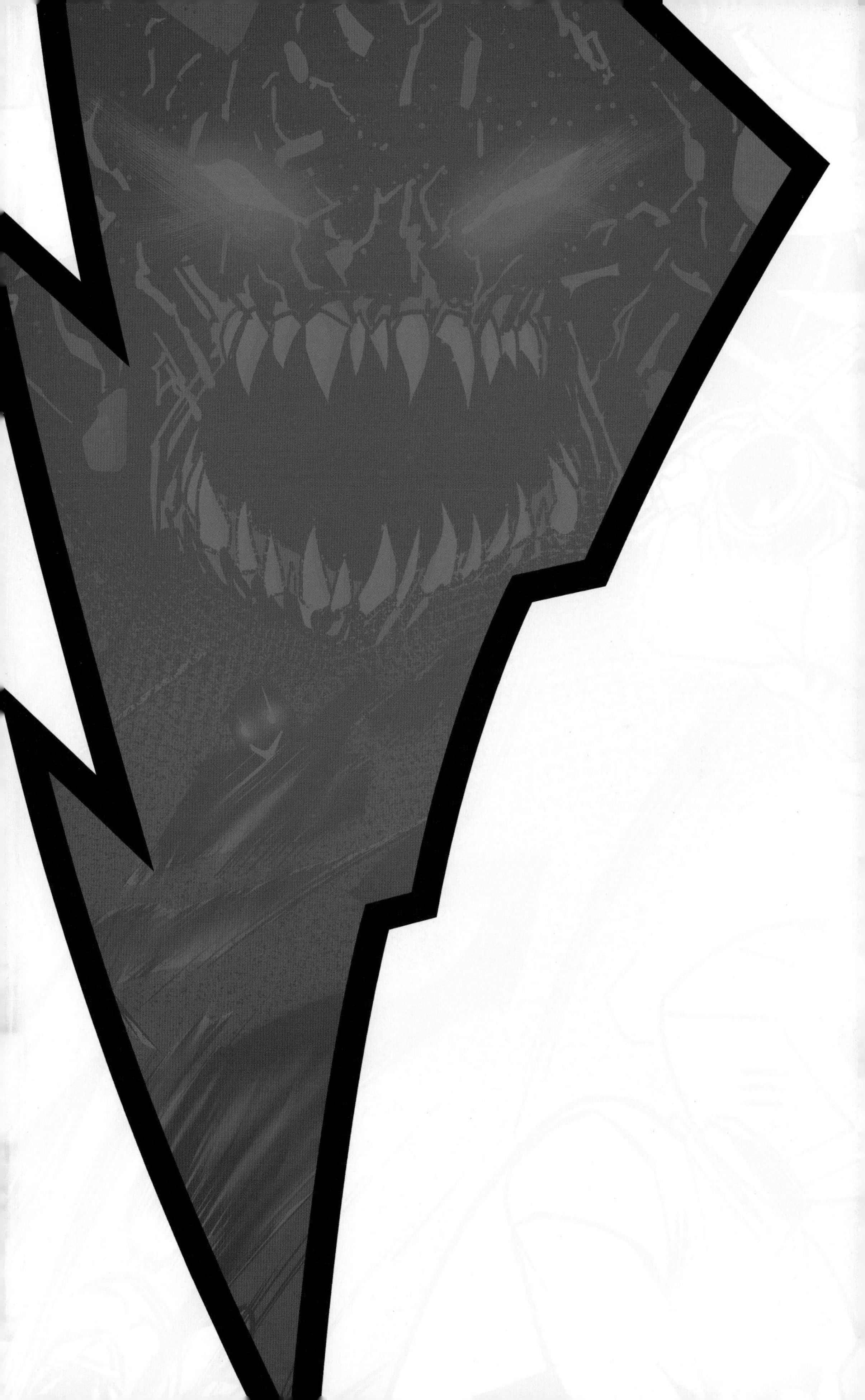

SPECIAL PREVIEW

Power Rangers

VOLUME SIX

WRITTEN BY

RYAN PARROTT

ILLUSTRATED BY

MARCO RENNA

COLORED BY

WALTER BAIAMONTE &
SARA ANTONELLINI

LETTERED BY

ED DUKESHIRE

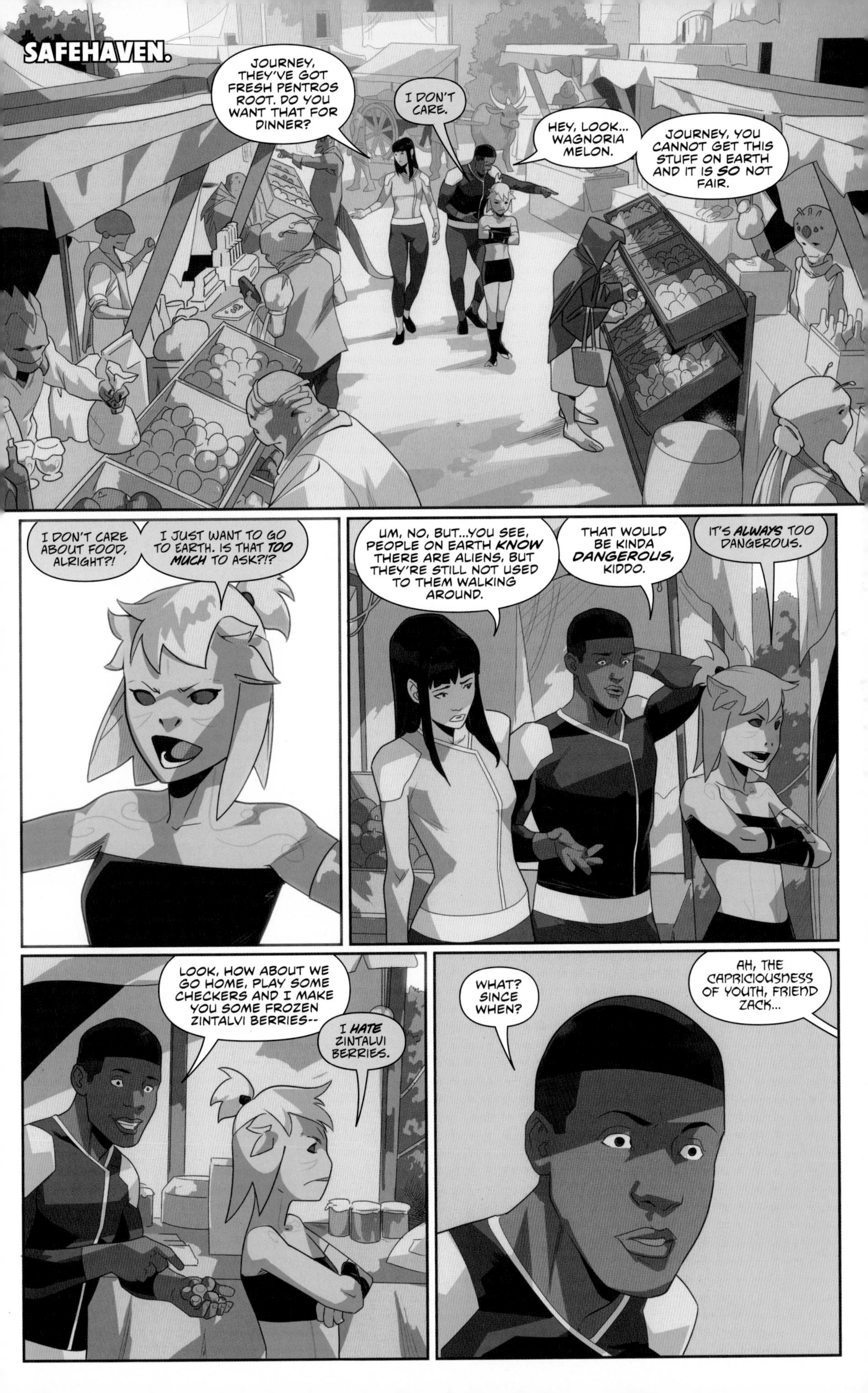
SAFEHAVEN.
JOURNEY, THEY'VE GOT FRESH PENTROS ROOT. DO YOU WANT THAT FOR DINNER?
I DON'T CARE.
HEY, LOOK... WAGNORIA MELON.
JOURNEY, YOU CANNOT GET THIS STUFF ON EARTH AND IT IS SO NOT FAIR.
I DON'T CARE ABOUT FOOD, ALRIGHT?!
I JUST WANT TO GO TO EARTH. IS THAT TOO MUCH TO ASK?!?
UM, NO, BUT...YOU SEE, PEOPLE ON EARTH KNOW THERE ARE ALIENS, BUT THEY'RE STILL NOT USED TO THEM WALKING AROUND.
THAT WOULD BE KINDA DANGEROUS, KIDDO.
IT'S ALWAYS TOO DANGEROUS.
LOOK, HOW ABOUT WE GO HOME, PLAY SOME CHECKERS AND I MAKE YOU SOME FROZEN ZINTALVI BERRIES--
I HATE ZINTALVI BERRIES.
WHAT? SINCE WHEN?
AH, THE CAPRICIOUSNESS OF YOUTH, FRIEND ZACK...

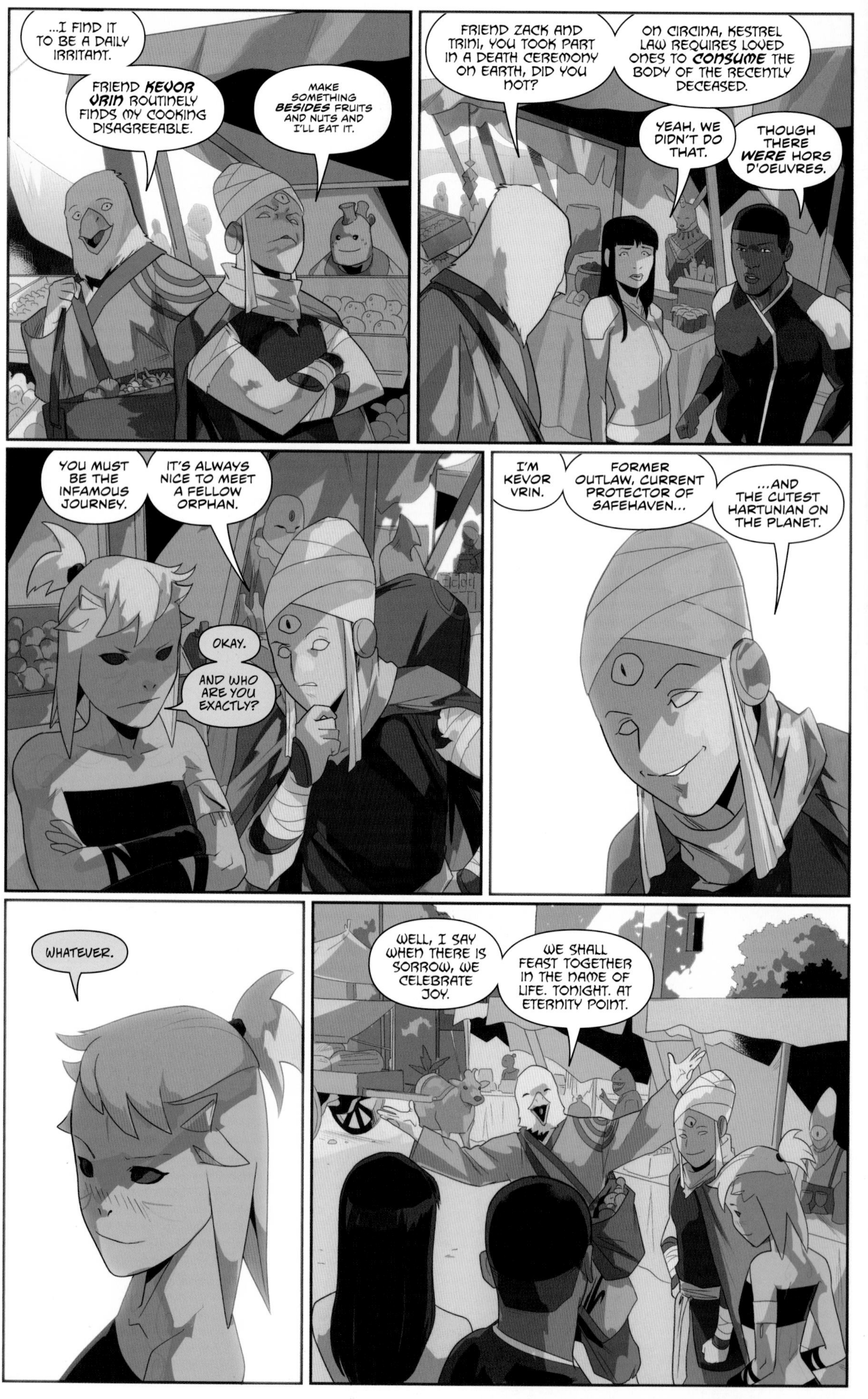
...I FIND IT TO BE A DAILY IRRITANT.
FRIEND KEVOR VRIN ROUTINELY FINDS MY COOKING DISAGREEABLE.
MAKE SOMETHING BESIDES FRUITS AND NUTS AND I'LL EAT IT.
FRIEND ZACK AND TRINI, YOU TOOK PART IN A DEATH CEREMONY ON EARTH, DID YOU NOT?
ON CIRCINA, KESTREL LAW REQUIRES LOVED ONES TO CONSUME THE BODY OF THE RECENTLY DECEASED.
YEAH, WE DIDN'T DO THAT.
THOUGH THERE WERE HORS D'OEUVRES.
YOU MUST BE THE INFAMOUS JOURNEY.
IT'S ALWAYS NICE TO MEET A FELLOW ORPHAN.
OKAY.
AND WHO ARE YOU EXACTLY?
I'M KEVOR VRIN.
FORMER OUTLAW, CURRENT PROTECTOR OF SAFEHAVEN...
...AND THE CUTEST HARTUNIAN ON THE PLANET.
WHATEVER.
WELL, I SAY WHEN THERE IS SORROW, WE CELEBRATE JOY.
WE SHALL FEAST TOGETHER IN THE NAME OF LIFE. TONIGHT. AT ETERNITY POINT.

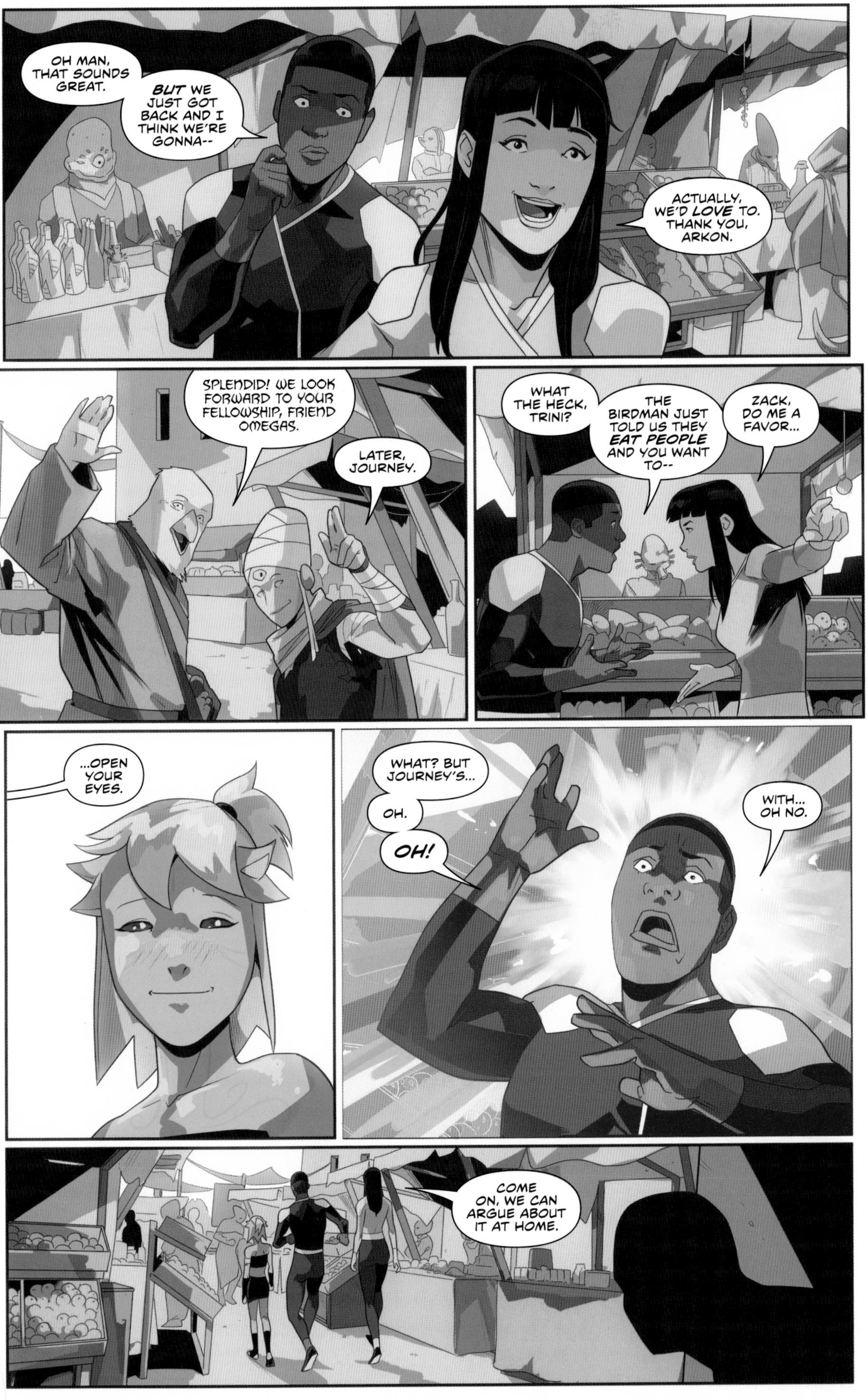
OH MAN, THAT SOUNDS GREAT.
BUT WE JUST GOT BACK AND I THINK WE'RE GONNA--
ACTUALLY, WE'D LOVE TO. THANK YOU, ARKON.
SPLENDID! WE LOOK FORWARD TO YOUR FELLOWSHIP, FRIEND OMEGAS.
LATER, JOURNEY.
WHAT THE HECK, TRINI?
THE BIRDMAN JUST TOLD US THEY EAT PEOPLE AND YOU WANT TO--
ZACK, DO ME A FAVOR...
...OPEN YOUR EYES.
WHAT? BUT JOURNEY'S...
OH.
OH!
WITH... OH NO.
COME ON, WE CAN ARGUE ABOUT IT AT HOME.

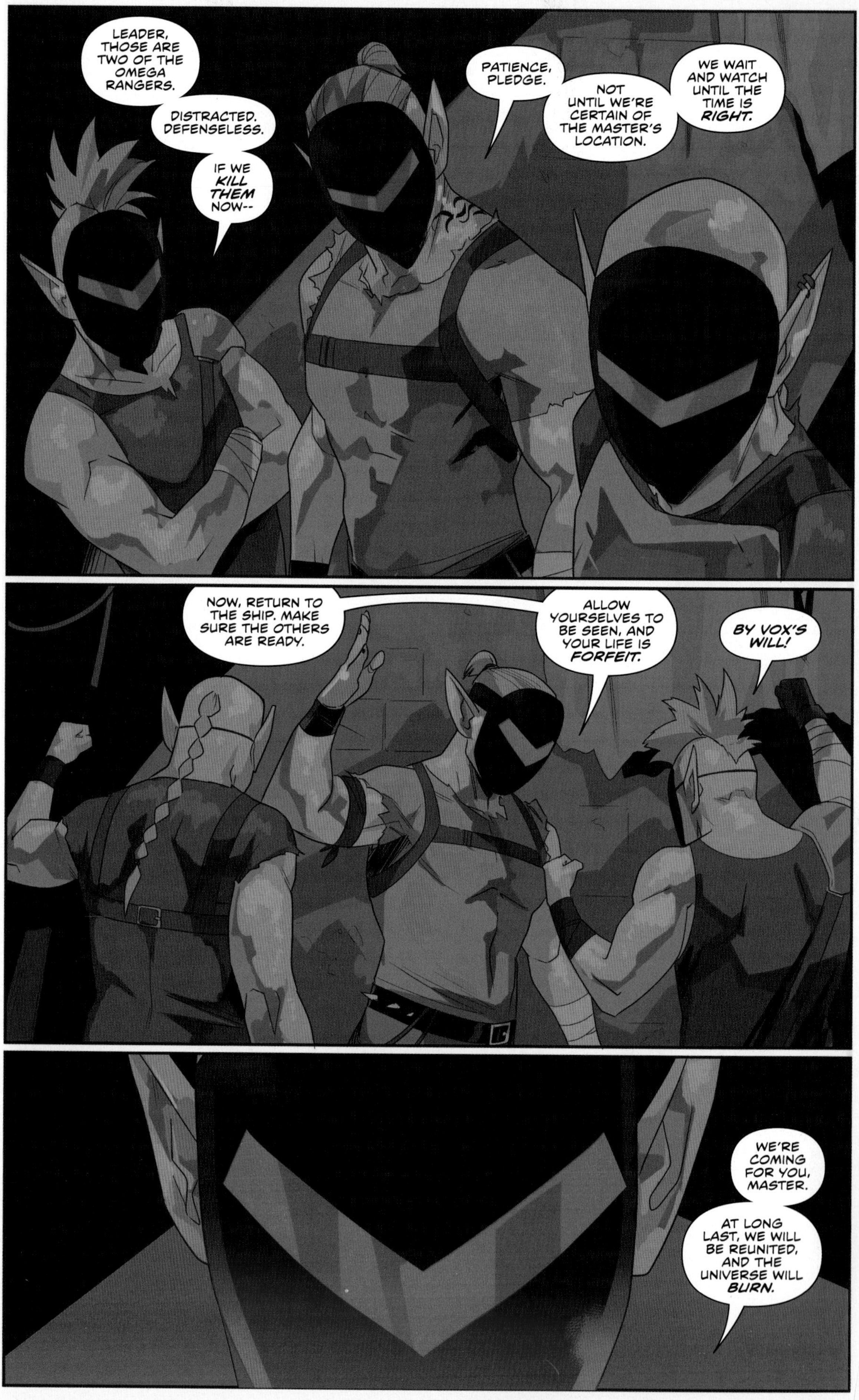
LEADER, THOSE ARE TWO OF THE OMEGA RANGERS.
DISTRACTED. DEFENSELESS.
IF WE KILL THEM NOW--
PATIENCE, PLEDGE.
NOT UNTIL WE'RE CERTAIN OF THE MASTER'S LOCATION.
WE WAIT AND WATCH UNTIL THE TIME IS RIGHT.
NOW, RETURN TO THE SHIP. MAKE SURE THE OTHERS ARE READY.
ALLOW YOURSELVES TO BE SEEN, AND YOUR LIFE IS FORFEIT.
BY VOX'S WILL!
WE'RE COMING FOR YOU, MASTER.
AT LONG LAST, WE WILL BE REUNITED, AND THE UNIVERSE WILL BURN.

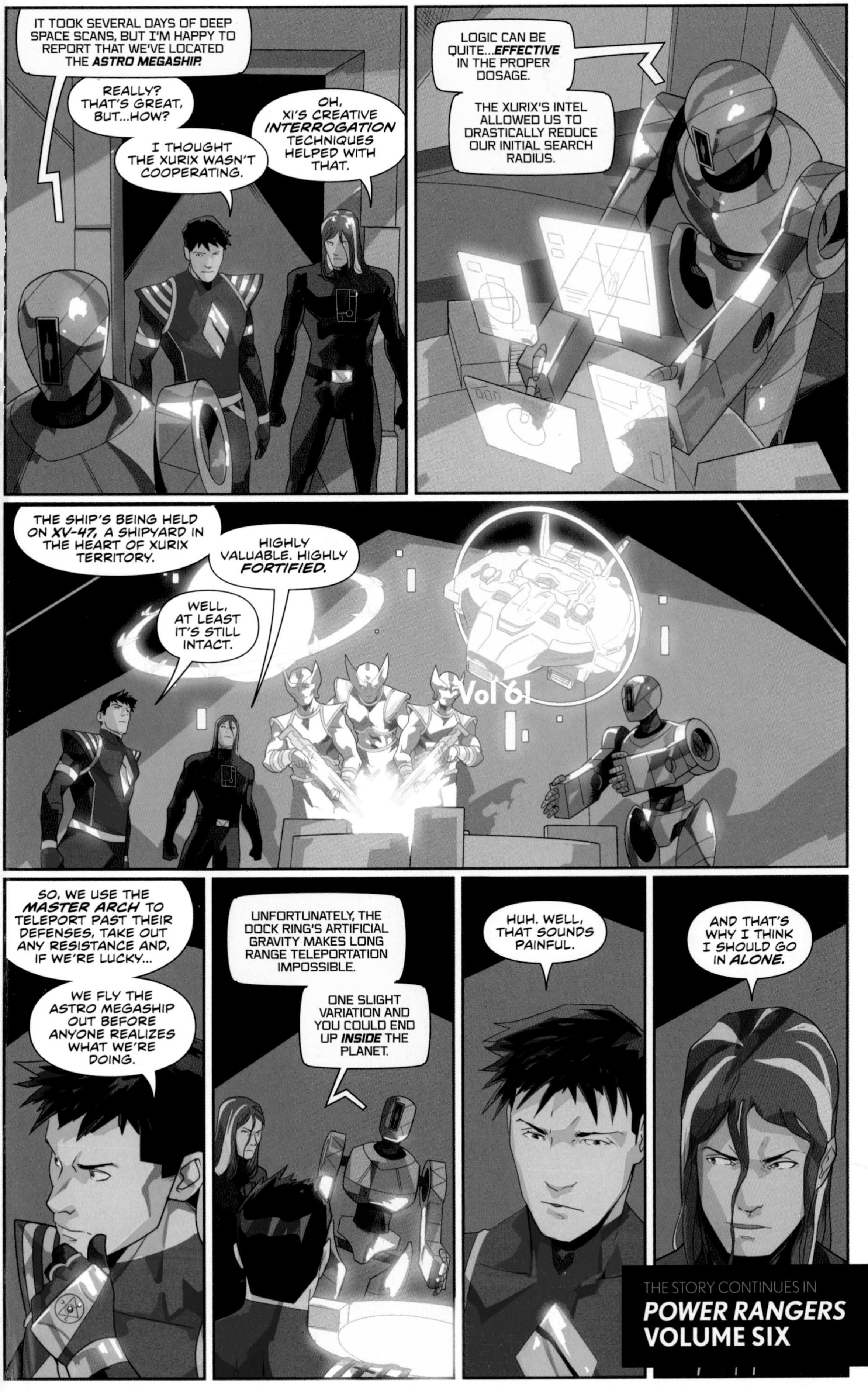
IT TOOK SEVERAL DAYS OF DEEP SPACE SCANS, BUT I'M HAPPY TO REPORT THAT WE'VE LOCATED THE ***ASTRO MEGASHIP.***
REALLY? THAT'S GREAT, BUT...HOW?
I THOUGHT THE XURIX WASN'T COOPERATING.
OH, XI'S CREATIVE ***INTERROGATION*** TECHNIQUES HELPED WITH THAT.
LOGIC CAN BE QUITE...***EFFECTIVE*** IN THE PROPER DOSAGE.
THE XURIX'S INTEL ALLOWED US TO DRASTICALLY REDUCE OUR INITIAL SEARCH RADIUS.
THE SHIP'S BEING HELD ON ***XV-47,*** A SHIPYARD IN THE HEART OF XURIX TERRITORY.
HIGHLY VALUABLE. HIGHLY ***FORTIFIED.***
WELL, AT LEAST IT'S STILL INTACT.
SO, WE USE THE ***MASTER ARCH*** TO TELEPORT PAST THEIR DEFENSES, TAKE OUT ANY RESISTANCE AND, IF WE'RE LUCKY...
WE FLY THE ASTRO MEGASHIP OUT BEFORE ANYONE REALIZES WHAT WE'RE DOING.
UNFORTUNATELY, THE DOCK RING'S ARTIFICIAL GRAVITY MAKES LONG RANGE TELEPORTATION IMPOSSIBLE.
ONE SLIGHT VARIATION AND YOU COULD END UP ***INSIDE*** THE PLANET.
HUH. WELL, THAT SOUNDS PAINFUL.
AND THAT'S WHY I THINK I SHOULD GO IN ***ALONE.***
THE STORY CONTINUES IN
POWER RANGERS VOLUME SIX

DISCOVER
MORE POWER RANGERS!

HIGGINS • PRASETYA • HERMS
ORLANDO • HOWELL • LAWSON
MIGHTY MORPHIN
POWER RANGERS
VOLUME ONE
INTRODUCTION BY POWER RANGERS EXECUTIVE PRODUCER JUDD "CHIP" LYNN

HIGGINS • PRASETYA
SILAS • HERMS
VALENZA • ORLANDO
HOWELL • LAWSON
MIGHTY MORPHIN
POWER RANGERS
VOLUME TWO

FLETCHER
THOMPSON
HOWARD
DI NICUOLO
STERN
MIGHTY MORPHIN
POWER RANGERS
PINK
INTRODUCTION BY AMY JO JOHNSON KIMBERLY HART, THE ORIGINAL PINK RANGER

POWER RANGERS
AFTERSHOCK
RYAN PARROTT
LUCAS WERNECK
JOANA LAFUENTE

MIGHTY MORPHIN
POWER RANGERS
POSTER BOOK
FEATURING 20 REMOVABLE POSTERS

PARROTT • MORA • ANGULO
SABAN'S
GO GO POWER RANGERS
VOLUME ONE

Mighty Morphin Power Rangers
Kyle Higgins, Hendry Prasetya, Matt Herms
Volume 1
ISBN: 978-1-60886-893-3 | $19.99
Volume 2
ISBN: 978-1-60886-942-8 | $16.99
Volume 3
ISBN: 978-1-60886-977-0 | $16.99
Volume 4
ISBN: 978-1-68415-031-1 | $16.99

Mighty Morphin Power Rangers: Pink
Kelly Thompson, Brenden Fletcher, Tini Howard, Daniele Di Nicuolo
ISBN: 978-1-60886-952-7 | $19.99

Saban's Go Go Power Rangers
Ryan Parrott, Dan Mora
Volume 1
ISBN: 978-1-68415-193-6 | $16.99

Saban's Power Rangers: Aftershock
Ryan Parrott, Lucas Werneck
ISBN: 978-1-60886-937-4 | $14.99

Mighty Morphin Power Rangers Poster Book
Goñi Montes, Jamal Campbell, Joe Quinones
ISBN: 978-1-60886-966-4 | $19.99

Mighty Morphin Power Rangers Adult Coloring Book
Goñi Montes, Jamal Campbell, Hendry Prasetya
ISBN: 978-1-60886-955-8 | $16.99

Mighty Morphin Power Rangers Year One: Deluxe HC
Kyle Higgins, Hendry Prasetya, Steve Orlando
ISBN: 978-1-68415-012-0 | $75.00

BOOM! STUDIOS™

AVAILABLE AT YOUR LOCAL COMICS SHOP AND BOOKSTORE
Find a comic shop near you at www.comicshoplocator.com
WWW.**BOOM-STUDIOS**.COM

Licensed by: Hasbro